50 YEARS OF
RANGERS
IN EUROPE

THE ENDURING DREAM

50 YEARS OF
RANGERS IN EUROPE

THE ENDURING DREAM

ROBERT McELROY

Cover illustrations courtesy of Eric McCowat, who provided many of the photographs for this book.

First published 2007

Stadia is an imprint of
Tempus Publishing Limited
The Mill, Brimscombe Port,
Stroud, Gloucestershire, GL5 2QG
www.tempus-publishing.com

British Library Cataloguing in Publication Data.
A catalogue record for this book is available from the British Library.

ISBN-10: 0 7524 4151 5
ISBN-13: 978 0 7524 4151 1

Typesetting and origination by Tempus Publishing Limited
Printed in Great Britain

Contents

Introduction

For fifty years Rangers Football Club have been participating in European competition against the best that the Continent has to offer. Generations of Ibrox patrons have feasted on clashes with the cream of Europe – Real Madrid, Juventus, AC and Inter Milan, Bayern Munich and Manchester United have all graced the Glasgow ground in European competition.

Competitive European football arrived at a time when the frequency of visits to these shores by foreign opposition had increased primarily due to the introduction of floodlighting. There had been the occasional game in the 1930s, and the arrival of Dinamo Moscow to play a four-game tour of the UK following the end of the Second World War had attracted massive attendances, including 95,000 to witness a 2-2 draw with Rangers at Ibrox in November 1945. A decade later British football fans, weaned on a diet of domestic football, were flocking to the glamour friendlies. The British Press, never a group to countenance modesty, had proclaimed Wolverhampton Wanderers European Champions in the wake of victory at their very own Molineux against Honved of Budapest, a side containing the likes of Puskas, Hidgekuti, Kocsis and Czibor. The challenge was taken up by Gabriel Hanot of the distinguished newspaper *L'Equippe*, who argued, with considerable logic, that such a claim could only be justified if Wolves fulfilled, and triumphed in, a return fixture in Hungary. Thus the European Cup was born, and with it the concept of competitive football between the champion clubs of different countries.

For Rangers, the dominant club in Scottish football for so long, the new horizons presented new challenges and new opportunities. Home and away challenge matches during the 1930s against the mighty Arsenal under the managership of the legendary Herbert Chapman had indicated that at that time the Ibrox men were the best in Britain – and by proxy therefore the best in Europe – but that was the 1930s, and this was the 1950s.

Legendary names including those of the great Alfredo Di Stefano, Ferenc Puskas, Franz Beckenbauer, Gerd Muller, Juan Alberto Schiaffino, Kurt Hamrin,

Danny Blanchflower, Dave Mackay, John White, Jimmy Greaves, Luis Suarez, Giacinto Facchetti, Sandro Mazzola, Wolfgang Overath, Wlodzimierz Lubanski, Johan Cruyff, Dino Zoff, Roberto Bettega, Rainer Bonhof, Mario Kempes, Franco Baresi, Karl Heinz Rummenigge, Oleg Blokhin, Georghe Hagi, Marius Lacatus, Eric Cantona and Ronaldinho feature amongst the myriad stars to have entertained capacity audiences at Ibrox since then – from the days of the old oval bowl that held so many memories to the modern arena, beyond question the finest in Scotland and one of the best in the UK.

Not that the world-class footballers have been confined to visiting teams by any means – this book will narrate the story of the Ibrox greats who stood against the might of Europe, reaching three finals at a time when the true giants of European club football bestrode the world stage and, after two frustrating setbacks, achieving the Holy Grail in a memorable campaign that culminated in one of the world's great sporting arenas – the Nou Camp in Barcelona.

There have been triumphs and tragedies, great nights and grim nights, heroes and villains. The story of Rangers' fifty years in Europe is the continuing search for a dream that has endured for half a century: the quest for glory on a global scale.

ONE

The Early Years

Rangers were the first Scottish Champions to qualify for the European Champions' Cup. In the inaugural tournament, held in 1955/56, Hibernian represented Caledonia despite Aberdeen having won the Scottish League in the previous campaign, entry to the first competition being by invitation only. A first-round bye meant that the Light Blues were paired with French Champions OGC Nice in the second round, with the first leg scheduled for Wednesday 24 October 1956 at Ibrox. Sixty-five thousand spectators produced an electrifying atmosphere on a night of heavy rain and hailstones. The contrast in styles made for an engrossing contest. Rangers were the more direct and powerful, playing very much in the traditional British fashion; their opponents exhibited the Latin style that would provoke so many flashpoints throughout not just this tie but all the early years of European competition, when the different interpretation of the laws of the game created so much ill-feeling in clashes between British clubs and Continental sides.

The French struck first blood in the twenty-third minute when Jacques Faivre opened the scoring – but only a superb display of goalkeeping by Dominique Colonna, aided by resolute defending from his colleagues and some atrocious finishing, kept Nice ahead until shortly before the interval when a Max Murray header levelled the scores.

A second-half siege produced just the one goal through Ulsterman Billy Simpson on the hour, but that forty-five minutes was long remembered for two other remarkable incidents. The first came when the scores were still tied at 1-1. English referee Arthur Ellis, who had taken charge of the previous year's final in Paris, dramatically called both sets of players together to deliver a lecture, later admitting that his main concern was the blatant body-checking of the French. Even more unusually, Ellis signalled for full time after just eighty-five minutes' play. Realising his error, he recalled the players to complete the game. One Ranger, Eric Caldow, was already in the dressing-room and later recalled the incident:

I had my boots off at the time. That was the day of my brother's wedding, and I was best man. I had to rush off back to the reception, but George Young came in and told me to get back on the park – the game hadn't finished.

One week later the Scottish Champions travelled to the Cote d'Azure expecting blue skies and warm sunshine on the Riviera. Instead, dark skies and torrential rain greeted them – conditions were so bad that the game had to be postponed and rearranged for 14 November when, incredibly, Rangers were once again greeted by rain. The host club were apologetic to their guests, but this time the game went ahead on a quagmire of a pitch.

Rangers dominated play during the first half with the heavy conditions suiting the visitors. The referee was brave enough to award the Light Blues a penalty after forty minutes for Cesar Gonzales' foul on Murray. Protests from the entire Nice team were to no avail and spot-kick expert Johnny Hubbard made his customary efficient job to notch the opening goal. A second goal would have killed the tie stone dead, and only the referee's precise timing denied Murray, who stabbed home a corner kick just as the interval whistle sounded. Three-one ahead on aggregate, the Ibrox men were well on top as the second half progressed, only for a mishit shot by Ruben Bravo to find the net on the hour, then within two minutes Jacques Foix converted a Jacques Faivre cross to level the aggregate score.

Both sides were reduced to ten men in the closing stages when Alberto Muro fouled Willie Logie and followed up by throwing a punch at the Ranger, who put his arm up to protect himself. Bravo ploughed in to flatten Logie and the Italian referee sent both players off – while the original perpetrator Muro incredibly got off scot-free.

The game ended with fireworks exploding around George Niven's goal, spectators attempting to scale the wire fence around the pitch and the referee receiving a police escort at the final whistle.

There was to be no extra time and no penalty shoot-out. Instead, the tournament regulations allowed a third game to be staged – a ruling that would do much to enhance European football today. The Stade Olympique de Colombes in Paris was the venue. This was an historic venue, having hosted the 1938 World Cup final, not to mention the football match in the film *Escape to Victory*.

For the third game, Rangers were without their inspirational captain George Young, who was injured, but again dominated play in the first half only to be denied by some outstanding goalkeeping from Colonna. A sucker-punch breakaway by Nice in the forty-third minute saw Joseph Ujlaki release Foix, who netted from twelve yards. The Scots levelled matters five minutes after the restart when Sammy Baird's low driven cross was turned into the Nice goal by Gilbert Bonvin. The French side regained the advantage, however, when Muro restored the lead within two minutes, and Faivre added a third before the end to seal victory for Nice.

There was yet another explosion after seventy-five minutes when Bobby Shearer followed through with a wild tackle on Muro that threw him two yards across the touchline. He appeared to be unconscious even before he hit the ground. Bravo and Shearer then exchanged punches before being dragged apart by teammates. The still-unconscious Muro was wheeled away on a trolley by an estimated fifty people, including two gendarmes, and Belgian referee M. van Nuffel incredibly booked only Ian McColl – although his official report later indicated that he had ordered off both Shearer and Bravo. Both these players finished the game, with 'Captain Cutlass' being roundly jeered by the home fans in the closing stages.

Elimination at the hands of Nice was the first indication for friends of Rangers that the Continentals had caught up with the British clubs in the game that this island claimed to have invented. Previously, tour games, friendlies and flood-lit challenge matches had all suggested that the British still reigned supreme, although such a fallacy had been exposed at international level by the World Cup of 1954. Rangers, in all probability, should have defeated the French Champions, but Nice were themselves eliminated by the holders, and eventual champions, Real Madrid, 6-2 on aggregate (3-0, 3-2), but Rangers had by no means been disgraced.

1956/57 European Champions' Cup, second round, first leg
Wednesday 24 October 1956, Ibrox Stadium, Glasgow
Rangers 2 (Murray, Simpson) OGC Nice 1 (Faivre)
Attendance 65,000
Niven; Shearer, Caldow; McColl, Young, Logie; Scott, Simpson, Murray, Baird, Hubbard
Second round, second leg
Wednesday 14 November 1956, Stade Municipal du Rey, Nice
OGC Nice 2 (Bravo, Foix) Rangers 1 (Hubbard pen)
Attendance 12,000
Niven; Shearer, Caldow; McColl, Young, Logie; Scott, Simpson, Murray, Baird, Hubbard
Second round, decider
Wednesday 28 November 1956, Stade Olympique de Colombres, Paris
OGC Nice 3 (Foix, Muro, Faivre) Rangers 1 (Bonvin o.g.)
Attendance 15,000
Niven; Shearer, Caldow; McColl, Davis, Logie; Scott, Simpson, Murray, Baird, Hubbard

Season 1957/58 saw Rangers enter the European Champions' Cup for the second successive season, and for the second time be drawn against the Champions of France. Ibrox on the night of 4 September 1957 presented a wonderful sight under the floodlights as Rangers and St Etienne ran out for the first leg of their tie. There had been a frantic rush for tickets, and a British record crowd for a floodlit match of 85,000 was there to roar encouragement, with thousands more locked out.

What a shock there was for Rangers in the fourteenth minute. Harold Davis had possession near his own goal, with plenty of time to part with the ball, only to be robbed by the eager Yves Goujon. Fast as an arrow, the ball was passed to Rachid Mekloufi, an Algerian who was to prove one of the most brilliant inside forwards ever to grace Ibrox. In a flash, Mekloufi had shot, giving George Niven no chance. It was a glorious goal – a goal by an outstanding opportunist.

The quick, accurate football of the French was troubling the home team, but South African Don Kichenbrand came to Rangers' rescue within five minutes. Fellow Springbok Hubbard lobbed the ball into the French goal area to be headed on by Billy Simpson and then nodded backwards past the bewildered Claude Abbes by 'Kich'.

The excitement mounted and, displaying greater determination, Rangers took the lead early in the second half when Davis atoned for his earlier mistake by winning possession before sending the ball across to Scott for the winger to score with a thundering drive from the corner of the penalty area. That was better for Rangers, but the crowd weren't satisfied, realising that a 2–1 lead had not been enough against Nice the year before.

Rangers rose to the occasion, inspired by the outstanding Sammy Baird, and added a third in the eighty-second minute when a Hubbard cross was headed down by Kichenbrand to Simpson, who slotted the ball home. The big question remained: was a 3–1 score enough to see Rangers through the second match in France? The young St Etienne side had demonstrated individual skill of high quality and their teamwork was slick and accurate. Rangers had fought hard but they didn't have the precision of their opponents.

The Stade Geoffroy Guichard, a ground at the very heart of an industrial city, with iron, steel and football as its very lifeblood, was the venue three weeks later for the second leg. In temperatures which touched 88°F in the shade, the Scottish Champions lost Johnny Hubbard through illness, replacing him with Davie Wilson, and introduced Billy Ritchie, John Valentine, and Jimmy Millar in place of George Niven, Harold Davis, and Don Kichenbrand, the absence of the Springbok perhaps indicating that the Rangers directors, after a long meeting with manager Scot Symon, had decided that discretion was the watchword bearing in mind the flashpoints of Nice and Paris one year earlier. The tearaway style of 'Kich' could have been misinterpreted as intimidation.

It proved yet another dramatic match and the real hero was Valentine, who inspired his colleagues in the rear and pulled down an old-style Ibrox iron curtain. It was a hot, breathless night when the match began and right from the start the shirt-sleeved crowd of 35,000 cheered, whistled and shouted encouragement to St Etienne, making a great bid to save the tie. Rangers, immaculate in blue with satin shorts to match, won the toss, but almost at once were jerked back into desperate defence. The French came close to opening the scoring four times in the first ten minutes – a goal had to come, so penetrating were their onslaughts, and after eleven minutes Njo-Lea was allowed to run unchallenged to the edge of the penalty area. His cross was met on the half-volley by Oleksiak, giving Ritchie no chance from fifteen yards.

It was fifteen minutes before Rangers mounted their first attack as 'Les Verts' mounted attack after attack, with Billy Ritchie making several fine saves and both Rene Domingo and Rachid Mekloufi missing clear-cut chances. It seemed only a matter of time before the aggregate scores were levelled yet, suddenly, on the hour, in a rare attack, Davie Wilson stooped low to head an Alex Scott corner into the net. After that goal St Etienne lost heart – and also their heads, eventually leading to the award of a penalty when Francois Wicart fouled Wilson in the seventy-fifth minute. Amidst exploding fireworks (some of which were thrown on to the pitch) Abbes pulled off a magnificent one-handed save from Ian McColl, touching the ball against the post, and the chance was lost. A second goal for Rangers would have killed the tie stone dead, but the home side gained renewed vigour from that let-off, and Rene Fevrier scored in the eighty-seventh minute. The dying minutes were frenetic, with only a wonder save by Ritchie preventing a third match, and the final whistle brought immense relief for the visitors. In cultured football terms, St Etienne had been ahead of Rangers but they appeared to lack the courage and directness of the Scots, and they failed to take their chances.

The luck of the draw was far from kind to the Scottish Champions when the ballot paired them with Italian aces AC Milan, semi-finalists in the inaugural tournament where they had gone under to eventual winners Real Madrid (4-2, 1-2). Indeed, in the second season of the European Cup, Italian Champions Fiorentina had made it all the way to the final where they were unfortunate enough to face the holders in their own Estadio Chamartin in Madrid, losing 0-2.

Milan were European aristocrats without question and included in their ranks, amongst many other international stars, was a certain Cesare Maldini – yet Rangers led at the interval through a Max Murray goal scored on the half-hour mark in the first leg played before a packed Ibrox of 85,000 spectators. Alex Scott's cross from the right had been only partially cleared by goalkeeper Lorenzo Buffon and Murray lashed a left-foot shot into the net. That one-goal lead was still intact as the clock reached the seventy-five-minute mark, yet the Ibrox men, wearing a dazzling change strip of white with red and blue hoops, were growing more and more frustrated at their failure to add a second goal. That frustration eventually manifested itself in a loss of discipline and composure and the visitors took the opportunity to cut loose, with the magnificent Juan Alberto Schiaffino, the

Milan captain (who had also played for Uruguay in their 7-0 mauling of Scotland during the 1954 World Cup finals), orchestrating play. Another South American, Argentinian Ernesto Grillo, equalised after seventy-five minutes, weaving his way through the home defence before scoring with a superb shot. Rangers were then cut to pieces, with both Dario Baruffi and Grillo again netting from tight angles with questions being asked about the positioning of Billy Ritchie. Baruffi's goal – when he skinned Johnny Little wide on the left before striking – left the crowd stunned. Gastone Bean added a fourth in the eighty-sixth minute to leave the Scottish Champions floundering.

The first ever encounter with an Italian club had looked promising for seventy-five minutes but by the end the Scots had sunk without trace – an apt description as the return tie was played in monsoon conditions, with Milan demonstrating Rangers' pulling power in Italy by switching the game from the San Siro to The Arena (a small sports ground still in use in Milan to this day) with a paltry 3,000 spectators attending.

Rangers' visit to the fashion capital of Europe was a miserable one. It was December, the weather was as cold as it was back in Glasgow, and the charter flight that carried them across the Alps was diverted to Torino with Milan fogbound. It took an additional four-hour coach journey for the visitors to reach

Max Murray scores against AC Milan.

their destination. If Rangers' journey had been fraught with problems, one fan had undertaken an even longer and more stressful journey, having driven across the Alps to Milan. That supporter was Matt Taylor, who would become chairman in 1973.

Manager Scot Symon made no fewer than four changes from Ibrox, while the hosts made just two – introducing Swedish international Nils Liedholm who, having played for Italy in the 1956 Olympics, would be a key component for his native Sweden when, against all odds, they reached the final of the 1958 World Cup played in their own country.

It was touch and go as to whether the game would be played at all with a waterlogged pitch being constantly pitchforked before kick-off at a venue that dated back to Napoleonic times. The game started ten minutes late and Milan went on to win 2-0 with goals from Baruffi and Carlo Galli.

The Rossoneri went on to the final, losing somewhat unluckily to Real Madrid 2-3 after extra time at the Stade du Heysel, Bruxelles, and Rangers could at least console themselves with the thought that they had been outclassed by one of the true giants of European football.

1957/58 European Champions' Cup first round, first leg
Wednesday 4 September 1957, Ibrox Stadium, Glasgow
Rangers 3 (Kichenbrand, Scott, Simpson) St Etienne 1 (Mekloufi)
Attendance 85,000
Niven; Shearer, Caldow; McColl, Davis, Baird; Scott, Simpson, Kichenbrand, Murray, Hubbard
First round, second leg
Wednesday 25 September 1957, Stade Geoffroy Guichard, St Etienne
St Etienne 2 (Oleksiak, Fevrier) Rangers 1 (Wilson)
Attendance 35,000
Ritchie; Shearer, Caldow; McColl, Valentine, Millar; Scott, Simpson, Murray, Baird, Wilson.
Second round, first leg
Wednesday 27 November 1957, Ibrox Stadium, Glasgow
Rangers 1 (Murray) AC Milan 4 (Grillo 2, Baruffi, Bean)
Attendance 85,000
Ritchie; Little, Caldow; McColl, Telfer, Millar; Scott, Simpson, Murray, Baird, Hubbard
Second round, second leg
Wednesday 11 December 1957, The Arena, Milan
AC Milan 2 (Baruffi, Galli) Rangers 0
Attendance 3,000
Niven; Shearer, Caldow; McColl, Telfer, Baird; Scott, Millar, Kichenbrand, Wilson, Hubbard

There was no European football for Rangers in 1958/59 with Hearts as Scottish Champions making a brief sojourn into the Champions' Cup – no Scottish club as yet had participated in the Inter-Cities Fairs Cup – but the Ibrox men secured the title that season in a dramatic last-day duel with the Tynecastle club to qualify for the 1959/60 European Cup.

The Royal Sporting Club Anderlechtois (Anderlecht), coached by Englishman Bill Gormlie, were Rangers' first-round opponents. For the fourth successive occasion the first leg was to be staged at Ibrox. It would prove to be as hostile and explosive a tie as any ever encountered by a Scottish side in Europe, with Rangers making a sensational start with two goals in the opening three minutes. An Alex Scott free-kick was met by the head of Jimmy Millar after just two minutes, the ball curling into the net with thirty-nine-year-old goalkeeper Henri Meert rooted to the spot, then sixty seconds later flying winger Scott was released by a pinpoint pass from Harold Davis and fired home from twelve yards.

Rangers were in command, but the Belgians lost all semblance of discipline, with Millar, Scott and Matthew the victims of outright assaults. The game boiled over utterly on the half-hour when a Pierre van den Bosch goal was disallowed for offside – the entire Anderlecht side surrounded the referee, manhandling him to the extent of holding him in a half-nelson and forcing him to consult first one linesman and then the other. Dane Leo Helge bravely stood by his decision.

As the interval approached, the Flemish side became even wilder as first Bobby Shearer and then Harold Davis were kicked to the ground. Very few opponents dared meddle with Davis, a Korean War veteran, and the bespectacled Josef Jurion, a class player by any reckoning, soon regretted his illegal challenge when the enraged Harold gave chase following yet another foul, pursuing him behind the goal before stopping dead in his tracks and laughing at the sight of his opponent haring away from him.

Remarkably, a tolerant referee had booked just two Anderlecht players – but more trouble erupted early in the second half when the home side were awarded a penalty after Ian McMillan had been crudely fouled. Matthew's spot-kick was parried by Meert, only for the winger to head home the rebound, yet within two minutes the Belgian Champions had struck back when Jacques Stockman, sixteen yards out, pivoted with the ball and shot past George Niven following a Fritz van den Boer cross. The loss of the goal scarcely knocked Rangers out of their stride, but as Baird and Matthew both squandered chances there was anxiety in the air when Gaston de Waele added a second for the visitors. However, the Light Blues' superiority was re-established within three minutes when Sammy Baird lashed home an Ian McMillan cross, and Baird, a player who relished games against the Continentals, then added a fifth from a second penalty in the seventy-third minute.

These early European ties had at times seemed to be more akin to guerilla warfare than to football, and the second leg in Brussels' Stade Emile Verse (or Parc

Astrid as it is more commonly known, after the adjacent public park) was apprehensively anticipated as a potential repeat of the Ibrox bloodbath. So it proved, for Anderlecht set out to intimidate the Scots at every opportunity. Rangers' defence held steady in the face of wave after wave of Belgian attacks and the game, played at a red-hot pace, exploded as the interval approached when Alex Scott was sent crashing against the boundary wall and was stretchered off with blood pouring from a head wound. The winger bravely returned to the fray in the second half and in a lightning breakaway in the sixty-fifth minute laid on a cross for Matthew to head home the opening goal. Ten minutes later Ian McMillan added a second and the tie was won.

The next round would send Rangers to Eastern Europe for the very first time in European competition. The destination was the beautiful city of Bratislava.

The Cold War was at its height in 1959 and Bratislava, the second city of Czechoslovakia, was under Communist occupation behind the Iron Curtain that split Europe in two. The opposition came under the banner of Ruda Hvezda (Red Star) or CH Bratislava. Red Star today are known as Inter Bratislava, and in the intervening years have been known by such names as Slovnaft, TJ Internacional, Internacional ZTS, and, since 1990, ASK Inter Slovnaft Bratislava.

The Scottish Champions welcomed Red Star Bratislava to Ibrox Stadium for the second-round first-leg game on 11 November 1959. The Czechoslovakian Champions had defeated FC Porto home and away in the previous round. A packed Ibrox held 80,000 spectators inside the oval bowl, and they witnessed a sensational opening when Ian McMillan opened the scoring from sixteen yards out after ninety seconds following an Alex Scott cross. The game then degenerated into a kicking match as CH quickly identified Scott as the danger man – the winger was body-checked, tripped and harassed at every opportunity.

Red Star turned the match on its head when Adolf Scherer (one of four Czech internationals in their team) equalised in the sixteenth minute, then on the half-hour Milan Dolinsky put the visitors ahead. CH were an accomplished, skilful side who were controlling the tempo of the game.

The game had been simmering throughout the opening forty-five minutes, and it exploded on the cusp of the interval when a mazy run on the left by Davie Wilson ended with a cross that led to Sammy Baird colliding in mid-air with goalkeeper Frantisek Hlavaty, the loose ball falling to Scott who lobbed it into the unguarded net with the goalkeeper lying prostrate on the penalty spot. Swiss referee Daniel Mellet awarded the goal, to the fury of the visitors, and when the Czech goalkeeper was stretchered off after a considerable delay, it fell to Dezider Cimra to replace him in goal; these, of course, were the days before substitutions were allowed.

The drama was far from over – before the interval Red Star were reduced to nine men after Sammy Baird was felled by a wild kick from Jiri Tichy. Mayhem ensued, and amidst the confusion it was Stefan Matlak who was ordered off.

The game restarted after the interval with Hlavaty resuming between the posts with his head heavily bandaged. The visitors regained the lead in the sixty-eighth minute when, after a period of sustained Rangers pressure, a lightning-quick counter-attack, taking full advantage of a Johnny Little slip, saw Dolinsky cross for Scherer to net at the culmination of a slick passing move that had encompassed virtually the full length of the park.

It had been Red Star's first attack of the second half, and the Scottish Champions were quick to respond; five minutes after falling behind they were awarded a penalty when Baird, who revelled in games against Continental opposition and Celtic alike, was sent sprawling.

The spot-kick was a drama in itself, with a line of defenders indulging in excessive gamesmanship by standing in front of Eric Caldow as he prepared to take the penalty. They danced around the ball, pointing at it and then at the corner flag, and when order was eventually restored the distraction had worked, for Hlavaty, with a dive to the left, diverted the full-back's effort wide for a corner.

The Light Blues would not be denied, however – sixty seconds later a superb dummy from Ian McMillan (another who revelled in European games) wrong-footed the Red Star defence before the 'Wee Prime Minister' crossed for Davie Wilson to hook in the equaliser.

Fully aware that the second leg awaited in Bratislava, Rangers went all out for the winner. Baird missed two good chances, and a momentous game looked certain to finish all square until the final minute when Jimmy Millar grabbed the winner following a neat Scott–McMillan move.

The Bratislava of 1959 was not by any stretch of the imagination the city that Rangers visited in 2005. With the Iron Curtain in place, Czechoslovakia was very much in the grip of a Soviet-backed government that would not tolerate free speech or freedom of expression.

Into such a depressing and hostile environment the Ibrox men travelled with such a narrow lead for the second leg one week later to be played not in Red Star's own ground (now Stadion Inter), but across the road in the very same Stadion Tehelne pole, home of Slovan, where Rangers faced Artmedia in 2005.

The Tehelne pole (or Brick field, named after the district) is an historic venue. Czechoslovakia was, of course, wholly annexed by Adolf Hitler's Germany in 1939, with Bratislava renamed Pressburg. The stadium was built in 1940 and opened on 22 October with the visit of Hertha Berlin. Two years later, on 22 November 1942, the ground witnessed the Third Reich's last-ever international fixture, a 5–2 win over Slovakia, which was ruled by a semi-autonomous government known as the Hlinka Guard during the German occupation. Such considerations were far from Ibrox minds in 1959 however – the job in hand was to qualify for the last eight of the European Champions' Cup for the first time.

The absence of floodlights necessitated an afternoon kick-off and, with a massive 60,000 spectators present, both sides made one change from Ibrox, the visitors replacing Eric Caldow with Bobby Shearer. Rangers were forced back into defence for most of the second leg but gave a composed, disciplined performance in the face of intimidation – a collision between Baird and Vladimir Weiss led to the Ranger being surrounded by several Red Star players. However, all was smoothed over by the referee, another Swiss official, S. Gelde, but not before blood flowed from a face wound suffered by Sammy. Weiss' son of the same name, incidentally, would face Rangers in the 2005/06 Champions' League as coach of Artmedia Bratislava.

Baird would have the last laugh in 1959, however – breaking out of defence in the seventieth minute he released Wilson down the left, the winger's cross being headed home by Scott at the far post. Twelve minutes later, Rangers were reduced to ten men when Millar, provoked and obstructed throughout by his direct opponent Tichy, finally retaliated after yet another foul by punching the centre half in the back and was ordered off. Red Star equalised in the eighty-ninth minute when the selfsame Tichy hooked home a Kazimir Gajdos corner, but Rangers were through 5-4 on aggregate.

The tale of that triumph in Bratislava would not be complete, however, without the story of two Light Blue followers who travelled to the game by somewhat irregular means. In 2005, some 3,500 Gers fans were present at Tehelne pole for the Champions' League fixture, having travelled to the Slovakian capital by various routes and methods – some more orthodox than others – but it is fair comment that none would have had to undertake the journey that Ross Bowie and Joe Walsh embarked upon in 1959.

The early days of European competition had understandably witnessed precious few of the 'Follow Follow' brigade travelling to away games – but Ross and Joe were frequently paying guests on the club's official flight. To visit the Soviet satellite state of Czechoslovakia in 1959 one required a visa, and when Ibrox manager Scot Symon studied the documentation received from the Czech Embassy in London he quickly realised that the visas were all there for the official party and press, with just two exceptions – for Messrs Bowie and Walsh. No reason was given for the exclusion, whether it was a simple oversight or otherwise, but there was little that could be done about it – or so it seemed.

At the last minute, very much on a whim, Ross and Joe (both sadly no longer with us) decided to fly to Vienna, just 45km from Bratislava. Indeed, this correspondent followed in their footsteps in 2005, travelling by precisely the same route. Hiring a car in the Austrian capital, they drove to the Czech border on the day before the game in an attempt to somehow be granted permission to enter Czechoslovakia. Armed guards and blank stares greeted the two Scots who vainly tried to explain that 'football' and 'Glasgow Rangers' was the purpose of their visit, the universal passport that should open all doors. Sadly, however, the only answer forthcoming was a request for 'papers' which meant visa as well as passport.

Undaunted, the intrepid two turned back to Vienna only to return the next day, the day of the game, when a new set of border guards were on duty, including, crucially, at least one who was a football fan. There remained a language barrier, but gifts of a Rangers pennant and lapel badge together with a bottle of Scotch whisky somehow persuaded a sympathetic guard to allow them to cross the border without visas with the stipulation, by way of sign language, that they return by 6p.m.

Ross and Joe drove straight to Bratislava and straight to the stadium, where a new problem presented itself – a lack of match tickets with kick-off rapidly approaching. This was a problem soon overcome by boldly walking straight up to the main entrance where, by dint of their Rangers blazers and ties, they were assumed to be club officials and waved straight through to trackside where an incredulous Scot Symon greeted them.

Incredibly, at the height of the Cold War, Messrs Bowie and Walsh had made it, and they watched the game from the trainer's bench before setting off back to the border at the final whistle. They made good time and, passing through a small village not far from the border, it was decided that a quick beer was the order of the day. Who should our two friends find in the tavern but the selfsame border guard who had permitted them passage – and a convivial evening was spent toasting Rangers, Red Star, Robert Burns and so on. It was well past midnight before Ross and Joe were spirited back out of Czechoslovakia to the West – and a day to remember was at an end.

As far as the European Champions' Cup was concerned, Rangers were now through to the quarter-finals where the draw would for the first time send them on their travels for the first leg – to a location much closer to home. It is a remarkable statistic that in fifty years of European competition Rangers have visited the bustling port of Rotterdam just twice. The first occasion was in 1959/60 when the Light Blues' visit was to play not Feyenoord (perhaps the more famous of the two major clubs from that city) but their neighbours Sparta. The European Champions' Cup quarter-final was to be the occasion of three memorable games between the two. Sparta had won their fifth (and to date most recent) Dutch Championship in 1959 to secure entry to Europe's premier tournament; the title success was their first since their heyday almost half a century earlier when four out of five championships had been won between 1909 and 1913.

The Rotterdam side had qualified for the last eight of the European Cup in 1959/60 with a 3-1 play-off victory over IFK Göteborg in Bremen after each side had won their home leg by the same 3-1 scoreline (mercifully, there was no extra time nor penalty shoot-outs in those days). The Stadion Feyenoord was the venue for the first leg rather than Sparta's own ground, Het Kassel (The Castle), presumably because of its greater capacity and floodlighting, and a 50,000 audience proved testimony to the wisdom of that decision. Sparta had a strong British Isles connection – their manager was Englishman Denis

Neville, while Irishmen Johnny Crossan and Peter Fitzgerald were forwards of some repute, particularly Crossan who had been banned from British football and whose path would again cross that of the Ibrox men some two years later when the Light Blues met Standard Liege in the same tournament. Crossan had fallen foul of the authorities when accused of accepting illegal payments by the Irish League, who consequently cancelled his transfer from Coleraine to Bristol City in 1960, suspending him *sine die* from playing in the British Isles. Even in 1960, the Rangers fans 'Follow Followed' to Rotterdam – and they were rewarded with a sparkling display from the Light Blues in the opening thirty minutes which threatened to sweep the Dutch Champions into the North Sea. Davie Wilson opened the scoring after just four minutes and the Ibrox men thereafter turned on the style only for Max Murray and Ian McMillan to squander chances aplenty. Baird did put a more realistic slant on the scoreline when he notched the second goal ten minutes from the interval, only for Sparta to reduce the deficit within three minutes when George Niven collided with Peter Fitzgerald as he rose to meet a cross from Tony van Ede, the loose ball being converted by Peter de Vries. The Rotterdam club found new strength with that goal and at the start of the second half pressed for the equaliser. Within five minutes a twenty-five-yard shot from Fitzgerald had cannoned off Niven's post, the diminutive goalie saving the rebound from Van Ede with his outstretched foot. It was 'hammer and tongs' as both sides strove for advantage, but Max Murray eased the pressure with a third in the sixty-third minute. Three-one ahead, Rangers eased off, believing the battle was won – a fatal error at any time and one for which the Light Blues would have cause for regret. Fitzgerald struck the crossbar before De Vries flicked the ball almost out of Niven's grasp from a corner in the dying seconds.

Nevertheless a 3-2 win in an away leg of a European Cup quarter-final tie is a good result by any standard, and Rangers would have had few worries as they flew home from Amsterdam the next morning.

Ibrox was packed with 82,587 spectators inside the huge oval bowl, all surely confident that the return leg was little more than a formality, even though Rangers' domestic form was less than impressive – five League fixtures since the turn of the year at home had all been drawn. Sparta had obviously learned from the Stadion Feyenoord encounter, anticipating right-winger Alex Scott as the main danger man, they played outside left Tinus Bosselaar in a withdrawn role to nullify the threat from the 'Flying Scot'.

The game was one of unrelenting Rangers pressure, yet the visitors' goal remained intact with Andries van Dijk seldom tested. A goalless draw would, of course, have been enough to see Rangers through, but the Dutch side broke upfield with just seven minutes remaining when Jimmy Millar lost possession midway inside the Sparta half. Jan Villerius quickly released Peter Fitzgerald who swept a long pass out to Tony van Ede wide on the right and he played a one-two with Peter de Vries before stabbing the ball home. There was no 'away goals' rule in those fledgling days of European competition; a third match was required – a regulation that would greatly enhance the tournaments of the present-day but one which is extremely unlikely to be resurrected due to overwhelming fixture congestion.

Highbury was agreed as the venue for the play-off; the Arsenal Stadium was eminently suitable for Rangers, who had won 3-0 there almost exactly one year earlier in a friendly against Arsenal and indeed the Light Blue legions comprised the majority of the 34,176 audience present in North London two weeks later in the shape of either exiled Scots or those who had made the journey south. Some 1,500 Sparta fans had travelled from Holland but the Dutch side must have felt that they were facing another away game, even though the venue was in actual fact closer to Rotterdam than Glasgow. Sparta had amused the Scottish fans with their enthusiastic celebrations following a goal – nothing that would raise an eyebrow today but in 1960 the football supporter was more

Action from Rangers *v.* Sparta at Ibrox.

accustomed to a simple handshake – and there was great joy again when the Dutch side took the lead for the first time in the tie in the seventh minute at Highbury, when Adrian Verhoeven bulleted home a flying header from a corner that found the Rangers' defence somewhat statuesque. The Ibrox men took that setback in their stride, however. Ian McMillan had returned and was the midfield orchestrator at the heart of almost every Rangers attack. The equaliser finally arrived in the twenty-sixth minute when Sammy Baird flicked a low free-kick from Davie Wilson into the net despite the despairing attempts of Verhoeven to prevent a goal. Although the interval arrived with the score still deadlocked at 1-1, Rangers were in command – then Sammy Baird took control in the second half, covering every inch of the wet Highbury pitch and sending the Scots into the ascendancy twelve minutes after the interval when a headed clearance from Jan Villerius found Wilson who fed a simple pass to Baird, who took the ball in his stride to crack home a twenty-five-yard left-foot drive. The tie seemed to have been won in the seventieth minute when a curling Ian McMillan cross was turned home by Jimmy Millar despite the efforts of Freek van der Lee to deny him, yet within five minutes Van Ede was sandwiched between Johnny Little and Harold Davis in the penalty area and Tinus Bosselaar converted the resulting spot-kick.

Rangers, however, ran out 3-2 winners and two-goal hero Sammy Baird was carried off shoulder-high by the jubilant fans at the final whistle. Had those fans known what awaited their heroes in the semi-final they may well have felt less inclined to celebrate! For Sparta Rotterdam that quarter-final represents the furthest that the club have thus far journeyed in Europe.

Nevertheless, those three games with the Ibrox side remained so much in the memory that an invitation to officially open Sparta's newly renovated ground was forthcoming. The fact that Rangers' manager Dick Advocaat had played for Sparta from 1980 to 1982 – making 61 competitive appearances and scoring 6 goals – also helped. The Eneco Stadion (as Sparta's ground is now officially called) is today a modern all-seated arena with a modest capacity of some 11,000, but to the traditional follower of Sparta it will surely always remain 'Het Kassel' – and thankfully the original 1916 clubhouse, built in the form of a fourteenth-century moated castle (Slot van Spangen, which once stood nearby) has been retained and lovingly restored.

Somewhat ironically, the semi-final draw which paired Rangers with West German Champions Eintracht Frankfurt was generally viewed as a kindly one in that the Ibrox men had avoided the two Spanish giants Real Madrid and Barcelona, but reality soon set in when the Light Blues were taken apart in the first leg in the Waldstadion. Eintracht squandered a golden opportunity to open the scoring after eight minutes when Richard Kress shot wide with a penalty after he had been upended by Johnny Little. The opening goal was delayed a further twenty minutes, but when it arrived George Niven was left

Eintracht Frankfurt supporters carry their banner before the Rangers *v*. Eintracht tie at Ibrox.

helpless as Dieter Stinka's drive ripped into the roof of the net. Rangers struck back immediately, with Eric Caldow netting from the spot after Ian McMillan was upended. The second half would prove to be a different story as the Light Blues were overwhelmed – the dam broke in the fifty-second minute when Alfred Pfaff netted following a goalmouth scramble, then three minutes later the German captain added a third from a twenty-yard free-kick. Rangers were up against it as Eintracht went for the kill. The Scots could only keep the tide at bay for so long and a Dieter Lindner header made it 4-1 with fifteen minutes remaining.

Such a deficit going into the second leg in Glasgow would have been daunting enough, but the roof fell in on the Ibrox men in the dying minutes when firstly a long shot from Lindner was misjudged by Niven, then Paul Stein made it six with a magnificent solo run that encompassed all of forty yards.

One Rangers player, Jimmy Millar, who had arranged to meet a friend later that evening for a few beers, was too embarrassed by the heavy defeat to do anything other than retire to his hotel room.

A 6-1 defeat is pretty conclusive by any standards, but in later years Ian McMillan was scathingly critical of manager Scot Symon's failure to respond to the situation at half-time, when the score stood at 1-1. McMillan described how Symon simply sat drinking a cup of tea, offering no thoughts or tactical alterations which might stem the tide of the sweeping Eintracht attacks. Rangers were level at the interval due more to good fortune than anything else, and it was clear that the German pace and power would soon breach the Ibrox defences – and so it proved. Rangers had reached the European Cup semi-finals in spite of poor domestic form, but they did win the Scottish Cup between the two legs of the tie against Eintracht with a 2-0 triumph over Kilmarnock.

There were those, including a certain ten-year-old youngster attending his very first European tie, who believed that the deficit could be overturned. Most certainly, the Scottish Champions could scarcely have had a greater incentive with the final scheduled for Hampden Park.

The second leg would, however, merely underline that the Germans were in a different league as far as athleticism, skill and tactical awareness were concerned. It was Lindner who opened the scoring as early as the eighth minute when he was allowed to advance fully fifty yards with the defence retreating in front of him before playing a one-two with Pfaff and then netting with a twenty-five-yard shot. Just like in Frankfurt, Rangers hit back almost immediately, McMillan equalising three minutes later from a Wilson cross. Eintracht regained the lead in the twentieth minute when Pfaff netted, as in the Waldstadion, with a twenty-yard free-kick, this time with the aid of a deflection. Kress added a third after Niven had blocked a Lindner effort. McMillan reduced the deficit eight minutes into the second half from a Harold Davis pass, but any hopes the home side had of salvaging even this single game evaporated midway through the second half when Erich Meier scored twice in as many minutes. A Wilson backheel from a Millar pass did add a third for the Scots, but Pfaff hammered the final nail in the coffin when he strode imperiously through the centre of the Ibrox defence to make it 6-3. Eintracht were simply much too good for a poor Rangers team, but at least they were a side out of the top drawer of European football, as they undoubtedly demonstrated in that magnificent Hampden final against Real Madrid, despite ultimately losing 7-3. For Rangers, it would be another thirty-three years before they would again compete in the last four of Europe's premier club tournament.

1959/60 European Champions' Cup, first round, first leg
Wednesday 16 September 1959, Ibrox Stadium, Glasgow
Rangers 5 (Baird 2, 1 pen, Millar, Scott, Matthew) Anderlecht 2 (Stockman, De Waele)
Attendance 80,000
Niven; Shearer, Little; Davis, Telfer, Stevenson; Scott, McMillan, Millar, Baird, Matthew

First round, second leg
Wednesday 23 September 1959, Stade Emile Verse, Brussels
Anderlecht 0 Rangers 2 (Matthew, McMillan)
Attendance 40,000
Niven; Shearer, Little; Davis, Telfer, Stevenson; Scott, McMillan, Wilson, Baird,
Matthew
Second round, first leg
Wednesday 11 November 1959, Ibrox Stadium, Glasgow
Rangers 4 (McMillan, Scott, Wilson, Millar) Ruda Hvezda Bratislava 3 (Scherer 2,
Dolinsky)
Attendance 80,000
Niven; Caldow, Little; Davis, Telfer, Stevenson; Scott, McMillan, Millar, Baird,
Wilson
Second round, second leg
Wednesday 18 November 1959, Stadion Tehelne pole, Bratislava
Ruda Hvezda Bratislava 1 (Tichy) Rangers 1 (Scott)
Attendance 60,000
Niven; Shearer, Little; Davis, Telfer, Stevenson; Scott, McMillan, Millar, Baird,
Wilson
Quarter-final, first leg
Wednesday 9 March 1960, Stadion Feyenoord, Rotterdam
Sparta Rotterdam 2 (De Vries 2) Rangers 3 (Wilson, Baird, Murray)
Attendance 50,000
Niven; Caldow, Little; Davis, Paterson, Stevenson; Scott, McMillan, Murray,
Baird, Wilson
Quarter-final, second leg
Wednesday 16 March 1960, Ibrox Stadium, Glasgow
Rangers 0 Sparta Rotterdam 1 (Van Ede)
Attendance 82,587
Ritchie; Caldow, Little; Davis, Paterson, Stevenson; Scott, Baird, Millar, Brand,
Wilson
Quarter-final, decider
Wednesday 30 March 1960, Arsenal Stadium, Highbury
Rangers 3 (Baird 2, Millar) Sparta Rotterdam 2 (Verhoeven, Bosselaar pen)
Niven; Caldow, Little; Davis, Paterson, Stevenson; Scott, McMillan, Millar, Baird,
Wilson
Semi-final, first leg
Wednesday 13 April 1960, Waldstadion, Frankfurt
Eintracht Frankfurt 6 (Pfaff 2, Lindner 2, Stinka, Stein) Rangers 1 (Caldow pen)
Attendance 80,000
Niven; Caldow, Little; Baird, Paterson, Stevenson; Scott, McMillan, Murray,
Millar, Wilson

Semi-final, second leg

Thursday 5 May 1960, Ibrox Stadium, Glasgow

Rangers 3 (McMillan 2, Wilson) Eintracht Frankfurt 6 (Pfaff 2, Meier 2, Lindner, Kress)

Attendance 70,000

Niven; Caldow, Little; Davis, Paterson, Stevenson; Scott, McMillan, Millar, Baird, Wilson

TWO

The Golden Age

That Scottish Cup victory meant that Rangers received an invitation to participate in the inaugural European Cup for National Cup Winners tournament in season 1960/61, with the Ibrox team one of just ten participating, the others being Austria Vienna, Borussia Moenchengladbach, Dinamo Zagreb, Ferencvaros, Fiorentina, Lucerne, Red Star Brno, Vorwarts East Berlin and Wolverhampton Wanderers.

The sparsity of competing clubs was testament to the lack of domestic cup competitions in many European nations – indeed, when the idea was first proposed in 1958, only six associations expressed interest and in 1960 the likes of Belgium, Holland, Poland, Sweden and Turkey had no such tournament, but the immediate success of the inaugural event changed all that. One interesting point to note was that in 1960/61 the Cup-Winners' Cup was organised under the auspices of the Mitropa Cup Committee and not by UEFA, who assumed control the following season when the number of entrants had risen to twenty-three. Similarly, the initial European Champions' Cup tournament of 1955/56 had been instigated by the French newspaper *L'Equippe* – albeit with the permission of FIFA – and of course the forerunner of the UEFA Cup, the Inter-Cities Fairs Cup, was controlled by an independent committee. These details are conveniently overlooked by those pedantic enough to dispute that the 1973 meeting of Rangers and Ajax deserves its rightful recognition as the first of the European Super Cup matches, a statistic which even UEFA acknowledges! The Mitropa Cup, incidentally, was a Central European club competition founded in 1927 encompassing teams from Austria, Czechoslovakia Hungary and Yugoslavia, subsequently joined by entrants from Italy and Switzerland but of course marginalised by the sweeping introduction of the European Champions' Cup in 1956.

Rangers' first opponents in the new competition were Ferencvaros Torna Club of Budapest with the first leg played at Ibrox Stadium on 28 September 1960 with a 36,000 crowd in attendance. The Light Blues had suffered defeat in their two previous European home fixtures to Sparta Rotterdam and Eintracht Frankfurt, and there were many who feared another reversal when, with Ian McMillan having already struck the woodwork, the great Hungarian centre forward Florian Albert created an opening in the seventeenth minute for Orosz to shoot low past an unsighted Billy Ritchie. Ferencvaros were ruthless in defence yet displayed immense skill in attack where the class of both Albert and Dr Mate Fenyvesi shone through, but two goals in five minutes early in the second half sent Rangers into the ascendancy. The first was a Harold Davis header from an Alex Scott free-kick, the second a Jimmy Millar strike following a one-two with Ralph Brand – and it was Millar and Brand who added two more with Friedmansky's strike sandwiched in between to leave Rangers with a two-goal cushion for the return trip to Budapest.

The twin city on the Danube was to prove no jaunt for Rangers, despite the absence of Florian Albert from the home line-up. The Magyars staged the game in the Nepstadion – People's Stadium, the national venue – instead of their own ground Ulloi Ut and Ferencvaros opened at pace, their sweeping attacks throwing the visitors back on their heels, with Orosz again opening the scoring from a Rakosi pass in the eighteenth minute. The marksman then turned provider three minutes into the second half for Friedmansky to level the aggregate score. The toss of a coin loomed until Davie Wilson took advantage of indecision between Horvath and Kiss to net the vital goal on the hour mark.

Rangers were through, but a trip to West Germany just seven months after the Frankfurt debacle at the hands of Eintracht was a daunting prospect, even though the Rangers outfit of 1960/61, having added Jim Baxter, seemed light years removed from their immediate predecessors. Borussia Moenchengladbach were Rangers' opponents this time round, and with the Bokelberg Stadion deemed unsuitable for such a major tie the game was switched to Dusseldorf's Rheinstadion. The Ibrox men buried the memory of Frankfurt with a devastating display of attacking football that overwhelmed their hosts, with Ian McMillan – who was always at home in the European arena – in quite superlative form, creating the first goal after twenty-two minutes with a bewildering run through the heart of the Borussia defence that left four Germans in his wake before squaring the ball for Jimmy Millar to net. Just three minutes later Alex Scott went one better by finishing off his own scintillating run with a left-foot shot. Borussia were offered a clear chance to reduce the deficit with the award of a penalty kick on the half-hour, but Karl Heinz Mullhausen shot straight at George Niven and the chance was lost. The home side, alas, did not take their drubbing in a sportsmanlike manner, with their roughhouse tactics causing the night to be dubbed the 'Battle of the Rhine' by the Scottish Press, but Rangers kept their cool and Ian McMillan rounded off a memorable display with a magnificent shot twelve minutes into the second half. Incidentally, there were old friends present that glorious night in the Rheinstadion – the Eintracht Frankfurt squad who had overwhelmed Rangers just six months earlier. They expressed their amazement at the improvement in Rangers' football after so short a period of time.

If the Ibrox return was a foregone conclusion, few who were present will ever forget it. Of all the glorious nights that enriched the era of the early 1960s, this was arguably the finest. Torrential rain – the worst Glasgow had seen for many years – cascaded down from the heavens and on the field the floodgates opened as early as the second minute when Jim Baxter opened the scoring. By midway through the second half Rangers were eight goals up and coasting, with Ralph Brand achieving the distinction of being the first Ranger to net a European hat-trick. Borussia on this occasion took their defeat like sportsmen and the 38,174 spectators gave both sides a standing ovation at the end. The Ibrox crowd revelled in the slaughter, with both the national anthem and 'Follow Follow' reverberating in the night air.

Rangers were now in the last four, and for the first time in their four European campaigns they faced English opposition in the shape of Wolverhampton Wanderers, FA Cup winners in 1960 and League Champions the two preceding years. Ibrox was bursting at the seams for the first leg, in the spring of 1961, and the 79,229 spectators were witness to a display of grit, determination and raw courage from the Light Blues, who were already severely handicapped by the absence through injury of Ian McMillan and Jimmy Millar, necessitating the selection of centre half Doug Baillie at centre forward. As if that were not bad enough, a leg muscle injury rendered Harold Davis a mere passenger (in the days before substitutes) as early as the ninth minute, handing the initiative to Wolves, who pulverised the home goal, Murray striking the crossbar and both Bobby Shearer and Eric Caldow clearing off the line. Remarkably, just when a Wolves goal seemed inevitable one was scored at the other end when Alex Scott outpaced Ron Flowers to send a twenty-yard shot crashing into the net in the thirty-third minute. Rangers were under extreme pressure throughout the second half, yet held out until the eighty-third minute when Ralph Brand seized on a mistake by Edwin Clamp – in playing the ball across his own area – to net a vital second.

A snowstorm greeted 15,000 Rangers fans at Molineux on 19 April, just four days after England had overwhelmed Scotland 9-3 at Wembley. Rangers caught the eye with a brand new strip – the blue and white 'butcher's stripes'. Wolves piled on the pressure in the first half but the Scots hit on the break to devastating effect two minutes from the interval when Alex Scott converted a Ralph Brand opening. Wolves responded immediately, with Ron Flowers forcing Billy Ritchie into a breathtaking save with a thirty-yard piledriver. Peter Broadbent did level matters on the night midway through the second half following work by Durandt, but the Rangers defence – with Bill Paterson immense at its heart – stood firm to the end and the Light Blues had created history by advancing to the inaugural European Cup-Winners' Cup final.

Wilson in the goalmouth as Ritchie punches over the bar against Wolves at Ibrox.

Rangers faced the formidable barrier of Italian aces Fiorentina while still missing the crucial influence of Jimmy Millar in the two-legged final, and were confronted by a cynical display of body-checking and blatant obstruction throughout the game as the Florence side displayed the dark side of Italian football. Eighty thousand spectators at Ibrox looked on aghast as a basic error in defence presented Gianfranco Petris with a clear opening when Harold Davis' back pass fell woefully short of Billy Ritchie, the Italian presenting his colleague Luigi Milan with a simple chance to open the scoring. Seven minutes later Rangers had a golden opportunity to equalise when they were awarded a penalty as Alberto Orzan swept the feet from Ian McMillan as he weaved his way through the Fiorentina defence. A heated debate on the merits of the award followed between the referee and an Italian coach, not to mention several Fiorentina players, but when the dust had settled Eric Caldow sent the ball well wide of goal with custodian Enrico Albertosi prancing about on the six-yard line! No retake was ordered, and Rangers spent the rest of the evening in frenzied attack, throwing high ball after high ball into a packed defence to no avail, and the die seemed cast in the closing seconds when a muddle between Davis and Shearer gave Milan possession; he played a one-two with Swedish winger Kurt Hamrin before firing into the net for his second goal of the night. In later years, Eric Caldow would rate Hamrin as second only to Gento among the wingers he had faced, and Rangers would have cause to remember his name after the second leg in the Renaissance city of Florence, celebrated as the most beautiful in Italy, where the tie was to be played, uniquely, on a Saturday evening.

The Fiorentina coach was none other than the legendary Hungarian international Nandor Hidegkuti. With Jimmy Millar restored to the ranks, Rangers had every reason for renewed optimism and almost struck an early blow only for the chance to be spurned by Davie Wilson, but that man Milan again struck early when he chested home a Hamrin cross after the Swede had eluded both Baxter and Caldow in the twelfth minute. The Scots at last breached the Florentine defence on the hour when Alex Scott blasted home an eighteen-yard volley after Ralph Brand's shot was blocked by a defender. Inspired by this strike, Rangers piled on the pressure with Jimmy Millar coming perilously close to adding a second and a strong penalty appeal denied when Alex Scott was bowled over, but with the sands of time running out a breakaway by Hamrin saw the winger evade three Rangers defenders on the right, cut along the goal line and crash home a magnificent shot from a tight angle before falling spreadeagled amongst the photographers. Rangers received a standing ovation from the 50,000 spectators in the Stadio Comunale, but to the Italians went the spoils of victory in the shape of the inaugural European Cup-Winners' Cup, and their fans lit bonfires on the darkened terraces as their heroes embarked on a lap of honour to celebrate their triumph. Fiorentina, incidentally, had entered the tournament as beaten finalists in the Italian Cup, having lost to League Champions Juventus 3-2. This feat was to be emulated by Rangers in 1972. Hamrin's winner meant that he finished the season as the competition's joint leading goalscorer alongside Ralph Brand with five goals.

Meanwhile, Rangers had ended the European campaign with precisely the same line-up as had commenced operations. Indeed, eight of that side had been ever-present throughout the competition: Messrs Shearer, Caldow, Davis, Paterson, Baxter (i.e. both full-backs and all three half-backs), Scott, Brand and Wilson.

1960/61 European Cup-Winners' Cup, first round, first leg
Wednesday 28 September 1960, Ibrox Stadium, Glasgow
Rangers 4 (Millar 2, Davis, Brand) Ferencvaros 2 (Orosz, Friedmansky)
Attendance 36,000
Ritchie; Shearer, Caldow; Davis, Paterson, Baxter; Scott, McMillan, Millar, Brand, Wilson
First round, second leg
Wednesday 12 October 1960, Nepstadion, Budapest
Ferencvaros 2 (Orosz, Friedmansky) Rangers 1 (Wilson)
Attendance 25,000
Ritchie; Shearer, Caldow; Davis, Paterson, Baxter; Scott, McMillan, Millar, Brand, Wilson
Quarter-final, first leg
Tuesday 15 November 1960, Rheinstadion, Dusseldorf
Borussia Mönchengladbach 0 Rangers 3 (Millar, Scott, McMillan)
Attendance 50,000
Niven; Shearer, Caldow; Davis, Paterson, Baxter; Scott, McMillan, Millar, Brand, Wilson
Quarter-final, second leg
Wednesday 30 November 1960
Ibrox Stadium, Glasgow
Rangers 8 (Brand 3, Millar 2, Baxter, Davis, Pfeffier o.g.) Borussia Moenchengladbach 0
Attendance 38,174
Niven; Shearer, Caldow; Davis, Paterson, Baxter; Scott, McMillan, Millar, Brand, Wilson
Semi-final, first leg
Wednesday 29 March 1961, Ibrox Stadium, Glasgow
Rangers 2 (Scott, Brand) Wolverhampton Wanderers 0
Attendance 79,229
Ritchie; Shearer, Caldow; Davis, Paterson, Baxter; Scott, Wilson, Baillie, Brand, Hume
Semi-final, second leg
Wednesday 19 April 1961, Molineaux Grounds, Wolverhampton
Wolverhampton Wanderers 1 (Broadbent) Rangers 1 (Scott)
Attendance 45,163
Ritchie; Shearer, Caldow; Davis, Paterson, Baxter; Wilson, McMillan, Scott, Brand, Hume

Final, first leg

Wednesday 17 May 1961, Ibrox Stadium, Glasgow

Rangers 0 Fiorentina 2 (Milan 2)

Attendance 80,000

Ritchie; Shearer, Caldow; Davis, Paterson, Baxter; Wilson, McMillan, Scott,
Brand, Hume

Final, second leg

Saturday 27 May 1961, Stadio Comunale, Firenze

Fiorentina 2 (Milan, Hamrin) Rangers 1 (Scott)

Attendance 50,000

Ritchie; Shearer, Caldow; Davis, Paterson, Baxter; Scott, McMillan, Millar, Brand,
Wilson

Fate has not always been kind to Rangers in UEFA draws, but there were few complaints when the draw for the 1961/62 European Champions' Cup paired the Light Blues with French Champions AS Monaco. There are few more attractive options on the European map than a trip to the Cote d'Azure.

The sun-kissed tax haven of Monaco was the venue, an independent principality of just 195 hectares (thirty-one of which have been entirely reclaimed from the sea) housing a population of some 30,000, only five per cent of whom are local nationals (Monegasques). The ruling royal family, the Grimaldi dynasty, are well known as active supporters of the local club, the Association Sportive de Monaco, who have belied their status as the club with the lowest home attendances in the French Championship by winning the title seven times within the last forty years, the first occasion being in 1961.

Remarkably, out of the four occasions that the Light Blues had been involved in the competition this was the third time that they had met the French Champions in the opening round. The venue was the Stade Louis II, the ground standing literally in the shadow of Monaco's Royal Palace between the railway line and the harbour wall – indeed, Prince Rainier (grandson of the said Louis II) would have had a perfect view of the game from his home atop the adjoining rock face, although he chose to attend in person.

French clubs had acquitted themselves well in the first six years of the European Cup, with Stade Reims twice finalists and OGC Nice twice quarter-finalists, and Monaco had every reason to expect a prolonged run themselves. A key member of the Monaco side to face Rangers, incidentally, was one Michel Hidalgo who had played for Reims in the inaugural 1956 final and who would in later years achieve fame as the French national coach.

A virtuoso first-half display from Jim Baxter dictated proceedings before a 6,024 audience that was modest by European standards but double the average attendance of the host club. Slim Jim had been inspired by the unique setting and the royal presence into producing one of his finest performances in a Rangers jersey.

Indeed, it was Baxter who opened the scoring in the tenth minute when he took possession of the ball deep inside his own half before leaving several opponents in his wake and finishing off a stylish run with a low twenty-yard shot into the net. Unlike many of Rangers' early European opponents, Monaco did not believe in mixing it physically. They were a footballing side who allowed the other team to play as well – a situation which Jim relished. At his best, Baxter was world-class and he relished the big stage. On this occasion he totally dominated play and created a second goal in the twenty-fifth minute when his goal-bound lob was thwarted by Luis Hernandez only for Alex Scott to convert the rebound. Rangers were a class apart and would have at least doubled their lead before the interval were it not for superb goalkeeping by Hernandez. The second half was to be a different story, however. Complacency reared its ugly head amongst the visitors, so great had been their superiority, allowing the Monegasques back into the game, the ever-dangerous and graceful Hess reducing the deficit on the hour with a hook shot and then winning a penalty award when he was sandwiched between Bobby Shearer and Bill Paterson. Billy Ritchie brilliantly blocked Carlier's spot-kick but the Frenchman converted the rebound. Monaco now clearly believed they could snatch a winner, but it was Alex Scott who restored a semblance of sanity to the proceedings when he headed the winning goal with just five minutes remaining.

The Ibrox return attracted 67,501 spectators, and any feeling that the tie had been won in the South of France soon vanished when that man Hess opened the scoring after eighteen minutes. The scoreline remained at 0-1 until the interval but Rangers finally equalised three minutes into the second half when Jim Christie (replacing the injured Jimmy Millar) pounced on a Ralphie Brand flick from Alex Scott's free-kick to net his first goal for the club, and when the centre forward pounced on a weak back pass from Novak to add a second midway through the second half the die seemed cast. Monaco, however, had other ideas and ten minutes later Carlier beat Bobby Shearer wide on the left, his cross being headed home by Hess. The French Champions scented blood and pressed desperately for the third goal which would lead to another match, only to be hit with a classic counterattack in the eighty-first minute when Christie dispossessed Lubo on the halfway line, enabling Alex Scott to race through on a forty-yard run which ended when he rounded goalkeeper Garafalo to score.

Remarkably, Rangers were in action again twenty-four hours later when 20,000 patrons returned to The Stadium to witness a 3-1 home win over East Fife on League Cup business. The home side showed only one change from the Monaco match, Ian McMillan being replaced by a youngster by the name of John Greig who was making just his second first-team appearance.

Rangers found themselves paired with an either/or situation in the second round, a nightmare of a draw that could not have been any worse. The choice lay between Vorwarts East Berlin and Linfield. The East Germans had already won the first leg 3-0 at home, but had been unable to travel to Belfast for the second because they had been refused visas by the Allied Military Command to travel to the United Kingdom for the return match. In 1961 the Cold War was at its peak, with the building of the Berlin Wall just a few months earlier having raised tension to unprecedented heights. John F. Kennedy was President of the United States, Nikita Khrushchev led the Soviet Union and Harold Macmillan was British Prime Minister.

The only option available to the Belfast club was to switch the game to a venue to which the East German club would be able to travel – essentially, in a country that was not a member of NATO, but the financial considerations in such a move would be crippling for the Windsor Park club. The carrot of a tie with Rangers in the next round was obviously an attractive one, with a guaranteed sell-out at Windsor Park, but even if Linfield were able to somehow organise the second leg, the Northern Ireland Champions would still have to overcome that three-goal deficit.

Reluctantly, the Northern Ireland Champions were left with no option but to withdraw from the tournament. Interestingly, there were no penalties imposed by UEFA, although had Linfield opted out before travelling to East Berlin they may well have been hit with a hefty fine as at that stage Vorwarts were still claiming that they would be granted entry visas. UEFA promised Linfield compensation for the loss of gate receipts from the Windsor Park tie, but it took all of six years for the sum of £1,100 to be paid.

The exact same problems encountered by Linfield would obviously apply equally to Rangers – but one important difference was that the Ibrox club had greater financial strength and were prepared to reschedule their home game at a neutral non-NATO venue, in the belief that victory would mean a money-spinning quarter-final tie at Ibrox.

The choice was not an easy one to make. Vienna was one option under consideration, given Rangers' close friendship with SK Rapid that dated back to the 1930s. However, Vienna was a mere 400 miles from East Berlin, and the Ibrox directors determined that their opponents should be obliged to travel at least as far as they themselves would. Scandinavia came under consideration, with Copenhagen a favoured proposal given that Rangers had spent many a close-season break in the city of Hans Christian Anderson, the Little Mermaid and the Tivoli Gardens. Malmö however was the final decision – a location which, as it happened, was a lot closer to East Berlin than Vienna, but, significantly, was much closer to Glasgow than the Austrian capital.

Rangers firstly had to negotiate the away leg, which meant a trip behind the Berlin Wall to the bleak and barren political wasteland of East Berlin. Flying into West Berlin's Templehof Airport, the Ibrox men drove to 'Checkpoint Charlie' at the Freidrichsstrasse where American soldiers on guard duty met them. Documentation was thoroughly examined before the party was cleared to walk across 'no man's land' to the east, where a welcoming reception of Vorwarts' officials awaited them with garlands of flowers. Many Rangers fans of today may be interested to note that amongst the official party were True Blue fans Ross Bowie, Bob Moffat and Joe Walsh.

The Rangers party was accommodated in the Johannashof Hotel on Stalinalle, a showpiece hotel used by Communist party apparatchiks for entertaining VIPs, set amidst a drab concrete landscape. Wherever Rangers went during their few days' visit, 'tour guides' accompanied them – in effect the East German secret police, at that time the 'Vopos', in later years of course being renamed the 'Stasi'.

Soviet tanks, armed and jackbooted policemen and barbed wire entanglements formed a bizarre backdrop to the game, which was to be played on 15 November 1961 at the Stadion Der Walter Ulbricht, named after the infamous East German leader. A near-capacity attendance of 14,268 proved to be both sporting and appreciative of the skill and class of the Scottish Champions, proving that sport can indeed transcend political differences.

Vorwarts caught Rangers by surprise when Kohle strode through the middle after twenty minutes to open the scoring, with goalkeeper Billy Ritchie perhaps at fault, but within sixty seconds the Ibrox men were level when Krampe upended winger Alex Scott. Eric Caldow equalised from the penalty spot.

Rangers took the lead on the stroke of half-time when the majestic Jim Baxter carried the ball deep into enemy territory, ghosted past two defenders and sent a cross into the goalmouth, where Ralph Brand had the simple task of nodding the ball into the net.

Ralphie again had the ball in the net in the second half, but on this occasion the Rangers marksman's effort had ended up there via the side-netting, where a hole in the rigging had caused momentary confusion.

Rangers ended up comfortable winners, despite the narrowness of the margin, and were clear favourites for the Malmö return in seven days' time. A meagre attendance of just 3,012 was present on a cold and damp evening, witnessing a drab game played in a sepulchral atmosphere, the deadlock being broken five minutes before the interval when Davie Wilson's shot was blocked by goalkeeper Spickenagel only for the rebound to be controlled by teenage winger Willie Henderson, who slashed the ball home.

Rangers were well in control, 3-1 ahead on aggregate at the interval, but the weather intervened as fog descended on the Malmö Stadion. The game was held up for half an hour in the hope that visibility would improve, but the Scots were taken aback during this period when they saw their opponents walking past their dressing-room fully clothed. Clearly the East Germans had pre-empted any decision by the referee, and eventually both sets of officials were obliged to go into conference in an effort to resolve the situation. Both clubs were due to fly home the next day, and Vorwarts had the additional problem that their visas were due to expire on the Thursday. One solution suggested by the Berliners – that the tie should be decided on the toss of a coin – was dismissed out of hand by Rangers, and eventually it was agreed that the game would be replayed at 10a.m. the next day.

There were just 1,781 spectators present to see Rangers finally put this most difficult of ties to bed. Granted, it took the Light Blues all of fifty minutes to open the scoring, but in truth they were well on top with Willie Henderson and Ian McMillan outstanding on the right wing. Henderson it was who engineered the opening goal when his cross spun into the net off Kalinke as Ralph Brand was poised to strike. A superb individual effort by Ian McMillan produced goal number two when he waltzed past three defenders before netting with an angular drive from eighteen yards.

Vorwarts reduced the deficit when a Wirth cross was diverted past Billy Ritchie by the unfortunate Eric Caldow, but with ten minutes remaining the 'Wee Prime Minister' struck again from the edge of the box when Jimmy Millar cleverly touched a Davie Wilson cross into his path. Henderson completed the scoring three minutes later when he finished off a Brand–Millar move.

It had cost Rangers an estimated £6,000 to reach the quarter-finals but the Ibrox men were relieved to put the tie behind them. Vorwarts, meanwhile, would face an uncertain future – having originally hailed from Leipzig (where they were founded in 1953) they moved again to Frankfurt an der Oder in 1971, where they remain to this day, although they are now known as FC Victoria 01 following the collapse of both the Berlin Wall and the German Democratic Republic. One East German official in fact failed to return home, interpreter – Karl Ernst Zrem seeking political asylum in the west.

Rangers were in search of a third successive European semi-final when they were paired with Belgian Champions Standard Liege in the last eight. It is fair comment to state that the draw could have been less kind, for there were also clubs of the calibre of holders Benfica, English League and FA Cup double winners Tottenham Hotspur and of course Real Madrid.

Included in the Liege ranks was a certain Johnny Crossan, who had played against the Light Blues for Sparta Rotterdam at the same stage two years earlier. Rangers suffered a late injury blow before the first leg in Liege when captain Eric Caldow dropped out through injury to be replaced by youngster Bobby King – one of three teenagers in the Light Blues' line-up, along with a right-wing combination of Willie Henderson and John Greig. Any advantage Rangers may have expected to have owing to the inexperience of their opponents was thus lost.

The Light Blues found themselves in an intimidating atmosphere; the Stade de Sclessin was a tightly packed enclosure situated beside the River Meuse, surrounded by steelworks and a slag heap, underlining the status of Liege as an industrial city.

Standard took the initiative on a heavy pitch with direct football, played with great speed and skill, opening the scoring after six minutes when Billy Ritchie parried a fierce Istvan Sztani shot straight to Roger Claessen, who easily converted.

Rangers *v.* Liege at Ibrox. A cross from Scott passes the post.

Davie Wilson restored equality in the twentieth minute following a solo run from a Jimmy Millar pass, but the home side had regained the initiative by the interval courtesy of Crossan's twenty-yard diagonal shot. Both teams were introduced to Prince Albert of Belgium before the start of a second half that would be played in conditions of such fierce wind and rain that the proceedings were rendered almost unplayable. Crossan struck again six minutes after the restart when aerial uncertainty at the heart of the Scots' defence allowed Szanti to outjump Bill Paterson, his downward header allowing the Irishman to volley home despite Ritchie's valiant effort, touching the ball onto a post. Rangers were right up against it – even more so in the fifty-fourth minute when Joseph Vliers' free-kick deflected off Harry Davis and into the net, again via an upright.

Standard Liege should not have presented a huge obstacle to the Light Blues but defensive errors had gifted the Belgians four goals. Their pace and skill exposed Rangers' lack of preparation. The Scottish Champions had received no breaks in Liege, but it was still a bad result, and the three-goal deficit would be difficult to recover.

A 76,730 crowd for the return leg at Ibrox saw the home side besiege the Belgian goal from the start. A night of fire and fury saw Standard pack their goal. Ralph Brand opened the scoring after twenty-eight minutes, but when Ian McMillan's twenty-yard effort came crashing back off the crossbar in the fifty-seventh minute the visitors began to slow down the furious pace to frustrate the Scots, who had two strong penalty claims waved aside by the referee. The spot-kick, when it finally arrived in the eighty-eighth minute, was converted by Caldow – alas, too late.

It is a measure of how far Rangers' reputation has plummeted during the past forty-five years that this loss at the quarter-final stage was regarded as an early exit after runs in the two seasons immediately preceding this one that had taken them to the final and semi-final respectively. Rangers had lacked the skill to unlock the Liege defence, due in no small part to the absence of Willie Henderson, who failed to turn up in time for the game, having spent too long in the snooker rooms at Glasgow's Mitchell Street! Standard's European campaign was halted abruptly in the semi-finals by the mighty Real Madrid (4-0, 2-0).

1961/62 European Champions' Cup, first round, first leg

Wednesday 5 September 1961, Stade Louis II, Monaco

AS Monaco 2 (Hess, Carlier) Rangers 3 (Scott 2, Baxter)

Attendance 6,024

Ritchie; Shearer, Caldow; Davis, Paterson, Baxter; Scott, McMillan, Millar, Brand, Wilson

First round, second leg

Tuesday 11 September 1961, Ibrox Stadium, Glasgow

Rangers 3 (Christie 2, Scott) AS Monaco 2 (Hess 2)

Attendance 67,501

Ritchie; Shearer, Caldow; Davis, Paterson, Baxter; Scott, McMillan, Christie, Brand, Wilson

Second round, first leg

Wednesday 15 November 1961, Stadion Der Walter Ulbricht, East Berlin

ASK Vorwarts Berlin 1 (Kohle) Rangers 2 (Caldow pen, Brand)

Attendance 14,268

Ritchie; Shearer, Caldow; Davis, Paterson, Baxter; Scott, McMillan, Millar, Brand, Wilson

Second round, second leg

Wednesday 22 November 1961, Malmö Stadion

Rangers 1 (Henderson) ASK Vorwarts Berlin 0

Attendance 3,012

(Match abandoned after forty-five minutes due to adverse weather conditions)

Thursday 23 November 1961, Malmö Stadion (match restaged)

Rangers 4 (McMillan 2, Henderson, Kalinke o.g.) ASK Vorwarts Berlin 1 (Caldow o.g.)

Ritchie; Shearer, Caldow; Davis, Paterson, Baxter; Henderson, McMillan, Millar, Brand, Wilson

Attendance 1,781

Quarter-final, first leg
Wednesday 7 February 1962, Stade de Sclessin, Liege
Royal de Standard Liege 4 (Crossan 2, Claessen, Vliers) Rangers 1 (Wilson)
Attendance 35,891
Ritchie; Shearer, King; Davis, Paterson, Baxter; Henderson, Greig, Millar, Brand,
Wilson
Quarter-final, second leg
Wednesday 14 February 1962, Ibrox Stadium, Glasgow
Rangers 2 (Brand, Caldow pen) Royal de Standard Liege 0
Attendance 76,730
Ritchie; Shearer, Caldow; Davis, Baillie, Baxter; Scott, McMillan, Millar, Brand,
Wilson

Rangers returned the following season to the European Cup-Winners' Cup,
the tournament having by now been expanded to twenty-five entrants under
the control of UEFA while Dundee qualified for the European Champions' Cup
for, to date at least, the only time in the club's history. The Light Blues were
confronted with a daunting prospect, their first-round opponents being Sevilla
Futbol Club of Spain, beaten finalists (1-2) to the mighty, double-winning Real
Madrid in 1961/62, whilst Rangers had secured their qualification with a 2-0 win
over St Mirren in the Scottish Cup final. Any Spanish club would be regarded
as formidable in those halcyon days of the early 1960s – just two years earlier
Scottish football had been awestruck at the majestic performance of Real Madrid
at Hampden, while local rivals Atletico Madrid had succeeded Fiorentina as Cup-
Winners' Cup Champions in 1962.

Ibrox Stadium welcomed 60,500 spectators who would witness one of Rangers'
finest European nights, inspired by a devastating 'will o' the wisp' display from
Willie Henderson, whose mazy right-wing runs created two goals for Jimmy
Millar in the opening fifteen minutes. Sevilla were rocked, and did not hesitate
to attempt to impose their will with displays of bad temper and body-checking
– a portent of what lay ahead of Rangers in southern Spain, but the tie seemed
secure midway through the second half when the Scots struck twice inside a
minute through the old double act of Millar and Brand.

September in the south of Spain – then as now – is intensely hot, even with
a late-night kick-off as Rangers faced three weeks later. The Estadio Sanchez
Pizjuan of 1962 was just four years old, but incomplete – financial problems, as
always, having disrupted construction. Not until 1975 would the finished arena
that hosted the memorable 1982 World Cup semi-final between France and West
Germany be ready.

A crucial factor for any team facing an away European tie in a hostile setting
– even one with a four-goal lead – is to avoid the loss of an early goal, yet that
is exactly what happened when Argentinian Jose Dieguez opened the scoring

Millar scores Rangers' first goal in the tie against Sevilla.

Gers' second goal, also scored by Millar (out of shot).

after just six minutes. Rangers were now under siege, yet managed to weather the storm and gain a measure of control as the game wore on, slowing the pace in the intense heat. Enrique Mateos added a second in the fifty-fourth minute, but Sevilla became more and more frustrated as time wore on. Both Mateos and right-winger D'Arcy Canario had experienced European success with Real Madrid – indeed Canario had played at Hampden in 1960 – but this was light years removed from those glory nights, with Rangers' walking wounded reading more like a war report than a sporting occasion: Jim Baxter, who had secured the crucial control of midfield, was a constant target for the hatchet men, at one stage being knocked onto the track, blood spurting from a mouth wound, while three Sevilla players rained blows down on him. Ronnie McKinnon was bitten on the ear, John Greig and Davie Wilson were both head-butted and finally, with just two minutes remaining, all hell broke loose when all twenty-two players on the field seemed to become involved in running battles across the pitch, with Harold Davis at one stage rescuing Willie Henderson from a beating. The Portuguese referee was left with little alternative but to abandon the game – but the result stood and Rangers were through to the next round, where in all probability they were more than a little relieved, after all their trials and tribulations, to be facing Tottenham Hotspur.

Goalkeeper Mut denies a young John Greig at Ibrox against Sevilla.

'The Battle of Britain' was decided at White Hart Lane as Spurs took advantage of Rangers' defensive frailties in the air; four of the five goals came from corner kicks as Billy Ritchie and Ronnie McKinnon were exposed. Tottenham opened the scoring as early as the fifth minute when Scottish inside forward John White headed home a Jimmy Greaves corner. Four minutes later, the Ibrox men equalised when Ralph Brand released Davie Wilson down the left, the winger's cross being parried by home goalkeeper Bill Brown into the path of Willie Henderson, who netted from close range. Greaves made it 2-1 in the twenty-third minute direct from a corner kick, then Les Allen struck thirteen minutes later with a header from Terry Medwin's cross despite the valiant efforts of Bobby Shearer to clear off the line. Billy Ritchie denied both Greaves and Allen, but the roof was falling in on Rangers when Allen's shot was deflected into his own net by Shearer in the forty-first minute. A faint hope was restored before the interval when Jimmy Millar headed home a Henderson cross, and the visitors restarted on the offensive, Scottish international goalkeeper Bill Brown making a superb save from Wilson. The second half, however, was all Spurs; they demonstrated some superb flowing football, with wing-halves Danny Blanchflower and Dave Mackay dovetailing to perfection with inside forwards White and Greaves. Gers' goalkeeper Billy Ritchie was outstanding in this period, with notable saves from Mackay, Allen, Greaves and Cliff Jones. Maurice Norman, however, did add a fifth in the seventy-eighth minute when he prodded home yet another Greaves corner.

This tie may even have been won and lost before kick-off, when Rangers manager Scot Symon held his one and only team talk, which lasted all of eight minutes, consisting of an analysis of how good every individual Tottenham player was! Any hopes of salvaging the tie were killed stone dead in the return, when Jimmy Greaves scored a wonder goal in the eighth minute when he strode through the home defence following a flick by Bobby Smith almost on the half-way line, ghosting past Harold Davis, Ronnie McKinnon and Eric Caldow. It was one of the greatest goals ever seen at Ibrox, and it silenced the old ground. Ralphie Brand headed the equaliser from a Henderson cross in the forty-seventh minute, the culmination of a move started by Caldow deep in his own half, but within three minutes Smith put his side back in front from a White pass. Rangers fought back once again, with the capacity crowd roaring them on. Brand struck the crossbar, then Wilson's seventy-fourth-minute free-kick levelled matters again and Rangers pressed for the third goal that would at least salvage some pride on the night. Undeservedly, however, when the goal did come in the last minute it was Smith's header from a Mackay cross that won the game.

Tottenham had been worthy winners over the two legs, but they demonstrated their appreciation of the opposition when they lined up to applaud Rangers off the park at the final whistle. The Londoners went on to become the first British club to win a European trophy, with a convincing 5-1 triumph over Atletico Madrid in Rotterdam.

1962/63 European Cup-Winners' Cup, first round, first leg
Wednesday 5 September 1962, Ibrox Stadium, Glasgow
Rangers 4 (Millar 3, Brand) Sevilla 0
Attendance 60,500
Ritchie; Shearer, Caldow; Davis, McKinnon, Baxter; Henderson, Greig, Millar,
Brand, Wilson
First round, second leg
Wednesday 26 September 1962, Estadio Sanchez Pizjuan, Sevilla
Sevilla 2 (Dieguez, Mateos) Rangers 0
Attendance 25,000
Ritchie; Shearer, Caldow; Davis, McKinnon, Baxter; Henderson, Greig, Millar,
Brand, Wilson
Second round, first leg
Wednesday 31 October 1962, White Hart Lane, London
Tottenham Hotspur 5 (White, Greaves, Allen, Norman, Shearer o.g.) Rangers 2
(Henderson, Millar)
Attendance 58,859
Ritchie; Shearer, Caldow; Davis, McKinnon, Baxter; Henderson, McMillan, Millar,
Brand, Wilson
Second round, second leg
Tuesday 11 December 1962, Ibrox Stadium, Glasgow
Rangers 2 (Brand, Wilson) Tottenham Hotspur 3 (Smith 2, Greaves)
Attendance 80,000
Ritchie; Shearer, Caldow; Davis, McKinnon, Baxter; Henderson, McMillan, Millar,
Brand, Wilson

In the early 1960s no club provided more glamorous opposition than the great
Real Madrid – and when Rangers drew the Spanish giants in the opening round
of the 1963/64 competition a full house was guaranteed, so much so that the
Rangers directors controversially increased admission prices, with the terracing
being set at 10s. The increase in admission charges did not deter a near-capacity
crowd of 81,215, thus setting a precedent of increased prices for decades to come.

Veteran superstars Alfredo Di Stefano, Ferenc Puskas and Francisco Gento were
all still there. Rangers were well on top throughout the Ibrox game without being
able to penetrate the packed Real defence. Ralph Brand shot into the side netting
from a Davie Wilson cutback in the twelfth minute, and struck the inside of a post
with a back header in the second half, but chances were few and far between,
with goalkeeper Jose Araquistain dominant throughout. The Spanish Champions
remained composed and unbowed, however, orchestrated by the peerless Di
Stefano. The only goal of the game arrived in the eighty-seventh minute, and it
was a classic strike from the 'Galloping Major', who started the move in his own
half with a sweeping pass to Gento out on the left. The Real captain sped down

Battle of Britain 1962 – Rangers *v.* Tottenham Hotspur. Henry heads clear from Millar, with Brand, Baker and Blanchflower looking on.

the wing before curling a cross around Shearer for Puskas to meet on the volley from the edge of the box; the ball flashed past Ritchie and into the net.

The Estadio Bernabeu is amongst the most intimidating and atmospheric arenas in the global game – yet when Rangers entered that cauldron in front of a 90,000 audience they did so with a forward line of youngsters. Davie Wilson had suffered a broken leg between the two ties, but the absence of Ian McMillan, Jimmy Millar and Ralph Brand was inexplicable.

However, Rangers, wearing all blue, should have opened the scoring in the first minute when a Shearer cross found Jim Forrest who, caught by surprise, shot wide. That chance would prove to be virtually the only one of the game for the visitors, for this was a night when the maestros of Madrid turned in a virtuoso performance reminiscent of their glory days. The great Puskas it was who found the net as early as the fourth minute, taking a cross from Gento on his chest before striking a powerful drive home via the underside of the crossbar. Nine minutes later it was 2-0 when Puskas body-swerved the entire Rangers defence before squaring for Macedo Evaristo to net. Gento's goal, in the twentieth minute, came from all of thirty yards, the swerve totally deceiving Ritchie. Four minutes later it was four when Puskas, from the same distance, sent an absolute screamer home from an Evaristo cross.

Somehow, Rangers survived until the interval without further loss, but within four minutes of the restart Puskas completed his hat-trick with a grounder from all of forty yards. Thankfully there was no further scoring until the eightieth minute when Antonio Ruiz made it six from an inch-perfect pass from the majestic Alfredo Di Stefano.

The result is to date Rangers' heaviest defeat in a single European fixture, but at least the Ibrox men had the consolation of knowing that they had witnessed perhaps the last great performance of that superb Real Madrid side, who would go on to reach that campaign's final, going down 1-3 to Internazionale in Vienna.

1963/64 European Champions' Cup, first round, first leg
Wednesday 25 September 1963, Ibrox Stadium, Glasgow
Rangers 0 Real Madrid 1 (Puskas)
Attendance 81,215
Ritchie; Shearer, Provan; Greig, McKinnon, Baxter; Henderson, McLean, Forrest, Brand, Wilson
First round, second leg
Wednesday 9 October 1963, Estadio Bernabeu, Madrid
Real Madrid 6 (Puskas 3, Evaristo, Gento, Ruiz) Rangers 0
Attendance 90,000
Ritchie; Shearer, Provan; Greig, McKinnon, Baxter; Henderson, Willoughby, Forrest, McLean, Watson

That season of 1963/64 saw the Light Blues annexe the 'Triple Crown' – or Treble – for a second occasion and that triumph, together with the following campaign's European run, would prove to be amongst the last 'hurrahs' of the great Rangers team of the early 1960s.

Crevna Zvezda Beograd (or Red Star Belgrade) were as tough an opponent as one could possibly have foreseen when the first round draw was made. Rated as one of the finest teams in Europe, they had won seven championships in their short history – having been founded as recently as 1945 following the liberation of their country – and had reached the semi-final of the Champions' Cup in 1957, losing by a solitary goal to Fiorentina. It was Rangers' first ever clash with a Yugoslavian side, with 77,669 present at Ibrox for the first leg. The Light Blues started in impressive style with Ralph Brand opening the scoring in the tenth minute following a superb defence-splitting move between Jim Baxter and Davie Wilson. At times the home side threatened to steamroll the Serbs in the first half, with John Greig twice thundering shots against the crossbar, Wilson also hitting the inside of a post.

A 1-0 scoreline at the interval scarcely indicated the Scots' level of dominance, but shortly after the restart Jim Forrest prodded the ball home from close range from a Wilson cutback, the winger's pace having caught out the Red Star defence

Rangers *v.* Real Madrid. Brand leaps in the air as the ball goes over the bar. Also in the picture are Casado, Isidro, goalkeeper Ariquistain and, in the background, Santamaria.

as he chased a Baxter pass. A loss of concentration cost Rangers dear on fifty-five minutes, however, when Dragan Djazic netted from six yards, and suddenly it was an entirely different game as the visitors took control, Zvezdan Cebinac hitting a post. Now it was Red Star's turn to create and miss chances. There was to be a further twist in the tail when in the dying seconds Baxter, more in desperation than anything else, swung a long, high ball into the goalmouth where goalkeeper Vlada Dujkovic misjudged the flight of the ball, allowing Brand to net.

There were many shrewd judges who believed that a 3–1 lead was a tenuous one to take to Belgrade, given the quality demonstrated by the Serbs in Glasgow, and when one week later Rangers travelled east a tempestuous time awaited them. The Light Blues were under siege from the opening seconds, with the home side striking the crossbar twice and the post once. A goal just had to come, so intense was the pressure and after thirty-two minutes a mistake by Billy Ritchie presented Red Star with the opener, as he misjudged a forty-yard lob from Borivoje Kostic, dropping the ball at the feet of Zoran Prlincevic who stabbed the ball over the line. It was no more than they deserved – yet within eight minutes Rangers had equalised when, following a corner, Greig's lob from the edge of the box found the net via an upright. Undaunted, Red Star renewed their pressure after the interval but for twenty minutes the visitors held out, the

Forrest and Brand of Rangers go up for a high cross watched by Red Star keeper Dujkovic.

dam finally being breached when Kostic scored with a superb header; within two minutes the aggregate scores were level when Prlincevic netted. A glorious strike from Vojislav Melic after seventy-seven minutes appeared to signal the end for Rangers, but just as at Ibrox there was last-minute drama to follow when a Wilson corner was misjudged by Dujkovic, allowing Forrest to head against the crossbar. McKinnon's flying header from the rebound found the roof of the net.

A third game was required – with the venue of Highbury obviously suiting the Scots, although the prime consideration for Red Star would no doubt have been a financial one, with a half share of a healthy attendance generating welcome sterling currency for the Eastern European club.

Fixture congestion meant a delay of almost two months before the play-off could take place, with the vast majority of the 34,428 crowd being either exiled Scots or Rangers' massive travelling support and it was the Light Blues who took control from the opening minutes with Jim Baxter and Jimmy Millar both outstanding in the middle of the park. The opening goal arrived in the twelfth minute when a Brand corner was headed on by Millar for Forrest to net. Red Star came surging back for Djazic to strike the crossbar but Forrest added a second when he prodded home the loose ball after Dujkovic had parried a Brand shot. Rangers were now in supreme command, their skill and class underlined on

Red Star score in Belgrade in 1964 with Billy Ritchie and Bobby Shearer left on the ground. Davie Provan, Ron McKinnon and John Greig are also pictured.

seventy-three minutes when Baxter released Brand with a superb through-ball, allowing the forward to score with a controlled shot off Dujkovic. Milan Kop's header two minutes later was a mere consolation. Rapid Vienna – old friends of the Light Blues from the 1930s – provided the opposition in the next round with, once again, the first leg at Ibrox. They held the distinction of being the first foreign club side ever to visit Ibrox – a 3-3 draw being the outcome on 21 January 1933 before 56,000 spectators.

Rapid had a considerable European pedigree – semi-finalists in season 1960/61 when they fell to eventual winners Benfica, having in earlier campaigns taken both Real Madrid and AC Milan to three matches. Indeed the early history of the European Cup might have been entirely different had Rapid not succumbed to base and tempting gold in the form of a £25,000 bribe to agree that the 1956/57 second round play-off should take place at Real's home ground of Chamartin and not on neutral ground. Real duly won; however, what is fascinating if pointless is the fact that had the 'away goals' rule been in operation then the Spanish aristocrats would have been eliminated.

It had taken Rangers three games to negotiate the opening round while the Austrian Champions made more comfortable progress in defeating Shamrock Rovers twice (3-0, 2-0). Rangers welcomed Rapid to Ibrox on 18 November 1964 – the third visit by this particular club to the Stadium.

Domestic form was unusually grim for the Govan side as they prepared to welcome old friends – only thirteen points had been accumulated from the opening twelve League fixtures and Rangers were trailing badly in the title race. This was perhaps a factor in the disappointing attendance, only 50,788 spectators, at the time the lowest crowd for a European Champions' Cup match at Ibrox.

Rapid threw up a defensive barrier from the start of the match, an almost impenetrable wall which wave after wave of home attacks failed to breach until the fifty-fifth minute when Jim Baxter placed a superb pass inside Josef Hoeltl for Davie Wilson to race onto and shoot past Lubomir Veres from close range. Rangers were continually frustrated by the visitors' offside trap and were unable to build on that narrow lead.

The old city of Vienna – one of the most historic in Europe – was the destination for a Rangers side who had won two successive League games since that first leg, restoring some credibility to their domestic form. The city of Strauss, the Blue Danube and 'The Third Man' were rightly regarded as some of the great attractions of Central Europe, but Rangers were here on business guarding a precarious 1-0 lead to take into the return which had been moved from Rapid's own ground, the Pfarrwiese or Rapidplatz, to the Wiener Stadion, more commonly known (certainly amongst foreigners) as the Prater, the park in which the national stadium stands. A massive crowd of 69,272 spectators packed the Prater, an intimidating arena regarded as something of a graveyard for visiting sides. The Austrian winter had arrived with a vengeance – the game was played on 8 December – and the heavy snow had to be cleared from the pitch before the game could start on an icy pitch. The Scots adopted a cautious approach from the kick-off with Jimmy Millar dropping deep, but gradually the great Jim Baxter began to impose his authority on the game, retaining possession in a bid to frustrate the offside trap which Rapid had so perfected at Ibrox. Baxter struck with perfect precision and timing in the nineteenth minute, waltzing past three opponents before releasing Jim Forrest with a perfectly weighted pass to enable the striker to use his pace to great effect and blast the ball home beyond the reach of Lubomir Veres.

Rangers had struck a massive blow in their bid to reach the last eight. Rapid pressed desperately in search of an equaliser but the Ibrox defence stood firm on a quagmire of a pitch. Tempers flared and the atmosphere was fraught as the minutes ticked away with Rangers in command; the outcome was sealed ten minutes into the second half when the Light Blues struck with a classic counter-attack, seventeen-year-old Willie Johnston making a lightning break from his own half, evading three opponents before cutting the ball back for Davie Wilson to hammer home. The tie was won and Rangers were on the brink of one of their greatest ever results in Europe when tragedy struck in the closing seconds. The mercurial Baxter – at his world-class best on that afternoon – had entertained even the home support with his superb football; at one point he had coolly broken up an attack

Rangers *v*. Rapid Vienna 1964. Davie Wilson nets the only goal at Ibrox.

in his own penalty area, strolled past the Rapid forwards, then chipped the ball into the arms of his goalkeeper. There were just twenty seconds left for play on the giant clock inside the Wiener Stadion when 'Slim Jim' took the ball for a walk yet again on the heavy pitch, toying with the opposition as he alone could, only to be caught from behind with a late tackle by Walter Skocik, a totally dispirited figure in the vertical green-and-white stripes of Rapid who had been chasing shadows all night. The Ranger was caught just above the ankle, his leg fractured, and in the twinkling of an eye the Light Blues' greatest triumph had turned to disaster. Rangers' display that afternoon had been so stunning that, with a fit Baxter, they could that season have become the first British club to win the European Cup. A dream died in the Vienna snow that afternoon. The following summer Jim Baxter left Rangers for Sunderland and would arguably never again be the player he was that afternoon in the Prater Park. The club too would take perhaps twenty years to recover from his loss.

Rangers were through to the last eight – but the draw could not have been more difficult, pairing them as it did with the World Champions and European Cup holders Internazionale Milano. In 1965 there was no fixed calendar for European ties, competing clubs being allowed to negotiate suitable dates amongst them-selves, provided certain deadlines were adhered to. Inter very cleverly insisted on early dates for the two games with Rangers, thus nullifying any prospect of 'Slim Jim' being available. Manager Scot Symon had allowed himself to be outflanked by the wily Argentinian coach Helenio Herrera in the scheduling of the two games with 17 February and 3 March selected; clubs were allowed until 20 March to play the games, by which time Baxter would certainly have returned. A formidable task awaited Scot Symon's team – Herrera had achieved outstanding success both with the San Siro club and previously with Barcelona. He had built a team of all the talents in the fashion capital of Europe – attacking full-back Giacinto Facchetti, gifted inside forward Sandro Mazzola and winger Mario Corso were, together with Luis Suarez, midfield general and club captain, players of the highest class. Suarez in particular was Herrera's lieutenant on the field of play, the very fulcrum around which Inter's system revolved – he would be desperately missed when absent through injury in the 1967 Lisbon final.

Inter were at their very peak, yet in the first leg played in Milan the Ibrox men demonstrated composure and discipline throughout the first half, frustrating the World Champions who had pressed constantly without ever threatening Billy Ritchie's goal. The roof fell in on Rangers in the opening minutes of the second half, when ill luck and misfortune combined with a loss of concentration allowed Inter to run riot. The dam was breached after forty-eight minutes when Suarez took advantage of a cruel deflection off Jimmy Millar to volley home.

Sixty seconds later it was 2-0, and again the Italians received the break of the ball

Internazionale keeper Sarti rises to deny Jimmy Millar. Jim Forrest and George McLean are also in the picture.

– Corso, captain in place of the injured Armando Picchi, saw a speculative shot that was heading well wide deflected off the head of Joachin Peiro and past the helpless Ritchie. Rangers were rocking now and, unbelievably, straight from the kick-off the cup holders were on the attack again, Peiro taking full advantage of a loss of concentration in the visitors' defence to hit a dipping fifteen-yard shot into the net.

Inter appeared as good as in the semi-finals, for surely no club could pull back a three-goal deficit against the Italian giants, yet Rangers somehow regained their composure and should have reduced the deficit on the hour, Jim Forrest shooting wide of the target when clean through. The centre would not be denied, however, and four minutes later he rifled home a Wilson Wood pass to make it 3-1.

Such a deficit, whilst not insurmountable, was certainly formidable against the masters of the art of cattenachio (or bolt system). Rangers got off to a stunning start in the Ibrox return two weeks later on a bitterly cold night, visiting goalkeeper Giuliano Sarti allowing a Roger Hynd drive to rebound off his chest into the path of Forrest, who converted the rebound from close range.

The Italians demonstrated their experience, however, by shutting up shop after that early shock, with sweeper Picchi outstanding in central defence and the Light Blues ineffective on the flanks where the threat of Willie Henderson was negated by Facchetti. Rangers seldom looked like levelling the aggregate score until the eighty-fourth minute when George McLean's eighteen-yard shot from a Henderson cross slammed back off the crossbar with Sarti helpless.

A 2-0 win would have meant a third match in Brussels, but time ran out on the Scottish Champions and they were left with only dreams and regrets for the absence of Baxter. Even without the great man they had come within inches of taking the World Champions to a third game.

Internazionale, meanwhile, to no one's surprise, went on to retain the trophy when they defeated Benfica 1-0 in a final controversially staged in their very own Stadio San Siro, and two years later Glasgow's second club defeated an ageing Inter Milan missing four of their most important players, including their captain Luis Suarez, in Lisbon.

1964/65 European Champions' Cup, first round, first leg
Wednesday 2 September 1964, Ibrox Stadium, Glasgow
Rangers 3 (Brand 2, Forrest) Crevna Zvezda Beograd 1 (Djazic)
Attendance 77,669
Ritchie; Hynd, Provan; Greig, McKinnon, Baxter; Henderson, McLean, Forrest, Brand, Wilson
First round, second leg
Wednesday 9 September 1964, Stadion Crevna Zvezda, Beograd
Crevna Zvezda Beograd 4 (Prlincevic 2, Kostic, Melic) Rangers 2 (Greig, McKinnon)
Attendance 42,939

Ritchie; Shearer, Provan; Greig, McKinnon, Baxter; Henderson, Millar, Forrest, Brand, Wilson

First round, third leg

Wednesday 4 November 1964, Arsenal Stadium, Highbury

Rangers 3 (Forrest 2, Brand) Crevna Zvezda Beograd 1 (Kop)

Attendance 34,428

Ritchie; Provan, Caldow; Greig, McKinnon, Wood; Brand, Millar, Forrest, Baxter, Johnston

Second round, first leg

Wednesday 18 November 1964, Ibrox Stadium, Glasgow

Rangers 1 (Wilson) Rapid Vienna 0

Attendance 50,788

Ritchie; Provan, Caldow; Greig, McKinnon, Wood; Wilson, Millar, Forrest, Baxter, Johnston

Second round, second leg

Tuesday 8 December 1964, Wiener Stadion, Vienna

Rapid Vienna 0 Rangers 2 (Forrest, Wilson)

Attendance 69,272

Ritchie; Provan, Caldow; Greig, McKinnon, Wood; Wilson, Millar, Forrest, Baxter, Johnston

Quarter-final, first leg

Wednesday 17 February 1965, Stadio San Siro, Milano

Internazionale Milano 3 (Peiro 2, Suarez) Rangers 1 (Forrest)

Attendance 49,520

Ritchie; Provan, Caldow; Wood, McKinnon, Greig; Henderson, Millar, Forrest, Brand, Wilson

Quarter-final, second leg

Wednesday 3 March 1965, Ibrox Stadium, Glasgow

Rangers 1 (Forrest) Internazionale Milano 0

Attendance 77,206

Ritchie; Provan, Caldow; Greig, McKinnon, Hynd; Henderson, Millar, Forrest, McLean, Johnston

There would be no European campaign in season 1965/66 for the Ibrox men, but the dramatic 1966 Scottish Cup final replay triumph over Jock Stein's Celtic ensured qualification for the European Cup-Winners' Cup in 1966/67. The Oval in the heart of East Belfast was as welcoming a venue as one would find anywhere in Europe as far as Rangers were concerned – even with ex-Celt John Colrain in charge of Glentoran as player-coach. Fifty-five thousand spectators packed the old ground on 27 September 1966 with the visitors enjoying as much support as the host club. Colrain had been dismissive of the Light Blues – yet few doubted that Rangers would enjoy a comfortable win at the Oval and so it seemed when

George McLean opened the scoring in the fifteenth minute, yet on a night when Rangers attacked throughout, the Glens treated the match as a typical cup-tie, packing their defence, hustling and harrying their more illustrious opponents, and incredibly striking with literally the last kick of the ninety minutes. Ironically the goal was created by two Scots, Colrain releasing Billy Sinclair whose eighteen-yard shot went in off a post. A 1-1 draw in an away European tie is hardly a disastrous result, yet that is how almost everyone regarded the outcome. Rangers had spent £100,000 on Alex and Dave Smith and the draw with the Irish part-timers was viewed as an embarassment, yet one year later the mighty Benfica could only overcome Glentoran on away goals (introduced, for better or worse, in 1965/66) in the European Champions' Cup.

Nevertheless, the Ibrox return offered the Scots the chance to make amends and an early goal by Willie Johnston eased the pressure. Rangers eventually coasted home with further strikes from Dave Smith, Dennis Setterington and George McLean. The next round would be something else again – the cup holders Borussia Dortmund, who had won the trophy just six months earlier at Hampden Park with a 2-1 triumph over English League Champions Liverpool. The Germans were formidable opposition to say the least. Included in their ranks were three who had played in the World Cup final at Wembley that summer – namely forwards Sigi Held and Lothar Emmerich, together with goalkeeper Hans Tilkowski.

A night of drama in the Ibrox first leg centred around an outrageous refereeing blunder that gifted the Germans a vital away goal. Rangers had taken the initiative from the whistle, opening the scoring after just ten minutes when Kai Johansen of all people netted with a low drive from a wide angle. The home side were in command, but were shaken to the core by one of the most controversial decisions ever seen at the stadium. Held it was whose penetrating run down the left was partially cleared as far as Gerd Peehs, some thirty yards out. As the full-back advanced with the ball, the German centre, whose momentum had carried him behind the goal, deliberately stayed off the field of play to avoid being offside. Peehs' shot was deflected wide by John Greig, and was going out for a corner when Held incredibly returned to the field of play, gathered the ball, and squared for Horat Trimhold to net. Unbelievably, Spanish referee Daniel Zariquiegui awarded a goal, despite the home side's heated protests. These protests were fully justified on not one but two counts: namely that Held had been guilty of ungentlemanly conduct in deliberately staying off the park then returning whilst play was in motion without the referee's permission, and because he was certainly offside when the ball reached him.

Distinguished and respected former referee Jack Mowatt, who had refereed the 1960 European Champions' Cup final just six years earlier, observed on television later that evening that had he been in charge he would have disallowed the goal and cautioned Held for ungentlemanly conduct. The concession of that equaliser was a body blow to the Ibrox men, who found themselves consistently thwarted by the massive presence of the dominating Wolfgang Paul at the heart of the Borussia defence, but in the dying minutes a dipping header by Alex Smith from a Willie Johnston cross deceived Bernard Wessel to give Rangers a narrow but vital lead.

The Light Blues had been the better side at Ibrox, but the cup holders had every reason to be confident of victory in their own Stadion Rote Erde. On a night of drama and passion, however, Rangers produced one of their finest European performances in front of a capacity 40,000 crowd, defending resolutely against wave after wave of Borussia attacks with John Greig and Ronnie McKinnon outstanding at the heart of the visitors' defence. Even the loss of midfielder Bobby Watson with a broken ankle after just thirty-eight minutes, having been quite deliberately kicked off the ball by Emmerich, failed to daunt the visitors. The ten men produced a heroic backs-to-the wall stand with Alex Smith, an experienced and versatile player of no little quality, dropping deep to cover for the loss of Watson. Indeed, Jim Forrest missed the best chance of the night when, clean through from a Johnston pass, he somehow shot wide with the goal at his mercy – a miss that might have been costly, for Gers' goalkeeper Norrie Martin made a crucial save in the dying seconds from Reinhard Libuda, scorer of the winning goal at Hampden. Following Rangers' magnificent triumph they faced opponents whom John Greig later rated as the finest team encountered that season, Real Zaragoza of Spain, who had already proved their worth by eliminating Everton in the previous round and who clearly enjoyed confronting British opposition. En route to the Inter-Cities Fairs Cup final of 1965/66 (where they lost to Barcelona) Zaragoza had eliminated Hearts, Dunfermline Athletic and Leeds United. Rangers were desperate for cup success – they had already been eliminated from the Scottish Cup (passport, of course, to the selfsame competition in which they had now reached the last eight) by Berwick Rangers of all teams! Old friend D'Arcy Canario was in the Spanish ranks; the Brazilian winger was at the veteran stage by now, but still regarded with awe in Glasgow. Ibrox was bathed in a new Philips floodlighting system on the night of 1 March 1967 which was a vast improvement on the old, the system being identical to that which lit up the Rock of Gibraltar. As if that were not enough of an omen, the heavens opened to greet Zaragoza with rain, snow and sleet so intense throughout the ninety minutes that there are many to this day who would rate that night as the worst conditions under which they have spectated at a football match. However, these were conditions in which Rangers revelled, playing a standard of football which threatened to swamp the señors. It was Dave Smith who opened the scoring after ten minutes with a chance created by his namesake Alex, and when Alex Willoughby notched a second in the twenty-seventh minute the Spaniards were reeling. Midway through the second half Dave Smith again found the net with a free-kick only for Dutch referee Lauren van Ravens to order that the kick be retaken, this time to no avail, and Rangers had to be content with a 2-0 lead for the second leg, a result which they would certainly have accepted before the start. La Romareda was no place for the faint-hearted three weeks later, and Rangers suffered a pre-match blow with the absence of Ronnie McKinnon who had suffered a broken nose at Ayr the preceding Saturday, being replaced by a young and inexperienced Colin Jackson. Zaragoza pressed from the start and reduced the deficit after twenty-four minutes when Carlos Lapetra curled in a free-kick, the signal for intense pressure on the visitors' goal. Yet the Ibrox defence stood firm against the onslaught with 'Bomber' holding Marcelino well in check. Subsequently, an Alex Willoughby goal was disallowed for offside, but as the minutes ticked away it seemed that victory was in sight, only for French referee Michel Kitabjian to controversially award a penalty against John Greig for handball, although 'Greigy' to this day would maintain that the ball hit his chest. The eighty-sixth minute penalty was converted by Eleuterio Santos to ensure extra time. Rangers were presented with a golden opportunity to secure the tie in the opening stages only for Dave Smith to be just too obvious with his penalty, allowing Enrique Yarza to save. The Scots continued to dominate, but could not break the deadlock and it all came down to the toss of a coin – a French two-franc piece – between Severino Reija and John Greig. 'Tails' decided the Rangers captain and thus it was, as Reija walked in tears to his dressing-room. The Light Blues were through to the last four, with Slavia Sofia awaiting – the Scots' first ever visit to Bulgaria. A bumpy pitch and searing heat awaited the Light Blues at the Vasilij Levski Stadium (Bulgaria's national stadium) against opposition who, en route to the penultimate round, had eliminated Swansea Town, Racing Strasbourg and Servette Geneva. Slavia had the proud record of never having conceded a home European goal, yet that is exactly what occurred on the half-hour mark when Johansen's twenty-yard shot was turned onto the crossbar by goalkeeper Simeon Simeonov, the loose ball quickly gathered by Alex Willoughby who squared for Davie Wilson to net with a low shot off Petar Petrov's foot. The Bulgars fought back, however, Martin having to produce two instinctive saves from Alexander Vassilev's header and volley. It was a veritable siege at the start of the second half, yet the visitors were denied a second goal ten minutes in when, in a classic counter-attack, Henderson and Willoughby interpassed the length of the park before the winger's reverse pass found Dave Smith who curled the ball into the corner of the net only for the Russian referee B. Bachramov to mysteriously chalk the 'goal' off. Slavia continued to press for the rest of the game with Willoughby and Wilson running themselves into the ground up front to the extent that they later suffered from dehydration.

Two weeks later the Bulgarians arrived in Glasgow to be mystified by man-ager Scot Symon's pre-announced team changes. The return of Willie Johnston was more than a little premature, given that this would be his first game since breaking his leg at Berwick just over three months earlier. However, the inclu-sion of Roger Hynd in attack in place of Alex Willoughby was inexplicable,

Slavia Sofia goalkeeper Simeonov diverts Sandy Jardine's drive over the bar.

based as it was on his scoring four goals in a reserve fixture the previous Saturday. His selection for that game had been purely accidental, in that a last-minute call-off led to his inclusion as a makeshift centre (Hynd was a solid but one-paced full-back or wing half). Roger (the nephew of the Shankly brothers) had played one week earlier at centre half against Glasgow Corporation Transport at Helenvale Park – now he was playing up front in a European semi-final.

Hynd certainly troubled Slavia (although his lack of pace was painfully obvi-ous). Indeed, both he and Sandy Jardine forced Simeonov into outstanding saves. Rangers were well in command throughout, with Alex Smith and Willie Johnston both striking the posts and the only goal of the game was a spectacular affair when, after thirty-one minutes, Johnston's corner, headed downwards by Hynd, was spectacularly volleyed home by Henderson (in outstanding form throughout) from twenty yards. Rangers had qualified for their second European final in seven years, but would find themselves up against it even before the game kicked off, with the final against Bayern München scheduled for Nürnberg, just over 100 miles from Bayern's home city. The handicap of playing in Bayern's own backyard would prove too great, with Rangers' dreams of success bunkered in the Reichsparteitaggelande.

Bayern were a young side – they were excluded from the first National League Championship (Bundesliga) when it was formed in 1963/64. Not considered either a good enough or big enough club, they would remain in the 'Regionalliga Sud' for just one more season before gaining promotion and proceeding to take the Bundesliga by storm, finishing a remarkable third in their first season and annexing the DFB Cup for a second time with a 4-3 win over Meiderich in Frankfurt – a success that was a passport to the European Cup-Winners' Cup where, en route to the final, they eliminated Tartan Presov, Shamrock Rovers, Rapid Vienna and Standard Liege. Bayern's emergence had been built around a youthful group of players, all in their early twenties, who would develop into world-class performers over the next decade, specifically goalkeeper Sepp Maier, libero/midfield playmaker Franz Beckenbauer (already well known in Britain after starring in the 1966 World Cup), midfielder Franz Roth and a goalscorer who would go on to create all manner of records during his playing career, Gerd Muller. They were at full strength, unlike Internazionale Milano when losing to another Glasgow club six days earlier.

Some 7,500 Rangers fans travelled to Nürnberg for the game – there would undoubtedly have been considerably more had the tickets been forthcoming, but the presence of a German team in the final had restricted availability somewhat. Rangers were under considerable pressure prior to kick-off, having won no silverware thus far that season. Team selection for Nürnberg demonstrated the idiosyncratic management style of Scot Symon. Goalscorers had been jettisoned like confetti that season, with Jim Forrest and George McLean both discarded following the catastrophic Scottish Cup exit at the hands of Berwick Rangers, and Alex Willoughby dropped to accommodate defender Roger Hynd in attack, despite scoring 16 goals in 13 games in the second half of the season. Forrest's goalscoring record was exceptional – 145 goals in 163 competitive games for the club, including 6 in the Champions' Cup campaign of 1964/65. The self-imposed exile of all three forwards would cost the Ibrox club dear.

Rangers based themselves in Neundettelsau, some twenty miles outside of Nürnberg – a mistake as it turned out for the lack of atmosphere and distance from the city meant that the party lost the big-match feel of the occasion. The final

Rangers *v.* Bayern Munich in the 1967 European Cup-Winners' Cup final. The two teams line up before the kick-off.

itself was a dour struggle with defences well on top. A Hynd goal was disallowed for offside, and the centre also missed a golden opportunity from a Dave Smith pass after thirty-three minutes, his weak shot producing a fine one-handed save from Maier. An honest, wholehearted player lamentably lacking in pace and skill, Hynd was no match for the class of the young Beckenbauer. Rangers' wingers Henderson and Johnston were marked out of the game by the Bayern full-backs. The winner, deep into extra time, came from Franz Roth with a spectacular hook shot in the 109th minute from a long through-ball from Beckenbauer. The very same Roth, nine years later, would net the only goal of the game in the Champions' Cup final at Hampden against St Etienne. At the presentation ceremony Roger Hynd hurled his runners-up medal into the crowd, unaware that it was identical to the winners' gongs.

Defeat for Rangers was devastating – manager Scot Symon did not say a word after the game, locking himself in his hotel room without acknowledging a single person. Six months later, his thirteen-year reign as Ibrox boss would end. Chairman John Lawrence would in years to come lament Roger Hynd's miss, suggesting that it had cost him a knighthood. In all probability, he was right.

For Bayern, the triumph was to prove the launching pad to a glittering array of prizes over the next decade, including three Champions' Cups and a World Club Cup at club level, whilst at international level Messrs Maier, Beckenbauer and Muller would be World Cup winners in 1974.

1966/67 European Cup-Winners' Cup, first round, first leg

Tuesday 27 September 1966, The Oval, Belfast

Glentoran 1 (Sinclair) Rangers 1 (McLean)

Attendance 55,000

Ritchie; Johansen, Provan; Millar, McKinnon, D. Smith; Henderson, Greig,

McLean, A. Smith, Johnston

First round, second leg

Wednesday 5 October 1966, Ibrox Stadium, Glasgow

Rangers 4 (Johnston, D. Smith, Setterington, McLean) Glentoran 0

Attendance 33,473

Ritchie; Johansen, Provan; Greig, McKinnon, D. Smith; Henderson, A. Smith,

McLean, Setterington, Johnston

Second round, first leg

Wednesday 23 November 1966, Ibrox Stadium, Glasgow

Rangers 2 (Johansen, A. Smith) Borussia Dortmund 1 (Trimholdt)

Attendance 65,000

Martin; Johansen, Provan; Greig, McKinnon. D. Smith; Henderson, Watson,

Forrest, A. Smith, Johnston

Second round, second leg

Tuesday 6 December 1966, Rote Erde Kampfbahn, Dortmund

Borussia Dortmund 0 Rangers 0

Attendance 45,000

Martin; Johansen, Provan; Greig, McKinnon. D. Smith; Henderson, Watson,

Forrest, A. Smith, Johnston

Quarter-final, first leg

Wednesday 1 March 1967, Ibrox Stadium, Glasgow

Rangers 2 (D. Smith, Willoughby) Real Zaragoza 0

Attendance 65,000

Martin; Johansen, Provan; Jardine, McKinnon, Greig; Henderson, Willoughby,

A. Smith, D. Smith, Wilson

Quarter-final, second leg

Wednesday 22 March 1967, La Romareda, Zaragoza

Real Zaragoza 2 (Lapetra, Santos pen) Rangers 0

Attendance 40,000

Martin; Johansen, Provan; Jardine, Jackson, Greig; Henderson, Willoughby,

A. Smith, D. Smith, Wilson

Semi-final, first leg

Wednesday 19 April 1967, Stadion Vasilij Levski, Sofia

Slavia Sofia 0 Rangers 1(Wilson)

Attendance 48,000

Martin; Johansen, Provan; Jardine, McKinnon, Greig; Henderson, Willoughby,

A. Smith, D. Smith, Wilson

Semi-final, second leg
Wednesday 3 May 1967, Ibrox Stadium, Glasgow
Rangers 1 (Henderson) Slavia Sofia 0
Attendance 71,000
Martin; Johansen, Provan; Jardine, McKinnon, Greig; Henderson, A. Smith,
Hynd, D. Smith, Johnston
Final
Wednesday 31 May 1967, Nürnbergerstadion, Nürnberg
Bayern München 1 (Roth) Rangers 0
Attendance 69,500
Martin; Johansen, Provan; Jardine, McKinnon, Greig; Henderson, A. Smith,
Hynd, D. Smith, Johnston

That final setback meant that Rangers would have to settle for a place in the
Inter-Cities Fairs Cup in season 1967/68, their first entry into the competition.
The Ibrox men travelled to East Germany in the opening round, to face Dinamo
Dresden. Thankfully, there would be none of the problems associated with the
draw when Rangers had faced Vorwarts East Berlin six years earlier. The Cold
War had melted ever so slightly and Dinamo would have nothing to inhibit them
from travelling to Glasgow for the second leg.

Rangers travelled to Dresden via Kobenhavn and East Berlin, having just
inflicted the first defeat post-Lisbon on the European Cup holders, 1-0 at Ibrox
courtesy of a goal from Swedish International winger Orjan Persson.

Dinamo forced the visitors back into defence for the entire first half, with
Danish international goalkeeper Erik Sorensen outstanding. The Light Blues were
fortunate in the extreme to reach the interval at the Stadion Heinz Steyer with the
scoresheet blank, yet within sixty seconds of the restart a certain Alex Ferguson
– signed that summer for a £65,000 transfer fee from Dunfermline Athletic –
notched the opening goal following a fine build up by Sandy Jardine and Persson.

Undaunted, the East Germans renewed their attacks, and an equalising goal
after sixty-six minutes was no more than they deserved, Dieter Riedel levelling
the scores. Rangers hung on in the closing stages and a 1-1 draw was an acceptable result to carry forward into the second leg.

An early goal from Andy Penman was the perfect start at Ibrox, and for the
entire game Rangers attacked, forcing the visitors into deep defence, a defence
that was solid and organised with Klaus Sammer and Wolfgang Pfeifer outstanding at the heart of it. It seemed that Penman's goal would be enough to win the
tie, when suddenly in the eighty-ninth minute, in almost their first attack of the
game, Dinamo equalised when Hans Kreische netted with a twenty-yard drive.
Extra time loomed. The 60,000 crowd, many of whom were already heading for
the exits, were stunned – yet Rangers reacted immediately with John Greig volleying the ball home.

Rangers *v*. Dinamo Dresden. Alex Ferguson looks on as Kallenbach punches a Willie Johnston cross over the bar.

Germany awaited once again in the second round, but thankfully this time it was to the West that the Ibrox club would travel, to Köln, the Cathedral city on the Rhine, with the first leg in Glasgow.

Rangers were a club in turmoil as they prepared for the visit of the West Germans. Manager Scot Symon had been sacked just one week earlier after thirteen years in charge and assistant manager David White had been promoted – many felt prematurely – into the hotseat. The new boss had an immediate problem for the European tie as his predecessor, together with coach Bobby Seith who had resigned in the wake of Symon's dismissal, had spied on Köln. White had not, although he did have access to Seith's notes. The German club may well have been apprehensive about visiting Scotland – on the occasion of their only previous visit on European business they had been hammered 8-1 by Dundee in a European Cup-tie. The return had incredibly almost salvaged the tie – Köln winning 4-0 in a game dubbed the 'Battle of the Rhine' by the Scottish Press. They were, however, a formidable outfit, including in their ranks World Cup finalists Wolfgang Weber and Wolfgang Overath. The Light Blues carried the game to the Germans throughout the first half, but the closest they came to the breakthrough was a Greig shot that came crashing back off a post. The opening goal duly arrived on fifty-three minutes when that man Ferguson (an experienced combatant in the European arena with Dunfermline) swooped on the loose ball to net after Greig's powerful drive had been parried by goalkeeper Toni Schumacher. Fifteen minutes later a Persson corner was nodded down by Ronnie McKinnon for Willie Henderson to volley home from sixteen yards. A dazzling run by 'Wee Wullie' in the seventy-third minute produced a magnificent flying header from Ferguson to give Rangers a 3-0 lead to take to the Rhine. Incidentally, an injury to John Greig after seventy minutes led to the introduction of Alex Smith as Rangers' first ever European substitute just as the third goal was being scored. It was a night of torrential rain in the Müngersdorfer return, which incidentally occupied the same location as today, but bore no resemblance to the stadium utilised in the 2006 World Cup, having undergone not one but two redevelopments since 1967. One golden rule for any away European tie is to play it tight at the back in the opening stages, avoiding at all cost the loss of an early goal. The Ibrox men proceeded to ignore any such advice by conceding the opening goal inside thirty seconds when a miskick by Ronnie McKinnon allowed Overath to net.

Rangers were now under severe pressure as Köln relentlessly attacked, but somehow the visitors hung on and the tide began to turn with Greig, Penman and Johnston taking control of midfield as part of a fluent 4-3-3, underlining that under a new, young manager the Ibrox men were much more tactically aware than in days of yore. The score was 1-0 at the interval and as the second half wore on Rangers were controlling more and more of the game, yet on seventy-five minutes a twenty-yard drive from Wolfgang Weber skidded along the wet turf, catching Sorensen unawares to make it 2-0. Four minutes later, unbelievably, it was three when the referee controversially awarded a free-kick against Sorensen just outside the six-yard box allegedly for time-wasting. Overath touched the ball to Karl-Heinz Ruhl, who forced the ball home.

Rangers had their backs to the wall but fortunately somehow survived to full time (even having a Ferguson goal chalked off for an infringement) but in extra time it was the visitors who were the stronger on the heavy pitch with John Greig (anxious to avoid a repeat of Zaragoza) urging his team on and wingers Henderson and Persson becoming more and more prominent. Schumaker made one magnificent save from Greig, but the tie was decided after 117 minutes when Henderson netted the winner, celebrating with a series of cartwheels.

It had been too close for comfort, but Rangers progressed to the last eight courtesy of a bye in round three, where they would face English giants Leeds United, moulded by the ruthless and autocratic manager Don Revie. 'Revie's Robots' comprised players such as Billy Bremner, Norman Hunter, Johnny Giles, Jack Charlton, Paul Reaney, Terry Cooper, Mike Jones and Peter Lorimer – all good players, but a team that had strode across the football grounds of Europe bending the rules and exploiting the frailties of opponents and referees alike in a determined and unscrupulous drive to reach the very pinnacle of the English game – mercifully a peak they seldom achieved. Fixture congestion had hampered Rangers' progress on three fronts; unbeaten all season in League fixtures, they led Celtic by two points in the title race, and were clear favourites for the Scottish Cup until eliminated by Hearts in a Tynecastle replay two weeks earlier.

Rangers missed a plethora of clear chances against a packed Leeds defence in the first half at Ibrox. The absences of Andy Penman and Alex Willoughby. through illness and injury respectively, were crucial to Rangers' chances against opposition high on confidence thanks to a three-month unbeaten run and the securing of their first trophy success at Wembley in the League Cup final with a 1-0 win over Arsenal just three weeks earlier. A packed stadium with 85,000 spectators looking on saw Willie Henderson, in fine form on the right wing, lay on a cross that was somehow missed right in front of goal by both Alex Ferguson and Willie Johnston, then 'Bud' managed to scoop his shot from point-blank range into the arms of Gary Sprake after Orjan Persson's cross had been missed by Cooper. A titanic midfield battle between Greig and Bremner ensued throughout the match, but Leeds closed down play for most of the second half, the one outstanding chance of the night falling to Persson after eighty-eight minutes, Sprake producing a magnificent save to deny him.

Rangers officially received a 4,000 ticket allocation for the second leg at Elland Road, but in the time-honoured fashion countless numbers of Gers fans acquired briefs from other sources with many travelling to Yorkshire in the weeks before the tie where tickets were on public sale. At the end of the day an estimated 20,000 Light Blue followers were present amongst the 50,498 crowd with 43,177 following the action on closed-circuit television at Ibrox.

The visitors almost made the perfect start inside two minutes when Johnston headed wide with Scots goalkeeper David Harvey stranded following good work by Ferguson. That miss proved fatal, however, for with Bremner, Giles and Hunter controlling the middle of the park and launching fast, incisive raids, the opening goal arrived in twenty-five minutes when Giles converted a penalty awarded for handball against Ferguson. Six minutes later Leeds struck a killer blow when Scot Lorimer netted from a suspiciously offside position following a Giles cross. Rangers battled on, but the die was cast, and the home side might have added a third in the second half when Lorimer struck a powerful shot against an upright. Leeds were through to the semi-finals, and after defeating Dundee they annexed the trophy with a single-goal triumph in the two-legged final against Ferencvaros.

1967/68 Inter-cities Fairs Cup, first round, first leg
Wednesday 20 September 1967, Stadion Heinz Steyer, Dresden
Dinamo Dresden 1 (Reidel) Rangers 1 (Ferguson)
Attendance 50,000

Sorensen; Johansen, Greig; Jardine, McKinnon, D. Smith; Henderson, Penman, Ferguson, Johnston, Persson

First round, second leg

Wednesday 4 October 1967, Ibrox Stadium, Glasgow

Rangers 2 (Penman, Greig) Dinamo Dresden 1 (Kreische)

Attendance 60,000

Sorensen; Johansen, Mathieson; Greig, McKinnon, D. Smith; Henderson, Penman, Ferguson, Johnston, Persson

Second round, first leg

Wednesday 8 November 1967, Ibrox Stadium, Glasgow

Rangers 3 (Ferguson 2, Henderson) 1. FC Köln 0

Attendance 60,000

Sorensen; Johansen, Mathieson; Grieg (A. Smith), McKinnon, D. Smith; Henderson, Penman, Ferguson, Johnston, Persson

Second round, second leg

Tuesday 28 November 1967, Stadion Müngersdorfer, Köln

1. FC Köln 3 (Overath, Weber, Ruhl) Rangers 1 (Henderson)

Attendance 46,000

Sorensen; Johansen, Mathieson; Greig, McKinnon, D. Smith; Henderson, Penman, Ferguson (Watson), Johnston, Persson

Quarter-final, first leg

Tuesday 26 March 1968, Ibrox Stadium, Glasgow

Rangers 0 Leeds United 0

Attendance 85,000

Sorensen; Johansen, Mathieson; Greig, McKinnon, D. Smith; Henderson, B. Smith, Ferguson, Johnston, Persson

Quarter-final, second leg

Tuesday 9 April 1968, Elland Road, Leeds

Leeds United 2 (Giles pen, Lorimer) Rangers 0

Attendance 50,498

Sorensen; Johansen, Mathieson; Greig, McKinnon, D. Smith; Henderson, Willoughby (Penman), Ferguson, Johnston, Persson

The League Championship of 1967/68 was unjustly lost on the final day of the season, a 2–3 defeat at the hands of Aberdeen being the only loss of the entire season. For a second successive year, consequently, it was the Inter-Cities Fairs Cup. Rangers' destination in the opening round was the Balkans – that corner of Europe where the fuse that was to create the First World War in 1914 was lit, as the 'Lamps went out all over Europe'. Serbia, a name from the history books that almost disappeared in Tito's Yugoslavia, was the one enlightened regime in the Warsaw Pact. The city that would play host to the Glasgow club was Novi Sad (a NATO target more than thirty years later) where they would face Vojvodina

– a side which Jock Stein had rated as Celtic's most difficult opponents in their triumphant European Cup campaign of two years earlier.

Rangers played well at Ibrox, John Greig opening the scoring from the penalty spot on twenty-eight minutes after Dobrivoj Trivic had fouled Willie Henderson – a decision hotly disputed by the Slavs. Sandy Jardine's dipping header from an Orjan Persson cross with just six minutes remaining gave the Light Blues a healthy 2-0 lead to take to Serbia.

The return in Novi Sad would be a different story however; Vojvodina besieged the visitors' goal throughout, using rough-house tactics to intimidate their opponents. A sixty-sixth minute Nikezic free-kick reduced the deficit, but somehow Rangers held out. Both Greig and Trivic were ordered off in the eightieth minute, the Ibrox captain had been kicked throughout by his midfield opponent, yet as they both trudged off the Yugoslav star protected his foe from the shower of missiles that rained down upon his head. The second-round draw gave the Light Blues a tie much closer to home, but set in an environment and location just as alien and hostile as Serbia. It was to Dundalk in the Republic of Ireland that Rangers would journey, but not before first playing host to the Irish club, who had achieved the not inconsiderable feat of eliminating DOS Utrecht of the Netherlands in the opening round.

Dundalk created some problems pre-match with their insistence that the Irish Tricolour and national anthem be played as part of the pre-match ritual in the first leg at Ibrox, but in the event were persuaded that neither would be a good idea. The match itself was not much of a contest – former Celtic inside forward Paddy Turner was in an Irish side who defended in depth throughout the match. Both Willie Henderson and Alex Ferguson netted twice as Rangers romped to a 6-1 win making the return at Oriel Park, Dundalk, a formality. There was a massive Rangers support in Dundalk for the return, most having crossed the border from Northern Ireland. The visitors would have to cope without the presence of both John Greig and Ronnie McKinnon, suspended and injured respectively, but main interest in the game centred not on the outcome of the tie – that was a formality – but on whether Rangers' new £100,000 record signing Colin Stein from Hibernian would score three goals for a third successive match. He had already done so in his first two games for the Light Blues against Arbroath and his old club Hibs, but would have to settle for just two against the Irish, although Stein did miss a late chance for yet another hat-trick. Willie Mathieson notched the other in a 3-0 win.

The 'Venice of the North', Amsterdam, was Rangers' destination in round three, to face not Dutch giants Ajax but local rivals DWS who may not have been as illustrious a name as their city rivals but who certainly presented a very real threat having eliminated Chelsea in the previous round, and who, immediately prior to the European tie, with Ibrox manager David White an interested onlooker, defeated Ajax 2-1 in a League fixture. For once, the Light Blues travelled for the first leg, to be played in the historical Olympic Stadion, venue of the 1928 Olympic Games. Included in the home line-up was Norwegian international Finn Seeman, once of Dundee United, and both Jan Jongbloed and Rob Rensenbrink – mainstays of the Dutch National side for years to come. The Dutch side controlled the first half, yet Rangers struck a monumental blow after thirty-eight minutes when Willie Johnston gave Jongbloed no chance following a Henderson/Persson move. A tactical switch by David White at the interval changed the Ibrox side's system from 4-2-4 to 4-3-3 with the introduction of Dave Smith for Orjan Persson, enabling Rangers to control the midfield with John Greig outstanding. A second goal was added on fifty-three minutes when Henderson converted an inch-perfect Dave Smith pass.

The 2-0 win effectively ensured Rangers' progress, even if the formalities of the second leg had still to be concluded. An early Dave Smith goal after just eight minutes was the perfect start, even if the wing half injured himself in the process. Frans Geurtsen equalised three minutes later, but Colin Stein netted after twenty minutes to give the home side the lead and ensure a 2-1 win that was much more impressive than the score would suggest. Into the last eight for a second successive campaign, the club broke new ground in season 1968/69 when paired with Athletic Bilbao from the Basque region of Northern Spain. Bilbao, a club who signed only Basque players, were coached by Englishman Ronnie Allen. They had already eliminated Liverpool en route to the quarter-finals, and were clearly a skilful side.

The first leg in Glasgow attracted nearly 63,000 spectators, but Ibrox preparations were seriously disrupted by the harsh ordering-off of Colin Stein against Clyde the previous Saturday – a dismissal, and subsequent draconian five-match suspension, that would ultimately cost Rangers both that season's League Championship and Scottish Cup.

Stein was, of course, eligible to play against the Basques, and the Light Blues got off to the perfect start in just seven minutes when Alex Ferguson headed home a Willie Henderson corner. Rangers had rattled the visitors and went 2-0 ahead on twenty-seven minutes when Dave Smith's clever lob released Andy Penman clean through on goal, the midfielder expertly chipping the ball over the head of the advancing Angel Iribar, rated by no less an authority than Bill Shankly as the finest goalkeeper in Europe. The Light Blues appeared to be set fair for a comfortable win, yet within two minutes Bilbao had silenced the home crowd when a weak headed clearance by Ronnie McKinnon allowed Javier Clemente to volley home from the edge of the box following a corner kick. The Scots were rattled, but regained their composure before the interval only to find Iribar in the form that had so impressed the legendary Shankly.

Ibrox captain John Greig squandered an ideal opportunity to restore his side's two-goal advantage after forty-seven minutes when he fired a penalty kick wildly over after Jose Larrauri had upended Stein.

Rangers became more and more frustrated as the game wore on, with Allen later reflecting that he imagined the crowd to have gone home so quiet were the darkened terraces. However, a seventy-fourth-minute substitution that introduced Orjan Persson in place of Ferguson would prove crucial: with just five minutes remaining the Swede broke free on the left from a Stein pass, catching Iribar by surprise with a strike to his near post. Sixty seconds later the same combination struck again, Persson's cross, this time to the far post, finding Stein who drove the ball home.

A 4-1 lead appeared on the surface a comfortable one to take to the Campo San Mames, Bilbao, yet Rangers suffered an injury blow on the eve of the tie when Bobby Watson suffered a broken ankle in training – an injury that would render him a casualty for the remainder of the season. Watson had been earmarked for a holding role in midfield and his absence would mean the repositioning of John Greig to the middle of the park, his role in central defence being taken by Colin Jackson.

Bilbao was the birthplace of football in Spain with San Mames – nicknamed 'La Catedral' – one of the most distinctive of stadiums with its unique arch. Travel difficulties plagued the Ibrox men en route to Spain and they arrived just twenty-four hours before kick-off. To make matters worse, Bilbao opened the scoring as early as the tenth minute when Nicholas Estefano netted at close quarters from an Ibanez opening. Rangers survived incessant home pressure throughout the remainder of the first half, but were hit by a body-blow after fifty-five minutes when Ibanez scrambled the ball home.

The visitors were now just one goal from elimination, and in an increasingly tense and hostile atmosphere the game exploded with ten minutes remaining when Willie Johnston, chopped down by Betzuen, retaliated in a flurry of fisticuffs and both players were ordered off.

The closing minutes were fraught – and it took a last-minute interception by Kai Johansen to save Rangers and send them into the last four.

The journey home was as stressful as the outward one, with the official party finally ariving home at Glasgow Airport at 1.30a.m. on the Friday morning. A crucial League fixture at Tannadice the next day was lost 1-2, virtually gifting Celtic that season's title, and Rangers declared that any such undertakings in future would be by chartered aircraft. For the fourth time in a decade Rangers had reached the semi-finals of a European tournament where they would face Newcastle United. Season 1968/69 had been one of great promise for the Ibrox club with Rangers playing attractive attacking football as they strove for glory on three fronts – League, Scottish Cup and Fairs Cup. An attacking combination of Colin Stein and Alex Ferguson had produced a striking partnership second to none for, alas, all too brief a period, the pairing having been forcibly dissolved by Stein's ordering-off against Clyde. The Fairs Cup was all that remained to be won against a side packed with Scots, namely former Celt John McNamee, captain Bobby Moncur, Tommy Gibb, Jim Scott (brother of ex-Ranger Alex) and Jackie

Sinclair. The first leg at Ibrox took place in the wake of the Home International Championships, all played in the space of a week. Rangers, however, did not have their troubles to seek with Ronnie McKinnon and Willie Mathieson both absent through injury, Willie Johnston through suspension. It was a wholly one-sided ninety minutes which Rangers totally dominated only to be denied time and time again by a packed United defence with goalkeeper Iam McFaul outstanding. The Belfast-born keeper, a Gers fan as a boy, even saved an Andy Penman penalty after thirty-four minutes, and ten minutes later produced a quite stunning save from the same player from a thirty-five-yard thunderbolt.

The absence of Johnston had proved critical – his natural replacement, Alex Ferguson, was now considered 'persona non grata' by the Ibrox management. For Alex Ferguson, the 1969 Scottish Cup final would be his last game in Light Blue. No matter the extent of the Scots club's superiority, a goalless draw left them with a massive task on their hands for the second leg at St James' Park. An estimated 10,000 Light Blue followers travelled to the north-east of England and for forty-five minutes Rangers had the better of the play, only for the deadlock to be broken seven minutes after the restart when Scott netted with a raging shot from the edge of the box from a pass by Gibb. Another long-range effort from Sinclair after seventy-seven minutes sealed the tie, and the Ibrox gloom was heightened when the game was held up in the closing minutes as fans spilled onto the park. Rangers for the fourth time in succession at least had the consolation of knowing that they had been eliminated by the eventual winners, the Geordies surprisingly defeating Ujpesti Dosza of Hungary 3-0, 3-2 in the final. A season that at one time had promised so much ended in tears, with no luck, no trophies, and, to many friends of Rangers, no hope. Newcastle were no better than a moderate, mid-table English First Division side whose initial qualification for the tournament had been very much of the back-door variety, due to the 'one club per city' rule of the time that the previous season had denied Clyde their one opportunity (thus far at least) to compete in Europe.

1968/69 Inter-Cities Fairs Cup, first round, first leg
Wednesday 18 September 1968, Ibrox Stadium, Glasgow
Rangers 2 (Greig pen, Jardine) Vojvodina 0
Attendance 70,000
Martin; Jackson, Mathieson; Greig, McKinnon, Hynd; Henderson, Penman,
Jardine, Johnston, Persson
First round, second leg
Wednesday 2 October 1968, Stadion Gradski, Novi Sad
Vojvodina 1 (Nikezic) Rangers 0
Attendance 12,000
Martin; Jackson, Mathieson; Greig, McKinnon, Hynd; Henderson, Penman
(D. Smith), Jardine, Johnston, Persson

Second round, first leg

Wednesday 30 October 1968, Ibrox Stadium, Glasgow

Rangers 6 (Henderson 2, Ferguson 2, Greig, Brennan o.g.) Dundalk 1 (Murray pen)

Attendance 30,000

Martin; Johansen, Mathieson; Greig, McKinnon, D. Smith; Henderson, Penman, Ferguson, Johnston, Persson

Second round, second leg

Wednesday 13 November 1968, Oriel Park, Dundalk

Dundalk 0 Rangers 3 (Stein 2, Mathieson)

Attendance 10,000

Martin; Johansen, Mathieson; Hynd, Jackson, D. Smith; Henderson, Ferguson (Conn), Stein, Johnston, Persson

Third round, first leg

Wednesday 15 January 1969, Olympisch Stadion, Amsterdam

DWS Amsterdam 0 Rangers 2 (Johnston, Henderson)

Attendance 18,000

Martin; Johansen, Mathieson; Greig, McKinnon, Watson; Henderson, Penman, Stein, Johnston, Persson (D. Smith)

Third round, second leg

Wednesday 22 January 1969, Ibrox Stadium, Glasgow

Rangers 2 (D. Smith, Stein) DWS Amsterdam 1 (Geurtsen)

Attendance 62,000

Martin; Johansen, Greig; Watson, McKinnon, D. Smith (Jardine); Henderson, Penman, Stein, MacDonald, Johnston

Quarter-final, first leg

Wednesday 19 March 1968, Ibrox Stadium, Glasgow

Rangers 4 (Ferguson, Penman, Persson, Stein) Athletic Bilbao 1 (Clemente)

Attendance 62,842

Martin; Johansen, Mathieson; Greig, McKinnon, D. Smith; Henderson, Penman, Stein, Ferguson (Persson), Johnston

Quarter-final, second leg

Wednesday 2 April 1968, Campo San Mames, Bilbao

Athletic Bilbao 2 (Estefano, Ibanez) Rangers 0

Attendance 40,000

Martin; Johansen, Mathieson; Jackson, McKinnon, Greig; Henderson, Penman, Stein, D. Smith, Johnston

Semi-final, first leg

Wednesday 14 May 1969, Ibrox Stadium, Glasgow

Rangers 0 Newcastle United 0

Attendance 75,518

Neef; Johansen, Provan; Greig, Jackson, D. Smith; Henderson, Penman, Stein, Jardine, Persson

Semi-final, second leg
Wednesday 21 May 1969, St James' Park, Newcastle
Newcastle United 2 (Scott, Sinclair) Rangers 0
Attendance 61,000
Neef; Johansen, Mathieson; Greig, McKinnon, D. Smith; Henderson, Penman, Stein, Johnston, Persson

Despite the cataclysmic defeat in the 1969 Scottish Cup final, the first suffered by a Rangers team in forty years (0-4 *v.* Celtic), the Ibrox men entered the European Cup-Winners' Cup the following season (for the first time as runners-up) with the opening round breaking new ground – a visit to Romania to face army team Steaua Bucharest. It was a trip into the unknown for the Light Blues – no Scottish club had played in Romania before 1969, and travel difficulties meant that manager David White was unable to watch the Bucharest side. Nevertheless, Steaua were clearly formidable opponents: five of their side had been in the Romanian national team that had eliminated Portugal in qualifying for the Mexico 1970 World Cup finals.

The Romanians had identified Willie Johnston as the principal danger and so it proved in the first leg at Ibrox when two opportunist goals just before the interval turned out to be decisive. The first was an individual goal as he went through on a Jim Baxter pass to beat goalkeeper Vasile Suciu, then three minutes later 'Bud' intercepted a bad pass-back to slot the ball home.

Baxter had returned home in the summer of 1969, and there can be no doubt that he relished the glamour and atmosphere that surrounded European ties. A 2-0 lead is normally a satisfactory one to take to most European destinations and the Scots club were more than happy with the scoreline. They would adopt a professional attitude to the Bucharest visit, chartering their own aircraft and taking hampers of their own food.

The date of the game was a national holiday in Romania and the Steaua–Rangers tie was to be the second of a double-header played at the National Stadium on 27 August, with a massive 90,000 spectators demanding and expecting a victory, even more so when in the first game Vittorio Setubal easily defeated Rapid Bucharest. There had been massive demonstrations in the streets of Bucharest on the morning of the match, celebrating their version of independence, tens of thousands marching past the hotel where Rangers were staying.

The stadium had been packed since midday, packed indeed to overflowing with even the passageways full and hundreds perched around the top of the massive terracings. The afternoon kick-off meant temperatures in the seventies, yet Rangers would display a cool professionalism that took the heat and passion out of the game. David White had set out a tactical plan that revolved around a 4-3-3 system that enabled the visitors to control the midfield with Sandy Jardine,

Bobby Watson and Jim Baxter the key players. Baxter stood head and shoulders above every other player on the park, dictating the pace of the game, with John Greig and Ronnie McKinnon solid at the rear. Both Jardine and Vasile Negrea struck the crossbar in quick succession midway through the second half, but that was the nearest anyone came to a goal, the home side losing heart as the game wore on, with the crowds departing in droves in the closing ten minutes. Rangers were through and would face a second consecutive trip behind the Iron Curtain in the second round when they were drawn against Poland's Gornik Zabrze. Sadly the professionalism and efficiency they had demonstrated in Bucharest would be lacking against the Poles. Rangers' first visit to Poland could not have occurred at a less opportune moment; arguably that country's finest ever side were the opponents in a tie that would prove such a focal point in the Ibrox club's history.

The first leg, staged in the Stadion Slaski, attracted a near capacity 72,000 spectators to the ground based in the town of Chorzow in the industrialised heartland of southern Poland, amongst the minefields of Silesia, a densely populated region of some eleven cities and towns of 2.5 million inhabitants. The Slaski (pronounced Shlonshi) or Wojewodzki Park of Culture and Recreation, to give the ground its full, formal title, was once upon a time named after Joseph Stalin, constructed in the style of the vast open bowls of the great socialist grounds of the post-war era, staging most major internationals and cup finals. Indeed this was the very stadium where England and Sir Alf Ramsey would in 1973 suffer their World Cup nadir. There are English fans who to this day believe that their defeat was suffered in Katowice (where they stayed before the match), rather than Chorzow, such is the proximity of the two locations (much in the same style as Glasgow and Paisley). Indeed, until as recently as 1918 Chorzow was part of Germany.

Sir Matt Busby had rated Gornik as the finest side Manchester United had encountered en route to their European Cup triumph in 1967/68, yet Davie White offered himself as a hostage to fortune in declining the opportunity to watch Gornik prior to the game, and furthermore declared an intention pre-match to attack the Poles from the off. Such a reckless decision was to prove catastrophic as Rangers conceded two goals in the opening twelve minutes through Wlodzimierz Lubanski and Zygfryd Szoltysik. Lubanski almost added a third soon afterwards when his close-range header narrowly missed the target.

The visitors were up against it, but gradually worked their way back into the game through the sterling defensive work of the experienced John Greig and Ronnie McKinnon, reaching the interval without further damage being done. Ten minutes into the second half Rangers reduced the deficit when Willie Henderson, for once operating on the left, crossed for Orjan Persson to smash the ball home.

The Ibrox men took heart from that breakthrough and might even, given an equal share of the breaks, have levelled the score, only to concede a late third when a lack of concentration at a quickly taken free-kick enabled Lubanski to net.

A 3-1 deficit to take into the Ibrox return was by no means an insurmountable one, yet the job in hand was scarcely helped when, with the team based at Largs, both Jim Baxter and Willie Henderson missed training on the day before the game, having overslept. White chose to field both players regardless, a decision that drew criticism from many Ibrox traditionalists.

The game started well for the Light Blues, when Baxter opened the scoring on eighteen minutes, and had Willie Johnston not shot wide from six yards early in the second half then the story of the night might well have been wholly different. As it was, in a lightning break Alfred Olek netted the equaliser from a narrow angle with Gerry Neef at fault and Rangers were right up against it.

A superb individual goal from Lubanski after seventy-seven minutes effectively ended Rangers' interest in the competition. Collecting the ball on the halfway line he left McKinnon trailing as he advanced towards the penalty area only to be forced wide by home goalkeeper Gerry Neef. Virtually on the goal line, Lubanski turned back as if to head towards his own goal only to wrong-foot two defenders as he swiftly changed direction, turning on a sixpence before rifling the ball into the roof of the net from a tight angle. It was a strike reminiscent of the famous counter by Ferenc Puskas at Wembley in 1953, and one worthy of winning any game, as was appreciated by the Ibrox legions, who sportingly applauded a class player and team. The tie was won – and five minutes later Skowroknok added a third with Neef found wanting as the Pole advanced through the middle before curling the ball home from twenty yards.

The superb Gornik side received a warm ovation from the 70,000 crowd as they left the field at the end of the game, and would go all the way to the final that season where they would go down, most unluckily, to Manchester City 1-2 in Vienna in a game played in appalling weather conditions that undoubtedly influenced the outcome.

The defeat led to demonstrations in Edmiston Drive demanding the head of David White. The criticism was to an extent justified – he had failed to break the iron grip exerted on Scottish football by Jock Stein, and, specifically relative to the Gornik game, he was accountable in that he had not taken the trouble to watch them beforehand; he was tactically inept in Chorzow and he was demonstrably lacking in authority and discipline when failing to take action against the Largs Two. The defeat had major repercussions for the club: David White was sacked the very next morning, to be replaced by Willie Waddell. Ironically, had a coin fallen on the other side in Lisbon that same evening, thus eliminating Celtic instead of Benfica, the Ibrox manager may well have survived.

1969/70 European Cup-Winners' Cup, first round, first leg

Wednesday 17 September 1969, Ibrox Stadium, Glasgow

Rangers 2 (Johnston 2) Steaua Bucharest 0

Attendance 43,346

Neef; Johansen, Provan; Greig, McKinnon, Baxter; Henderson, Jardine, Stein, Johnston, Persson (Smith)

First round, second leg

Wednesday 1 October 1969, Stadion 27 August, Bucharest

Steaua Bucharest 0 Rangers 0

Attendance 90,000

Neef; Johansen, Provan; Greig, McKinnon, Baxter; Henderson, Watson (Smith), Stein, Jardine, Johnston

Second round, first leg

Wednesday 12 November 1969, Stadion Slaski, Chorzow

Gornik Zabrze 3 (Lubanski 2, Szoltysik) Rangers 1 (Persson)

Attendance 72,000

Neef; Johansen, Heron; Greig, McKinnon, Baxter; Henderson, Penman, Stein, Johnston, Persson

Second round, second leg

Wednesday 26 November 1969, Ibrox Stadium, Glasgow

Rangers 1 (Baxter) Gornik Zabrze 3 (Olek, Lubanski, Skowroknok)

Attendance 45,000

Neef; Johansen, Heron; Greig, McKinnon, Baxter; Henderson, Penman, Stein, Johnston, Persson (A. MacDonald)

Willie Waddell's first European tie found Rangers encountering old friends Bayern München in the opening round of a tournament now known as the European Fairs Cup, in what would prove to be the last season of that competition, before it was replaced by the UEFA Cup.

There could scarcely have been tougher opposition at any stage than the Germans, the first club that Rangers had encountered for a second time in European competition. The young Bayern team of 1967 were still more or less together with Sepp Maier, Franz Beckenbauer and Gerd Muller having been key components of the West German side that had finished third in the Mexico World Cup that very summer. Franz Roth, scorer of the winning goal in 1967, was also still around.

The Light Blues were far from overawed, however, and if anything were the better team in the first leg at the Stadion Grunwalder in München. A superb Beckenbauer goal from twenty yards had given the home side the lead after twenty-two minutes following a one-two with Paul Breitner. The second half belonged to Rangers but a string of fine Maier saves denied them, as did the crossbar from a John Greig header.

A massive 82,743 attendance packed Ibrox for the return, with Rangers' manager Willie Waddell springing a tactical surprise by throwing central defender Colin Jackson up front in a bid to harrass and unsettle Beckenbauer. The move mirrored that of Roger Hynd and Nürnberg three years earlier and would ultimately prove to be equally unsuccessful as the home side struggled to break down a composed German defence. Despite incessant Light Blue pressure the deadlock was not broken until the eightieth minute when Gerd Muller scored in most controversial circumstances with a direct twenty-yard free-kick that many Gers players believed had been awarded as an indirect infringement – a claim strengthened by photographic evidence. With a priceless away goal, Bayern were now in the driving seat, despite Colin Stein equalising immediately thereafter. The Germans were through and would progress as far as the quarter-finals before being eliminated by Liverpool (0-3, 1-1).

1970/71 European Fairs Cup, first round, first leg
Wednesday 16 September 1970, Stadion Grunwalder, München
Bayern München 1 (Beckenbauer) Rangers 0
Attendance 30,000
McCloy; Jardine, Miller; Greig, McKinnon, Jackson; Fyfe, Conn, Stein (Henderson), A. MacDonald, Johnston
First round, second leg
Wednesday 30 September 1970, Ibrox Stadium, Glasgow
Rangers 1 (Stein) Bayern München 1 (Muller)
Attendance 82,743
McCloy; Jardine, Miller; Greig, McKinnon, Jackson (Johnstone); Fyfe (Henderson), Conn, Stein, A. MacDonald, Johnston

THREE

The Holy Grail

For the second time in three years Rangers qualified for the European Cup-Winners' Cup as beaten finalists to Celtic in the Scottish FA Cup. A sojourn which started somewhat cautiously in Brittany would in the final analysis explode into life in a glorious and memorable campaign that would go down in the annals of Ibrox folklore. The Breton tale that set it all off found Rangers travelling to face Stade Rennais (Rennes) with the storm clouds swirling around Ibrox. The Light Blues had been desperately unlucky to suffer defeat at the hands of Celtic by the odd goal in five just three days earlier, but it was nevertheless a third consecutive home defeat inside the space of just five weeks. The Scots set out their stall accordingly, with a conservative line-up that saw the French danger men Keruzore, Betta and Terrier man-marked by Alex MacDonald, John Greig and Willie Mathieson respectively.

Rennes attacked from the start, forcing a remarkable nine corners in the opening ten minutes, but somehow the visitors survived and began to threaten on the counter-attack. One such break after sixty-eight minutes provided the opener when Tommy McLean's corner was touched on by Colin Stein for Willie Johnston to net at the far post. One minute later 'Bud' should have killed the tie stone-dead when clear through, only to lose possession as he attempted to walk the ball around home goalkeeper Marcel Aubour; Rennes duly capitalised on seventy-eight minutes when Redon slid in at the back post to convert a right-wing cross from Berra.

Rangers had every reason to be satisfied with a 1-1 draw against a team currently sitting second top of the French League – even if the Stade Rennais coach Jean Prouff, an old foe from the clash with Standard Liege nine years earlier, had been severely critical of their negative tactics: 'Rangers did not play football. They came to defend. They removed the spectacle from the game and our fans were cheated.' Prouff continued the psychological warfare when arriving in Scotland for the second leg with the promise to attack, stating: 'I won't face the sack if we lose' – a dig at the under-pressure Ibrox manager whose side had lost three of their opening four League fixtures. The Scots controlled the game, however, with Willie Henderson in outstanding form, creating havoc on the wing. A Colin Stein header produced a fine save from Aubour, before the opening goal arrived on thirty-eight minutes when Johnston's shot was parried by Aubour, Alex MacDonald bundling home the rebound. That one-goal lead should have been enhanced in the second half, Stein striking the crossbar with an angled drive, and in the closing minutes Willie Henderson was denied a stonewall penalty when upended by Cosnard.

No matter; Rangers were through to round two, as were all five Scottish clubs (Aberdeen, Celtic, Dundee and St Johnstone) involved in Europe that week, for the first and only time (thus far at least). Prouff, so bitter after the game in Brittany, was gracious in defeat: 'Rangers played so much better tonight and Henderson and Johnston were the stars.'

Sporting Clube De Portugal (Sporting Lisbon) were Rangers' second-round opponents; at the time Portuguese League leaders, they were clearly going to be a force to be reckoned with. The first leg, for the only time that season, was to be played at Ibrox. Domestic form had revived in the weeks following the victory over Rennes, with a stirring 5-1 win at Tannadice over Dundee United on the Saturday before the visit of the Portuguese restoring confidence within the Ibrox ranks.

Inspirational Light Blue captain John Greig suffered a bizarre injury during pre-match training at Largs when he collided with a bench and required stitches to a chin wound. Unable to shave, Greig grew a goatee beard, vowing not to shave it off until Rangers were out of Europe.

A stunning first-half display by the home side threatened to bury Sporting before the tie was even half an hour old. Colin Stein it was who opened the scoring on nine minutes with a header from an Andy Penman free-kick, with Sporting goalkeeper Damas found wanting. Rangers suffered an injury blow soon afterwards when the experienced Penman (a European Cup semi-finalist with Dundee in 1962/63) limped off. Yet after twenty minutes another Stein header found the net, this time from a Dave Smith free-kick with Damas again struggling. The Scots were rampant and Willie Henderson added a third on the half-hour with a powerful twenty-yard drive. Sporting were on their knees but Rangers could not reproduce their stunning first-half form after the interval and faced the dilemma of whether to close the game down (never a popular option with a Scots crowd) or to go for more goals. In the event they did neither and the visitors reduced the deficit after seventy minutes when Hector Yazalde's shot was parried by Peter McCloy, the Brazilian forward Chico netting the rebound from a suspiciously offside position. With an away goal, the Portuguese took heart and struck a dagger to Ibrox hearts with a second goal in the eighty-sixth minute when substitute Pedro Gomes netted from a Dinnis pass.

The journey to Lisbon was long and tiring for the official Rangers party. Flying by scheduled air via Heathrow two days before the game they were caught up in a baggage handlers' dispute at the London airport. Delayed firstly for several hours in Glasgow, then again at Heathrow, they were forced to journey across the capital by coach to Stansted Airport where a chartered aircraft would fly them to Lisbon the following morning. The club finally arrived in Lisbon a mere twenty-seven hours before the scheduled kick-off.

The game itself in the Estadio Jose De Alvalade lived up to the drama of the Ibrox game. Rangers attacked from the opening minutes, calculating that Sporting were vulnerable in defence. It was the home side, however, who took the lead when Yazalde netted after McCloy spilled a long-range free-kick. Within sixty seconds Stein had equalised, but ten minutes later Tome put the home side 2-1 up and ahead on away goals. The stadium was a cauldron of noise throughout the game but the 70,000 spectators were silenced when Stein netted his second one minute after the restart. Sporting piled on the pressure as the second half wore on, with the visitors suffering a desperate injury blow on seventy-two minutes when Ronnie McKinnon suffered a broken leg. He was replaced by Dave Smith, but the injury would effectively end the centre half's Ibrox career. With time running out a Pedro Gomes goal in the eighty-third minute took the tie into extra time. Henderson, the scorer of so many vital counters in Europe, struck again on 100 minutes. Rangers were on course for the last eight, yet with just six minutes of extra time remaining the home side were awarded a penalty, converted by Perez, for an alleged handball against Colin Jackson. There was no further scoring and with the final whistle Rangers should have been through, but, unbelievably, Dutch referee Laurens van Ravens ordered a penalty shoot-out – directly against the tournament rules. In a hostile and intimidating atmosphere with the Portuguese fans spilling out from the vast terracings and standing on the touchline the Scots proceeded to miss the first four penalties with Dave Smith even failing twice after a retake was ordered. Colin Stein, Willie Johnston and Sandy Jardine were the other 'miscreants'.

In the stand, however, the UEFA delegate, Spaniard Andres Ramirez, had a better understanding of the rules. He attempted to go pitchside to stop the penalties but by then Damas had already saved the first one, and perhaps wisely decided not to intervene until it had concluded. Alerted by Scots journalist John Mackenzie of the *Scottish Daily Express*, Willie Waddell made certain that Ramirez knew that he was aware of the regulations. A top-level meeting between representatives of both clubs and the match officials confirmed that Rangers were through, despite bitter and heated Sporting protests, both on the night and in the days that followed.

It was not getting any easier when the quarter-final draw paired the Ibrox men with Italian giants Torino, at the time Serie A league leaders. Torino may have lived in the shadows of their more illustrious neighbours Juventus in recent decades, but they were a club with a proud history and tradition that had dominated

Italian football in the immediate post-war era, winning five successive titles until, in 1949, the tragedy of the Superga Air Disaster occurred when the entire team was wiped out as they returned from Lisbon, having played a friendly against Benfica. A bonus for Rangers before the first leg in Italy was that twenty-four hours earlier the Rangers party were able to attend a UEFA Cup-tie between Juventus and Wolverhampton Wanderers in the very same Stadio Comunale that would host the Ibrox men against Torino the following night. A 1-1 draw was an outstanding result for the Molineux club with Scottish international Jim McCalliog netting the crucial goal, giving the Scots every encouragement that they could follow suit the next day.

The visitors set out to play a holding game of containment with a young Derek Johnstone playing in central defence alongside Colin Jackson with Dave Smith sweeping behind them. Midfield playmaker Claudio Sala had been identified as the main danger in the Italian team but he would be man-marked out of the game by the dominant John Greig.

Rangers frustrated Torino from the start, and struck an early blow after twelve minutes when Willie Mathieson overlapped down the left before sending over a low, driven cross that was parried by home goalkeeper Castellinni, allowing the lurking Willie Johnston to stab the ball home. The Scots controlled the remainder of the half, but the 'Granata' (pomegranates, a nickname derived from their almost unique burgundy-coloured shirts) piled on the pressure after the interval, finally equalising in the sixty-first minute when quick thinking by Pulici saw him divert a Toschi drive past Peter McCloy. A second Pulici goal was disallowed for offside, and the visitors held out against furious Italian attacks with Dave Smith outstanding to finish

The non-existent penalty shoot-out in Lisbon, 1971/72.

the stronger with a superb 1-1 draw. Torino coach Gustavo Giagnoni bestowed on Rangers the ultimate praise: 'They played like an Italian team.'

The Ibrox return was no formality, of course, underlined when Willie Waddell fielded the same eleven and employed the same tactics. Nevertheless Rangers controlled the game, setting out at a furious pace to kill the tie as soon as possible. Italian defences are, however, accustomed to such pressure and Torino held firm until the interval. Indeed, the nearest thing to a goal had come at the other end when Toschi struck an upright from a Bui pass five minutes before the break, but when the deadlock was broken after forty-six minutes it was Alex McDonald who bundled the ball home from close range from a Tommy McLean cross, the winger's solo run encompassing half the length of the park. Johnston was denied a second by an upright, but this was a noteworthy victory for Rangers who were now through to their fifth European semi-final in thirteen years.

One of the potential winners had been removed from the competition, but still Rangers would receive no luck when the draw for the penultimate round paired them once again with Bundesliga giants Bayern München.

The semi-final destination might have been either East Berlin or Moscow, but it was to be West Germany yet again. Bayern were now an even more formidable force than before; within two months of the meeting with Rangers they would form the nucleus of the West German national side that would win the European Championships and go on two years later to annexe the World Cup. They were all there – Franz Beckenbauer (European Footballer of the Year), Gerd Muller ('Der Bomber'), Sepp Maier, Uli Hoeness, Paul Breitner and George Schwarzenbeck. This was truly a world-class outfit – they had already eliminated Liverpool earlier

Alex McDonald's winning goal at Ibrox against Torino in 1972.

in the tournament and would go on to success in three consecutive European Champions' Cup finals from 1974 to 1976.

München was busy preparing itself for the 1972 Olympic Games – which would be so marred by tragedy – when Rangers travelled to Bavaria for the first leg. Indeed Bayern would shortly be moving to the Olympic Stadion from their Grunwalder base, but it was the old ground with its 44,000 capacity that hosted the first leg on 5 April 1972.

The Light Blues found themselves under severe pressure in the early stages with Gerd Muller heading against the crosssbar in the eighth minute. The deadlock was finally broken fifteen minutes later when Breitner netted with a superb goal, running virtually the full length of the park. Somehow, the visitors survived without further loss until the interval, with Jackson and Johnstone keeping tight control of Messrs Muller and Hoeness and sweeper Dave Smith marshalling the defence behind them. Within three minutes of the restart Rangers struck back with a goal that would ultimately prove crucial to the outcome of the tie when Sandy Jardine fed Colin Stein who rounded Maier before crossing for the lurking Johnston. The ball never reached 'Bud' however, Zobel heading it into his own net. The loss of the away goal deflated Bayern, despite all their experience, and Rangers grew in confidence and strength as the game wore on with Willie Mathieson of all people twice forcing Maier into fine saves.

Once again Rangers had secured a magnificent result away from home, but the outcome was far from a formality and that hard truth was underlined just four days before the Ibrox return when inspirational captain John Greig received a bad ankle injury in the Scottish Cup semi-final at Hampden, drawn 1-1 against Hibernian. A virus also hit the club, undoubtedly affecting their performance at Hampden – and it had not fully cleared as the Light Blues prepared at Largs for the visit of Bayern. Youngster Derek Parlane replaced the injured Greig and Rangers could not have got off to a better start, opening the scoring after forty-five seconds when Willie Johnston's cross from the left was only partially cleared by Beckenbauer, Derek Johnstone passing to Sandy Jardine whose twenty-five-yard floated cross-cum-shot totally deceived Maier.

Ibrox was a cauldron of noise – and four minutes later it was almost 2-0 when Stein's header smacked off the crossbar. The second goal was merely delayed, however, and it was Parlane whose fifteen-yard volley found the net via the underside of the crossbar following a Johnston corner.

Rangers were running Bayern ragged and might have doubled their lead by the interval, although Peter McCloy produced a fine save early in the second half when turning a Hoeness shot onto the post. By this time the West Germans were rattled and squabbling amongst themselves, a beaten team. 'Barcelona here we come,' sang 80,000 Rangers' fans; with the final scheduled for the Catalan capital there was going to be a massive exodus to Spain.

The victory was sweet revenge in particular for Nürnberg, and on what was a remarkable night in Glasgow 75,000 spectators at Celtic Park witnessed a goalless

Derek Parlane nets the second goal at Ibrox in the semi-final against Bayern München.

draw with Internazionale Milano in the Champions' Cup semi-final, the Italians going through on penalties. Rangers had finally found light at the end of the long, dark tunnel they had found themselves in since 1967.

Old friends awaited the Light Blues in Barcelona – Dinamo Moscow, who had reached the final by eliminating Olympiakos Pireaus, Eskishehirspor of Turkey, Crevna Zvezda Beograd (Red Star Belgrade) and Dinamo Berlin, with the last two home ties being staged in Tashkent and Lvov due to the severity of the Moscow winters. The Russians had their own unique place in Ibrox folklore having visited the Stadium in 1945 in the slipstream of the Allied victory in the Second World War. Ninety-five thousand spectators were onlookers to a memorable 2-2 draw that is recalled with awe by those present to this day. The fixture marked the fourth and final game of a UK tour by the Muscovites to cement sporting relations between two nations that had fought the Axis powers as partners in the global conflict just concluded, but who would be on opposite sides of the Iron Curtain in the Cold War that was about to envelop Europe for the next forty-five years. Dinamo sought to go down in the annals of Soviet sporting history as the first club side from the USSR to win a European trophy. There was a massive exodus of Light Blue followers to Barcelona with almost 25,000 travelling. Belief was widespread that after two European final defeats in 1961 and 1967 to Fiorentina and Bayern München respectively it would be a case of third time lucky.

Rangers were not without their injury worries: John Greig had not played a competitive game for almost six weeks and despite featuring in two friendlies arranged in the run-up to Barcelona he had suffered a relapse in training one week before the game. Nevertheless, the Ibrox captain would play – it was unimaginable that he would not. As if that was not concern enough for manager Waddell, on the very eve of the final centre half Colin Jackson, one of the mainstays of the side, suffered an ankle injury in training and was forced to withdraw. That left one tactical decision for Waddell to make, one midfield berth to be filled with three possible candidates, namely Alfie Conn, Derek Parlane and Andy Penman. Many favoured the experienced Penman, but in the event the decision came down in favour of Conn. The Estadio Nou Camp is one of the world's great arenas and home to one of the world's great football clubs. In 1972 the stadium capacity stood at 100,000 and even if the ground was only one-quarter full it was still a colourful sight. Red, white and blue was everywhere, the Ibrox legions comprising at least ninety-five per cent of the 24,701 audience. Dinamo Moscow must have felt amongst the loneliest people in the world as none of their fans had been permitted to travel by the Soviet authorities, although this was a situation that their players must have been only too familiar with.

One hour before kick-off there was a wondrous, carnival atmosphere inside the ground with Rangers fans strolling at will across the pitch. From the front row of the seating to the level of the playing surface was literally one step. Unhindered by the presence of fencing, barriers, a ditch or a moat, and totally unobstructed by the local police, hundreds of Light Blue followers cavorted around, many even having their photographs taken with and by police officers. It was a totally relaxed situation, but one that would set a dire precedent. Dinamo midfield general and captain, the vastly experienced Josef Sabo, had been earmarked as the key to his team's play and was the subject of a hard, physical challenge from John Greig inside the opening five seconds. Greig had left the 'engine room' of the opposition aware of his presence, and would be a constant inspiration to his teammates as he drove them on to the Holy Grail that Ibrox teams had striven for during the previous sixteen years.

The Russians may not have been as glamorous a team as Rangers' semi-final opponents, but it did not take them long to demonstrate that they were every bit as dangerous, Yakubik shooting wide from a Baydachny cross after ten minutes. Seven minutes later Peter McCloy saved at the second attempt from a Makhovikov thirty-yard shot.

Rangers had the bulk of the play and of possession, but there was a cutting edge to Dinamo that carried a worying threat for the Light Blue legions. Nevertheless, the opening goal when it arrived on twenty-four minutes was for Rangers – a superb through-ball from Dave Smith releasing Colin Stein with the Dinamo defence hesitant. The Ibrox striker outpaced his marker Dolmatov and drove the ball unerringly home. The Ibrox legions were ecstatic and poured onto the pitch

Willie Johnston's header makes it 2-0 in the European Cup-Winners' Cup final.

in massive numbers to celebrate, once again, departing without the slightest hindrance.

Rangers were now thrusting forward at every opportunity with John Greig and Alex MacDonald the beating heart of a team that saw the ultimate goal in their sights. Five minutes before the interval it was 2-0 when the skilful Dave Smith, Scotland's Footballer of the Year, moved forward effortlessly before wrong-footing the Russian defence with a quick turn and cross for Willie Johnston to head home.

The Gers left the field to a massive ovation at half-time, and quite unbelievably were three up four minutes after the restart when a long, high clearance from Peter McCloy found Johnston clear and unmarked in front of goal, the goal-keeper's sky-high kickout having totally confused the Dinamo offside trap. 'Bud' executed his finish to perfection and, astonishingly in a major European final, Rangers led by 3-0.

The game was not yet over, however, as a misplaced pass by Willie Mathieson enabled Evryuzhikhin to feed the blatantly offside substitute Eshtrekov to net. Spanish referee Ortiz De Mendebel awarded the goal.

Dinamo came more and more into the game as the second half wore on, due to a combination of factors. They were much fresher, having played only six domestic League fixtures of their new spring/autumn season, whereas Rangers were at the end of a long, tiring campaign. The heat was also taking its toll on the Ibrox men, and undoubtedly the injury to John Greig was reducing the Ibrox captain's effectiveness.

Willie Johnston nets the third, and ultimately winning, goal against Dinamo Moscow.

McCloy had to make an instinctive save to prevent a Sandy Jardine own goal, yet Stein might have secured the trophy with a snap-shot. Frayed nerves were at boiling point after eighty-seven minutes when Sasha Makhovikov scooped the ball home from a Gershkovic pass, thus ensuring a tense closing few minutes. As Dinamo poured forward one could almost smell an equalising goal.

Ibrox worries were scarcely helped when, in the final minute, the referee, in awarding a foul, gave a long blast on his whistle, cue for a mini pitch invasion from many Gers fans, once again cleared without the slightest bother. When seconds later it was full time the 'Follow Follow' brigade poured on in their thousands to celebrate their club's great victory. This was Rangers' finest hour, uniquely achieved in their centenary year. Indeed, it is the only occasion when a club has won a European trophy exactly 100 years after their formation. The Light Blues had defeated the cream of Europe en route to their greatest triumph, the standard of opposition being far superior to that encountered by the two British clubs that until 1972 had won the Champions' Cup.

Thousands of Rangers' fans celebrated on the pitch, hugging their heroes. It was a good-natured celebration, exactly as Celtic fans had celebrated five years earlier in Lisbon. Indeed, the local police had positively encouraged the belief pre-match that the fans would be allowed to celebrate at will.

Tragically, it all went wrong, with disastrous consequences. In an effort to clear the pitch of the celebrating fans the police, instead of ushering them off as Strathclyde's finest would undoubtedly have done, chose to attack viciously and premeditately with batons flailing. The fans dispersed, regrouped on the far side of the ground and, to the absolute astonishment of the Spanish people, launched their own counter-attack. As the battle raged on, the trophy was presented to John Greig deep inside the bowels of the Nou Camp. The Rangers' fans had been denied the one sight they wanted to see above all others – their team with a European trophy.

It is, of course, true that the post-match incidents marred the achievement, but the damning publicity and condemnation heaped on Rangers by most of the Scottish Press was harsh in the extreme and surely unjustified. A more balanced media view came from broadcaster Archie McPherson in his fascinating book *Action Replays* published by Chapmans in 1991:

> A few minutes after the end of the match the crowd, in a considerable frenzy, had advanced right across the pitch to the Main Stand where they awaited the cup presentation. At that stage it was not much different from Lisbon... The police had by then merely retreated until they were standing with their backs to the stand... Disastrously, the police decided to act. It started slowly with the thin line of light brown uniforms pressing against the crowd... a martinet of a Spanish policeman, of some rank, was barking at his men. I remember him raising his arm and giving a signal... I saw a baton flailing just to my right... then it became like a threshing machine as the whirl of batons advanced on a crowd whose front ranks could not escape this onslaught because of the pressure of those at the back. They couldn't see the touchline, did not know what was happening, and weren't budging... As soon as the first real assault had taken place the Spanish television director turned his main camera away from the pitch... Not a single television picture was taken of the police in action.
>
> We thought it was over but to our astonishment we saw the supporters... regrouping in a remarkably spontaneous way... they mounted a counter-attack. The police broke ranks and retreated... the supporters were giving as good as they got. 'Any moment now the guns could come out, for God's sake' said Reuters' correspondent in the area. I recall his words vividly. 'What you're seeing down there are Franco's men. They are not Catalans. That is why they are so hated in this city.'

Macpherson vividly narrates the brutality he witnessed by the police, and recalls the media coverage back in Scotland:

> The emphasis was being placed naturally enough on the conduct of the Rangers supporters. In other words on the aftermath of the assault by the police. The riot was not fully described. Scandalously it never officially was. When we made efforts to try to rationalise and apportion blame fairly we were condemned by the public. There was one special reason for that. We had not shown the riot... we were discovering that trying to tell the truth was not enough.

Archie Macpherson's account will find sympathy and understanding with all who were present in the Nou Camp but the Rangers' support was unjustly condemned by the Scottish Press (some things never change!) and by many sections of society who had not been present in Barcelona. A statement from Glasgow's Labour Lord Provost John Mains defied belief – he showed his true colours as he described the behaviour of the fans as 'shameful and disgraceful'. Yet when questioned about the brutality of the Spanish police he replied: 'I would not want to criticise because I wasn't there'!

The club's treatment at the hands of UEFA was scarcely any better: a two-year ban reduced on appeal to one, although the governing body did also ensure that Spain would not host another European final for some ten years. No one could deny of course that the fans should not have been on the pitch in the first place, but there had been enough of a precedent to justify their belief that the celebration of a European triumph in this manner was customary (e.g. Lisbon 1967) and indeed some six weeks after that unforgettable night West German fans celebrated similarly in Brussels as their team overwhelmed the Soviet Union 3-0 in the European Championship final. Away from the Nou Camp there were a few regrettable but minor incidents in which a few windows were broken and plant pots smashed. Nothing, however, to justify the blatant exaggeration that was the Press reporting the likes of which happen most nights in Spanish holiday resorts. In a forerunner to similarly disgraceful media coverage of a friendly in Sunderland in 1993, these wholly minor events were hyped up to the extent that it appeared that the city of Barcelona and the whole stretch of the Costa Del Sol had been razed to the ground, at least according to sections of the anti-Rangers media. Meanwhile, for the local citizens of Barcelona there was unreserved

A European trophy is paraded at Ibrox – when will we see another?

praise and admiration for the Rangers fans who had achieved something no one had dared even to contemplate before – they had fought back against Franco's police.

1971/72 European Cup-Winners' Cup, first round, first leg
Wednesday 15 September 1971, Parc Des Sports, Rennais
Stade Rennais 1 (Redou) Rangers 1 (Johnston)
Attendance 13,993
McCloy; Jardine, Mathieson; Greig, McKinnon, Jackson; McLean, A. McDonald, Stein (Denny), Penman, Johnston
First round, second leg
Tuesday 28 September 1971, Ibrox Stadium, Glasgow
Rangers 1 (A. MacDonald) Stade Rennais 0
Attendance 42,000
McCloy; Jardine, Mathieson; Greig, McKinnon, Jackson; Henderson, Conn, Stein, A. McDonald, Johnston
Second round, first leg
Wednesday 20 October 1971, Ibrox Stadium, Glasgow
Rangers 3 (Stein 2, Henderson) Sporting Clube de Portugal 2 (Chico, Pedro Gomes)
Attendance 50,000
McCloy; Greig, Mathieson; Jardine, McKinnon, Smith; Henderson, Penman (Conn), Stein, Fyfe, A. McDonald
Second round, second leg
Wednesday 3 November 1971, Estadio Jose de Alvalade, Lisboa
Sporting Clube de Portugal 4 (Yazalde, Tome, Pedro Gomes, Perez pen)
Rangers 3 (Stein 2, Henderson)
Attendance 70,000
McCloy; Greig, Mathieson; Jardine, McKinnon (Smith), Jackson; Henderson, Conn, Stein, Johnston (McLean), A. McDonald
Quarter-final, first leg
Wednesday 8 March 1972, Stadio Comunale, Torino
Torino 1 (Pulici) Rangers 1 (A. MacDonald)
Attendance 40,000
McCloy; Jardine, Mathieson; Greig, Jackson, Smith; McLean, Johnstone, Stein, A. McDonald, Johnston
Quarter-final, second leg
Wednesday 22 March 1972, Ibrox Stadium, Glasgow
Rangers 1 (A. MacDonald) Torino 0
Attendance 75,000
McCloy; Jardine, Mathieson; Greig, Jackson, Smith; McLean, Johnstone, Stein, A. McDonald, Johnston

Semi-final, first leg

Wednesday 5 April 1972, Stadion Grunwalder, München

Bayern München 1 (Breitner) Rangers 1 (Zobel o.g.)

Attendance 44,000

McCloy; Jardine, Mathieson; Greig, Jackson, Smith; McLean, Johnstone, Stein, A. McDonald, Johnston

Semi-final, second leg

Wednesday 19 April 1972, Ibrox Stadium, Glasgow

Rangers 2 (Jardine, Parlane) Bayern München 0

Attendance 80,000

McCloy; Jardine, Mathieson; Parlane, Jackson, Smith; McLean, Johnstone, Stein, A. McDonald, Johnston

Final

Wednesday 24 May 1972, Estadio Camp Nou, Barcelona

Rangers 3 (Johnston 2, Stein) Dinamo Moskva 2 (Eschtrekov, Makovikov)

Attendance 24,701

McCloy; Jardine, Mathieson; Greig, Johnstone, Smith; McLean, Conn, Stein, A. McDonald, Johnston

Harshly denied the opportunity to defend their hard-won spoils the following season when Rangers would surely have retained the trophy, given the ability the team had demonstrated in defeating the cream of Europe over two legs, the Ibrox men had to content themselves with participation in the inaugural European Super Cup against Ajax.

It all started with an invitation to the Amsterdam giants (European Champions' Cup holders for the two previous seasons) by Willie Waddell (now general manager with coach Jock Wallace promoted to the post of team manager) to visit Ibrox in January 1973 as part of Rangers' centenary celebrations (albeit they were being marked one year late). Ajax were only too willing to accept and proposed a return match in Amsterdam. Thus the European Super Cup was born; UEFA readily adopted the idea, and the Rangers–Ajax meeting of 1972/73 is now accepted as the inaugural fixture in the series. Ibrox Stadium was awash with nostalgia on the evening of Tuesday 16 January 1973, with the colours of every club Rangers had faced in European competition displayed by pupils from local schools Bellahouston Academy and Govan High School. At the interval, both of Europe's two premier trophies were paraded before the 60,000 spectators by pupils from Hyndland Secondary School – one wonders when the Champions' Cup will make a reappearance in Govan.

Glasgow's Lord Provost William Gray was introduced to both teams prior to kick-off. Hard as it is to believe nowadays, Glasgow's leading citizen in 1973 had Light Blue leanings! Legendary former player Andy Cunningham ceremoniously kicked-off and the home side could have done with the presence of some of the

Rangers' European Cup-Winners' Cup side of 1972.

greats who had graced the Ibrox turf over the years, for Ajax were without question the finest club side in the world – Johan Cruyff, Johan Neeskens, Ruud Krol, Johnny Rep, Arie Haan, and Arnold and Gerry Muhren were all players of the highest class.

The Dutch masters produced an astonishing opening half-hour, displaying superb football at breathtaking speed, with the magnificent Cruyff at its epi-centre. Rangers were not dishonoured, however, somehow surviving that spell before succumbing in the thirty-fifth minute when Cruyff created the opening goal with a perfectly weighted pass to Rep who drew Peter McCloy off his line before stroking the ball home. Rangers' response befitted the occasion and saw them equalise within seven minutes when a long pass from John Greig found Alfie Conn who in turn released Alex MacDonald to shoot home on the turn, from a tight angle on the edge of the area, off Heinz Stuy's left-hand post. The game turned on the stroke of half-time, however, with a superlative goal scored by the majestic Cruyff – one of the finest ever seen at the old stadium – as the Ajax no.14 sped towards the home goal pursued by Derek Johnstone. DJ seemed to have closed his opponent down, blocking his road to goal, only to fall vic-tim to the classic Cruyff double-shuffle – a sudden drop in pace with the ball still under absolute control. Whilst the Ranger slithered helplessly past him, the Dutch maestro doubled back, swivelled, and as Tom Forsyth raced in to help, struck a vicious left-foot shot into the net.

Ibrox rose to a genius and Ajax were in command although Rangers pressed hard after the interval with Derek Parlane, John Greig and Tommy McLean all coming close, and one superb Johnstone run deserved better than to end with a shot inches wide. The classic sucker punch was struck on seventy-six minutes when that man Cruyff found Barry Hulshoff who touched on for Haan, who evaded Johnstone to crash home a great shot.

In truth, Ajax had been a class apart, as was perhaps underlined at the post-match press conference when coach Rinus Michels suggested that the second leg might be played at Ajax's own ground – Stadion Middleweg – as perhaps only 20,000 would attend. 'Why so few?' he was asked, 'Too easy,' was the reply.

However, the Olympisch Stadion was, in the event, the venue, with 43,000 in attendance. This was indicative perhaps that the citizens of Amsterdam – the city of the River Amstel, of fifty canals and 400 bridges, of the Rembrandt and Van Gogh Museums and of the Anne Frank House – recognised that Rangers remained one of the great names in the global game for, even at their peak, Ajax struggled to attract huge audiences in their own city.

A memorable game was just reward for the spectators with Rangers drawing first blood as early as the third minute when Alex MacDonald struck a glorious left-foot shot into the top corner of the net from twenty yards. It didn't take long for Ajax to respond, Arie Haan equalising with a great left-foot shot from a superb Cruyff pass, but there was another jolt for the home side after thirty-five minutes when Quinton Young stooped low to head a McLean free-kick past Stuy. Rangers now had real hopes of turning the tie on its head but a controversial penalty award two minutes later when Willie Mathieson was alleged to have fouled Neeskens allowed Gerry Muhren to convert low and hard past McCloy. The Scots gave their all, with Greig at the heart of every move, Derek Parlane covering every inch of ground and McCloy in outstanding form, only for another flash of genius from Cruyff on seventy-eight minutes to win the day when he broke free from midfield, beating Johnstone and netting with a sublime swerving shot low into the corner of the net.

Ajax had won the inaugural European Super Cup but Rangers could look back on the two games with pride, reflecting perhaps that were it not for the unjust ban on defending the European Cup-Winners' Cup they would, come May, have been heading for Thessaloniki and a second consecutive final. In the event, it would be AC Milan who would succeed Rangers as holders, defeating Leeds United 1-0 whilst Ajax secured their third consecutive Champions' Cup with a 1-0 win over Juventus in Belgrade.

1972/73 European Super Cup

First match

Tuesday 16 January 1973, Ibrox Stadium, Glasgow

Rangers 1 (A. MacDonald) Ajax 3 (Rep, Cruyff, Haan)

Attendance 60,000

McCloy; Jardine, Mathieson; Greig, Johnstone (Fyfe), Smith; Conn (McLean), Forsyth, Parlane, A. MacDonald, Young

Second match

Wednesday 24 January 1973, Olympisch Stadion, Amsterdam

Ajax 3 (Haan, G. Muhren pen, Cruyff) Rangers 2 (A. MacDonald, Young);
Attendance 43,000

McCloy; Jardine, Mathieson; Greig, Johnstone, Smith; McLean, Forsyth,
Parlane, A. MacDonald, Young

FOUR

Into the Shadows

Rangers qualified yet again for their favourite European tournament by winning the 1973 Centenary Scottish Cup final in the presence of HRH the Princess Alexandra after a long unbeaten run that stretched for more than half a season. The draw for the opening round of the 1973/74 European Cup-Winners' Cup was eagerly awaited and would send the Ibrox men further afield than on any UEFA expedition thus far, to the Asian continent to face Ankaragucu of Turkey.

The journey across the Bosphuras Straits to Ankara marked Rangers' first visit to Turkey, but whilst there was no hostile reception awaiting the Light Blues and the small band of some twenty fans who followed on, the journey was a long and tiring one via London and Istanbul – even more so for one supporter who had travelled overland only to arrive too late for the game! The official party – with four hours to kill in Istanbul between flights – were taken on a guided coach tour of the ancient city that included a visit to the Blue Mosque. Compiling a dossier on Ankaragucu had been even more of a problem for Jock Wallace; eventually he despatched experienced player Doug Houston (out of action through injury) to watch a League fixture against Galatasaray just four days before the first leg. Unfortunately, travel delays meant that Houston's first glimpse of the play was overhead as his plane came in to land. Eventually the former Dundee player would see thirty minutes' play standing on his suitcase at the back of the terracing.

The 19 Mayis (May) Stadium – so named after the date of Ataturk's revolution – was packed to its 45,000 capacity close to four hours before the 5p.m. kick-off on 19 September but the intense heat, altitude (Ankara is over 3,000ft above sea level) and the dry, dusty and bumpy pitch were more of a problem for the Scots than either the Turkish fans or their opponents. Indeed the visitors displayed a neat diplomatic touch before the start by distributing the bouqets of flowers they had each been presented with to the spectators. Supplementing the travel-ling support were the entire contingent of some 100 British Embassy staff who had entertained the Rangers directors at a reception, including the Ambassador himself, Sir Horace Phillips – a lifelong Rangers fan educated at Hillhead High School.

Ankaragucu had given Leeds United a difficult time the previous season when the two clubs met in the UEFA Cup (1-1, 0-1) but Rangers – even minus the suspended Alex MacDonald and the injured Derek Johnstone – were always in control after taking the lead as early as the eleventh minute when a Quinton Young cross was miskicked by Ismail Dilber allowing Alfie Conn to net from close range. A John Greig header from Tommy McLean's cross went close but Peter McCloy was not tested until the opening ten minutes of the second half when he kept the Turks at bay with excellent saves from Metin and Coskun. The tie was effectively sealed on the hour when a mazy run by Tommy McLean from inside his own half took him past five opponents before playing a one-two with Derek Parlane then curling the ball home from fifteen yards. A twenty-yard shot from Selcuk hit the post, but Rangers had secured a fine win with McCloy, Jackson and Young outstanding.

The Ibrox return was very much a formality and Jock Wallace took the opportunity to field youngster Alex O'Hara. Home form had been a major problem for the Light Blues: three games had already been lost even though September was barely over and not a solitary goal had been scored in three League fixtures. A ninth-minute twenty-two-yard thunderbolt from John Greig – finishing off a move involving McLean and O'Hara – settled any unease, however, and Rangers kept their heads as all around them lost theirs. Both Coskun and Errian were ordered off by Norwegian referee Rolf Nyhus for wild tackles on Tom Forsyth and Doug Houston. The home side eventually ran out comfortable winners with 3 goals in the last 10 minutes courtesy of Alex O'Hara (who had earlier struck the crossbar), John Greig (with another powerful drive) and Derek Johnstone.

The second round would be a different matter. Old friends Borussia Mönchengladbach awaited and the tie would to this day be remembered more than anything else for the loss of one of the most bizarre goals Rangers have ever conceded. Borussia were undoubtedly a class side, arguably the most difficult opponents Rangers could have encountered in the entire draw and second only to Bayern München (who had of course lost to the Light Blues just eighteen months earlier in the Bundesliga). Twice Champions – in 1969/70 and 1970/71 – Mönchengladbach had also reached the UEFA Cup final in 1972/73, losing to Liverpool. The previous season had seen them fall victim to one of the great injustices in European football history when their 7-1 annihilation of Internazionale Milano had been nullified by UEFA because Roberto Boninsegna alleged he had been struck down by a beer can. The great Gunter Netzer had departed for pastures new – to Real Madrid – but there was still a certain Berti Vogts (Scotland national coach, with disastrous consequences, three decades on), Jupp Heynckes, Rainer Bonhof, Ulli Stielike, Allen Simonsen and Henning Jensen. Quality indeed.

Rangers line up in Ankara.

The Ibrox men had nevertheless overcome even greater quality en route to Barcelona 1972 and many friends of Rangers believed passionately that the cup could be recaptured. The Light Blues had inaugurated the redeveloped Stadion Bokelberg in 1962 with a 1-1 draw and eleven years later the ground was a seething cauldron packed by 35,000 spectators, many of whom were travelling Gers fans whose numbers were swollen by the presence of many British soldiers stationed on the Rhine. The visitors made an impressive start, playing cautiously, confining the Germans to long-range efforts; the first twenty minutes in an away European tie are always tense yet Rangers had survived that opening spell and were looking comfortable when the roof fell in on Peter McCloy. A long ball out of defence had seen Bernd Rupp forlornly giving chase before his momentum carried him over the goal line and into the posse of photographers positioned behind the goal. McCloy had the ball safely in his possession and was rolling it out towards the edge of the penalty area with the Rangers defence turning upfield, awaiting their colleague's massive clearance from hand when a lapse in concentration by the goalkeeper allowed Rupp to come from behind him, steal the ball and roll it across goal for Jupp Heynckes to score easily. Belgian referee Robert Schaut dismissed Ibrox protests and, in all honesty, the goal was perfectly legitimate, as one suspects even McCloy would concede. The Light Blues were stunned by the loss of the goal and Borussia were very much in the driving seat, dictating the pace of the game. Rangers somehow survived for the remainder of the first half, yet were to suffer another blow on the hour when Tom Forsyth was adjudged to have fouled Jupp Heynckes. Penalty – and Heynckes himself took the kick but the 'Girvan Lighthouse' (who had already produced two outstanding saves from Horst Koppel) redeemed himself for his earlier aberration by pushing the ball wide. This escape should have offered Rangers a lifeline, but within five minutes Heynckes had atoned for his penalty miss by notching a second goal, leaving the Scots in desperate need of an away goal only to be hit with the classic sucker-punch breakaway goal in the dying minutes when Rupp added a third.

Such a deficit was a daunting task for the Ibrox return and with the home side already handicapped by the absence of the injured Derek Johnstone the last thing anyone needed was to hinder one's prospects with a self-inflicted wound – but so it proved as the Rangers directors incredibly set the admission prices so high for the Centenary Stand (never the most popular of locations at the best of times) that there was literally only a handful of spectators who were prepared to pay the admission price of £1.50. This was a staggering 200 per cent more than the rest of the ground, effectively meaning that virtually the entire covered stand (the site of the present Govan Stand) running the full length of one side of the pitch lay empty, thus destroying the atmosphere inside the ground!

Nevertheless, the 40,000 present in other parts of the ground were witness to a tumultous match as Rangers produced their finest display of the season, opening the scoring after ten minutes when a Willie Mathieson free-kick produced Alex O'Hara's glancing header against the post, Alfie Conn seizing on the rebound to shoot home. However, Borussia effectively clinched the tie on twenty-eight minutes when Henning Jensen outpaced Mathieson and saw his low shot from eighteen yards elude Peter McCloy. Within four minutes the Scots had regained the lead when Colin Jackson headed home a Doug Houston cross. The high ball was for once creating havoc in the visitors' defence and only a superlative save by Wolfgang Kleff from a Conn effort denied the Light Blues a third goal before the interval. It was end-to-end stuff, and when Alex McDonald's diving header from a 'Cutty' Young cross found the net after sixty-one minutes many believed that a miracle was at hand, but the dream evaporated ten minutes later when that man Heynckes released Jensen, the Danish striker sealing Rangers' fate when he slotted the ball home from close range after McCloy had blocked his first effort.

Rangers had traded goals with one of the finest sides in Europe and on the night had proved the better, but the reality was that they were out of Europe. Borussia Mönchengladbach meanwhile would advance to the semi-finals where they would be eliminated by AC Milan (0-2, 1-0).

1973/74 European Cup-Winners' Cup, first round, first leg

Wednesday 19 September 1973, 19 Mayis Stadium, Ankara

Ankaragucu 0 Rangers 2 (Conn, McLean)

Attendance 45,000

McCloy; Jardine, Mathieson; Greig, Jackson, Smith; McLean, Forsyth, Parlane, Conn, Young

First round, second leg

Wednesday 3 October 1973, Ibrox Stadium, Glasgow

Rangers 4 (Greig 2, O'Hara, Johnstone) Ankaragucu 0

Attendance 30,000

McCloy; Jardine, Mathieson; Greig, Johnstone, McDonald; McLean, Forsyth, O'Hara, Conn, Houston

Second round, first leg

Wednesday 24 October 1973, Stadion Bokelberg, Mönchengladbach

Borussia Mönchengladbach 3 (Heynckes 2, Rupp) Rangers 0

Attendance 35,000

McCloy; Jardine, Mathieson; Greig, Johnstone, McDonald; McLean, Forsyth, Parlane, (O'Hara), Conn, Houston

Second round, second leg

Wednesday 7 November 1973, Ibrox Stadium, Glasgow

Rangers 3 (Conn, Jackson, MacDonald) Borussia Mönchengladbach 2 (Jensen 2)

Attendance 40,000

McCloy; Jardine, Mathieson; Greig, Jackson, MacDonald; McLean, Forsyth (Young), O'Hara, Conn, Houston

Despite finishing third in the championship race in 1973/74, there would be no European football the following season. Rangers made up for that omission as the League flag came home for the first time in eleven years, thus sending the Light Blues into the Champions' Cup once again. More than forty years had passed since Rangers had last visited Dublin, but the Republic of Ireland was the destination in 1975/76 when the Ibrox men opened their campaign.

Manager Jock Wallace watched the Irish side twice before the tie, but surprisingly vetoed Bohemians' proposal to switch the first leg to Dalymount Park. Jock was not without his problems for the Ibrox meeting, being without Tommy McLean, Sandy Jardine and Tom Forsyth through injury, and Alex MacDonald through having been erroneously advised by UEFA of a one-match suspension on the player from two years previously – the governing body later admitted this was an administrative error on their part, but too late for Rangers.

Graham Fyfe was the key for the home side, easily opening the scoring after twenty minutes, although a Terry Flanagan equaliser in the thirty-seventh minute was a setback for the Scots. Two minutes later, however, Colin Stein harried Joe Burke into conceding an own goal, and second-half strikes from Alex O'Hara and Derek Johnstone, both laid on by Graham Fyfe, secured a comfortable lead for the trip to Dublin.

Many Light Blue followers in Dublin two weeks later had more than the football to entertain them; in the early hours of the morning on the day of the game they had the opportunity to watch the 'Thrilla in Manila' live on Irish television as Muhammed Ali retained the World Heavyweight Championship by defeating Joe Frazier in the Philippines. With the tie a virtual foregone conclusion, the return at 'Dalyer' attracted just 8,000 spectators and before kick-off Rangers were more concerned with IRA threats received at local newspaper offices than by the threat of Bohemians. In truth, Rangers dominated the return, but were consistently denied by goalkeeper Joe Smyth, who defied Quinton Young, John Greig and Tommy McLean before Derek Johnstone finally headed home a Greig free-kick after thirty-eight minutes. Turlough O'Connor equalised ten minutes into the second half to give the Dublin side a memorable draw, but it was Rangers who progressed to round two. As to the perceived threats, there was just one incident worthy of note, when a bottle was hurled through the window of the Rangers team bus as it was making its way along O'Connell Street, with Jock Wallace suffering a facial injury, thankfully not too serious.

The Scots now found themselves facing a return trip to the Stade Geoffroy-Guichard. St Etienne now had a considerable track record in Europe, having reached the semi-finals of the European Cup the previous season, disposing of Sporting Lisbon, Hajduk Split and Ruch Chorzow en route to a 0-2 aggregate defeat at the hands of the cup holders (and eventual champions) Bayern Munich. Indeed, in 1968/69 they had faced the outstanding Celtic team of that era, and after a 2-0 win in France were eliminated – mainly due to some quite appalling refereeing – 0-4 at Celtic Park.

Coach Robert Herbin had played in that game and his pre-match comments were revealing, to say the least: 'I am happy that we have this game instead of having to face perhaps Real Madrid, Bayern Munich, or Dinamo Kiev!' Pause for thought, perhaps, for many friends of Rangers who, three years after Barcelona, were expecting the ultimate success!

Jock Wallace, for his part, had watched St Etienne draw 2-2 at Nantes, pinpointing wingers Dominique Rocheteau and Patrick Revelli correctly as the danger men. Beset by injuries (some things never change), an electric atmosphere awaited the Light Blues in Loire, and pre-match nerves were scarcely helped when goalkeeper Peter McCloy was injured during the warm-up, being replaced by Stewart Kennedy.

'ALLEZ LES VERTS' was the battlecry of the home fans (St Etienne play in green shirts) and Rangers had their backs to the wall against a series of French attacks, before the first blow was struck in the twenty-eighth minute when Rocheteau lured Alex Miller out of position before crossing for Revelli to hammer the ball home. Gradually, however, Rangers tightened up on the wide pitch, gaining control of midfield, and the persistent attacks of Les Verts began to peter out. Indeed after sixty-three minutes only a brilliant save by Yugoslav goalkeeper Ivan Curkovic defied an Alex McDonald header, when Tommy McLean sped down the right wing, his cross being flicked on by Stein with a deft header. Rangers were in sight of a respectable result until disaster struck in the dying seconds when slackness in defence resulted in Alex MacDonald – a tireless worker throughout – misplacing a pass across the eighteen-yard line to Sandy Jardine, which was swiftly intercepted by Dominique Bathenay, who swept forward to net. The scoreline stood at 2-0 and all Rangers' hard work had been in vain.

'Doddie' would make amends for his aberration three days later with the goal in Rangers' 1-0 League Cup final victory over Celtic but it was another team in green who posed a much greater challenge for the Ibrox men. Guy Fawkes night in Copland Road produced a 45,000 attendance, but in truth Rangers never remotely looked like winning the match, far less the overall tie. Hurling themselves forward in wave after wave of attacks, the high ball to the two Dereks – Parlane and Johnstone – was counter-productive and only once was Curkovic troubled, when saving from Parlane. Rangers were wide open to the counter-attack, and in the sixty-third minute paid the penalty when Rocheteau went clear down the wing unchallenged to score and seven minutes later Herve Revelli (brother of Patrick) added a second.

'What a load of rubbish' chanted the Ibrox legions and, in truth, Rangers had been out-thought and outplayed. Alex MacDonald did net a crumb of consolation in the final minute, but by then it was all too late.

St Etienne went all the way to a Hampden Park final in 1975/76, losing somewhat unluckily to Bayern München 0-1 before 54,864 spectators.

1975/76 European Champions' Cup, first round, first leg
Wednesday 17 September 1975, Ibrox Stadium, Glasgow
Rangers 4 (Fyfe, O'Hara, Johnstone, Burke o.g.) Bohemians Dublin 1 (Flanagan)
Attendance 25,000
McCloy; Denny, Miller; Greig, Johnstone, Jackson; Fyfe, O'Hara (McDougall), Parlane, Stein, Young (Henderson)
First round, second leg
Wednesday 1 October 1975, Dalymount Park, Dublin
Bohemians 1 (T. O'Connor) Rangers 1 (Johnstone)
Attendance 8,000
McCloy; Miller, Dawson; Greig, Jackson, Young; McLean, MacDonald, Parlane, Johnstone, Fyfe
Second round, first leg
Wednesday 22 October 1975, Stade Geoffroy-Guichard, Saint-Etienne
AS Saint-Etienne 2 (P. Revelli, Bathenay) Rangers 0
Attendance 28,394

Kennedy; Jardine, Miller; Greig, Jackson, Forsyth; McLean (Young), Stein, Parlane (Henderson), MacDonald, Johnstone.
Second round, second leg
Wednesday 5 November 1975, Ibrox Stadium, Glasgow
Rangers 1 (MacDonald) AS Saint-Etienne 2 (Rocheteau, H. Revelli)
Attendance 51,000
Kennedy; Jardine, Greig; Forsyth, Jackson, MacDonald; McLean, Stein, Parlane, Johnstone, Young

A second successive League title meant another crack at the Champions' Cup and when the luck of the ballot paired Rangers with FC Zurich of Switzerland there were many friends of Rangers who regarded the draw as both a comfortable one and an omen, for had not Celtic met Zurich in the opening round ten years earlier?

It would be Rangers' first visit to Switzerland in a competitive European fixture, although the Light Blues had played four games in that country as part of a six-game summer tour in 1923. Twenty goals without loss had been the outcome of those four games, but more than half a century later the opposition would be made of sterner stuff.

Roger Federer may have achieved considerable sporting success in the world of tennis in recent years (particularly at Wimbledon) but three decades ago the country was more renowned for its magnificent scenery, cheese, banking and in the words of Orson Wells in the film *The Third Man*: 'In Switzerland they've had peace and harmony and 300 years of democracy – and what have they produced? The cuckoo clock.'

Rangers' Champions' Cup campaign could not have got off to a worse start, conceding the opening goal in the first leg at Ibrox inside fifty seconds. Careless passing in midfield allowed the visitors to gain possession, Botteron finding Risi with a neat pass, his swift shot hitting the post with Italian import Cucinotta netting the rebound.

In truth, the Scots never fully recovered, even when Derek Parlane equalised on the half-hour after Derek Johnstone had struck the crossbar, and Zurich comfortably held out for a 1-1 draw despite constant home pressure in the second half.

Two weeks later Rangers visited the Gnomes of Zurich fully aware that whilst the Stadion Letzigrund was not renowned as one of Europe's great football venues, Bayern München, Leeds United and Ujpesti Dosza had all suffered defeat there in recent years. Yet again, as in Glasgow, the Light Blues lost an early goal when Rosario Martinelli opened the scoring after just eight minutes. Rangers had an uphill struggle as they strove manfully to claw their way back into the tie only to be denied time and time again by goalkeeper Carl Grob, whose performance Ibrox manager Jock Wallace later described as the finest he had witnessed in Europe.

The equaliser appeared certain midway through the second half when a Tommy McLean cross found the head of Johnstone only for Grob to save low down just inside the post. The Swiss goalkeeper somehow defied the law of gravity in the closing minutes when he clawed out a twenty-yard volley from Parlane with the ball already behind him. The die was cast and Ibrox ignominy was complete when Johnstone was ordered off for dissent in the dying seconds. Rangers had exited Europe despite a much-improved performance in Zurich – the tie had been lost in Glasgow, but Zurich defied those who had labelled them as a poor team by progressing to the semi-finals, before succumbing to the might of eventual winners Liverpool (3-1, 3-0).

1976/77 European Champions' Cup, first round, first leg
Wednesday 15 September 1976, Ibrox Stadium, Glasgow
Rangers 1 (Parlane) Zurich 1 (Cucinotta)
Attendance 35,000
McCloy; Miller, Greig; Forsyth, Denny, MacDonald; McLean, Jardine, Parlane, McKean, Johnstone
First round, second leg
Wednesday 29 September 1976, Stadion Letzigrund, Zurich
Zurich 1 (Martinelli) Rangers 0
Attendance 28,500
McCloy; Jardine, Miller; Greig, Jackson (Denny), Forsyth; McLean, Hamilton (McKean), Parlane, MacDonald, Johnstone

It was a measure of Rangers' falling European standards that five years after Barcelona they found themselves playing in a preliminary-round tie of the European Cup-Winners' Cup against BSC Young Boys – a second consecutive visit to Switzerland for the Light Blues, having avoided the country for more than half a century. Rangers were in their favourite European tournament, despite season 1976/77 having been one of great disappointment, as Scottish Cup runners-up. Jock Wallace had restructured the team for the coming campaign, introducing a much-required touch of class and vision in the shape of three new signings, namely Davie Cooper from Clydebank, Gordon Smith from Kilmarnock and Robert Russell from Shettleston Juniors. The earliest ever entry to Europe for the club meant that the new team had not yet gelled when the Swiss visited Ibrox on 17 August, with Young Boys proving to be one of the most depressing and defensive outfits to visit the Stadium in a long time. Rangers, handicapped by the absence of the suspended Derek Johnstone, failed lamentably to spring the offside trap until the fortieth minute when John Greig seized on a Tom Forsyth pass to score with a powerful drive in off a post from fifteen yards. Incessant second-half pressure failed to add to that score with Sandy Jardine striking the crossbar, and Derek Parlane and Chris Robertson somehow between the two of them contriving to miss an open goal.

A 1-0 lead was certainly not the worst possible advantage to take to Berne and Rangers travelled in good heart following a 4-0 League win over Partick Thistle at Firhill, with new signing Smith netting twice.

The journey to Switzerland was not without its logistical problems – air traffic control disputes meant that the official party travelled by train from Glasgow to London. The good, solid burghers of the Swiss capital appeared more interested in the constant chess games that took place in the squares of the picturesque city than in a European tie. Light Blue followers quickly felt at home in a city where one of the main tourist attractions was a bearpit.

Defeat to the Swiss would have been a catastrophe following the loss to Zurich eleven months earlier, but Rangers were in command throughout the first half at the Stadion Wankdorf (venue of the 1954 World Cup final) with Johnstone finally opening the scoring after forty-three minutes when he outjumped goal-keeper Walter Eichenberger to head home Cooper's inswinging corner. The tie was surely won but the second half would be a different story, with Young Boys receiving a lucky break three minutes in when a low Josef Kuttel shot came back off the upright before rebounding off Jackson into the net. When substitute Jost Leuzinger added a second on the hour Rangers were right up against it, having already lost both McLean and Russell injured. Smith saved the day after seventy-five minutes with his third goal in two games from a Bobby McKean pass. Qualification was secured, yet the Ibrox men suffered a disappointment in the closing minutes when Johnstone was ordered off for retaliation, his second successive dismissal in European ties, both in Switzerland. The final word lay with the Italian referee who later stated that he had a degree of sympathy with the Ranger who had been kicked throughout the game!

Rangers were through to the first round proper, where they would confront Dutch side Twente Enschede, albeit handicapped by the absence of Johnstone, suspended for both legs due to his dismissal in Berne. Twente's European pedigree was considerable; twice in the 1970s they had lost to Rangers' old friends Borussia Mönchengladbach at a late stage of the UEFA Cup, in the penultimate round in 1972/73, going one better two years on. Clearly a side of some quality, numbered in their ranks were Frans Thijssen and Arnold Muhren; the latter had played in the 1972/73 European Super Cup against the Light Blues. Jock Wallace had plenty to think about before the first leg at Ibrox: apart from the suspended Johnstone, also missing were the injured Alex McDonald and Derek Parlane. Even more astonishing was the decision by the Rangers manager to leave captain John Greig and the experienced Tommy McLean on the substitutes' bench!

The Dutch side were disciplined and composed before 40,000 spectators at Ibrox, a defence orchestrated by their veteran skipper Epi Drost, frustrating the Scots time and time again. In truth, Rangers created just one clear chance throughout the ninety minutes when Jardine (captain on the night) surged through the defence to the byline, his low cutback being pushed wide from inside the six-yard box by Cooper. Many questioned why neither Greig nor McLean had come on at Ibrox and indeed neither would make an appearance in Enschede either, although both McDonald and Parlane would return. The small Dutch town of Enschede lies just five miles from the German border, and the Diekman Stadion presented its own particular problem – floodlights barely acceptable by UEFA standards and a pitch that at eighty yards wide was much bigger than anything at home. A score draw would of course have taken Rangers through on aggregate, but in reality the Ibrox side seldom looked capable of achieving such a result, although with half an hour on the clock the scoresheet remained blank. Alas, a goalkeeping blunder by Stewart Kennedy presented Twente with a golden opportunity in the thirty-fourth minute when Jaap Bos swung over a ball from the right which was missed in the floodlights by the Rangers custodian, allowing Ab Gritter the formality of heading into an empty net. The home side were now on the rampage and within six minutes Arnold Muhren rifled home a second from another right-wing cross from Cees van Irssel with the Rangers defence all at sea. The visitors were being overrun, and a powerful twenty-yard drive from Kick van der Vall completed the scoring in the sixty-fifth minute. Even the opportunity of a late consolation goal was squandered when Alex Miller missed from the penalty spot after Dutch goal-keeper Andre van Gerven fouled Smith.

It had been an abominable display by the Light Blues and Jock Wallace afterwards criticised his players, but in all honesty the tie with such a strong side had come far too early in the season for a Rangers side with three new players in their ranks. Twente went on to reach another semi-final before succumbing to eventual winners Anderlecht (0-1, 0-2).

1977/78 European Cup-Winners' Cup, preliminary round, first leg
Wednesday 17 August 1977, Ibrox Stadium, Glasgow
Rangers 1 (Greig) Young Boys 0
Attendance 30,000
McCloy; Jardine, Greig; Forsyth, Jackson, McDonald; McLean (Mackay), Russell, Parlane (Smith), Robertson, Cooper
Preliminary round, second leg
Wednesday 31 August 1977, Stadion Wankdorf, Berne
Young Boys 2 (Leuzinger, Jackson o.g.) Rangers 2 (Johnstone, Smith)
Attendance 21,000
McCloy; Jardine, Greig; Forsyth, Jackson, McDonald; McLean (McKean), Russell (Miller), Johnstone, Smith, Cooper
First round, first leg
Wednesday 14 September 1977, Ibrox Stadium, Glasgow
Rangers 0 Twente Enschede 0
Attendance 40,000

McCloy; Jardine, Miller; Forsyth, Jackson, Watson; McKean, Russell,
Henderson, Smith, Cooper

First round, second leg

Wednesday 28 September 1977, Diekman Stadion, Enschede

Twente Enschede 3 (Gritter, Muhren, Van der Vall) Rangers 0

Attendance 20,000

Kennedy; Jardine, Miller; Forsyth, Jackson, McDonald; McKean, Russell,
Parlane, Smith, Cooper

FIVE

Pride Restored

Season 1977/78 may have been a failure as far as Europe was concerned, but domestically the club secured its fourth treble, displaying a brand of football that no Scottish team had enjoyed since the Rangers team of the early '60s. Jock Wallace's new signings had blended into a team of class and vision, yet that very summer Ibrox Stadium was rocked to its very foundations by the shock resignation of manager Jock Wallace. His successor came from within in the form of club captain John Greig whose service to the club was legendary, but whose appointment carried a substantial risk, given that he had no managerial experience whatsoever.

Greig's immediate task was clear – continue the domestic dominance that the club had enjoyed (with two trebles in three years) whilst at the same time restoring some credibility to the club in Europe, where in the five years since Barcelona progress had been limited to say the least. With that in mind, the young Ibrox boss must have been cursing his luck when the first-round draw paired Rangers with Italian giants Juventus. The Italian Champions are always a difficult prospect at any time, but this Juventus team was regarded as the cream of Europe, containing as it did no fewer than nine players from the Italian side that had reached the World Cup semi-finals in Argentina that very summer. Indeed, it had been a tournament the 'Azurri' might well have won, given that they defeated the hosts and eventual winners in the group stages.

Rangers did have the benefit of travelling to Piedmonte for the first leg at the Stadio Communale, the tie being played during the brief reign of Pope John Paul I, and at a time when the Shroud of Turin was on public display – a rare event indeed.

The new manager's team selection was a cautious one with Sandy Jardine utilised as a sweeper and wingers Tommy McLean and Davie Cooper confined to the substitutes' bench. The visiting defence was nonetheless breached in the early stages when Pietro Virdis eluded Colin Jackson to hook the ball into the net.

The 'Zebras' surged forward in wave after wave of attacks, with 70,000 fans producing a hostile atmosphere in the oval bowl, rockets and firecrackers exploding in the night sky, but the Ibrox backline held firm with Colin Jackson and Tom Forsyth keeping a tight rein on twin strikers Pietro Virdis and Roberto Bettega. Shortly before the interval Jardine struck his own post with a desperate clearance, but as the game wore on Rangers pushed the Italians back until, with time running out and Juve growing more and more frustrated, Gordon Smith was the victim of a quite appalling foul by Romeo Benetti, who had already been booked. The tackle in itself merited an ordering-off, but the Romanian referee incredibly took no action other than the award of a free-kick. Peter McCloy saved the day in the dying seconds with a superb save when he tipped a Bettega header over the bar and Rangers could feel satisfied with the result, even if the 'Old Lady' remained favourites.

John Greig had outwitted Juventus coach Giovanni Trappatoni and would do so again at Ibrox, shrewdly altering his formation by switching McLean from right wing to left. Johnstone and Gentile both returned after suspension, but Benneti was relegated to the subs' bench. The Italian Champions arrived in Glasgow exuding confidence despite their narrow lead, and there were many Light Blue followers who doubted their team's ability to overhaul the one-goal deficit, given that no Ibrox side had ever overturned a first-leg loss in Europe. It was surely inconceivable that they could do so against the best that Serie A could offer.

Forty-four thousand spectators packed a stadium under reconstruction with the Copland Road end a building site. The night would go down in Ibrox folklore as Rangers produced one of the finest performances of any Scottish club in Europe. A cleverly worked free-kick unlocked the cattenachio defence in seventeen minutes, Smith's shot being punched out by goalkeeper Dino Zoff (Italy's 1982 World Cup-winning captain) only for Alex McDonald to head home from close range. The home side were now dictating the tactical direction of the play and added a second after sixty-eight minutes when a Robert Russell free-kick was met by Smith, his header soaring beyond the outstretched Zoff into the far corner of the net.

Juve were stunned but fought to the end with substitute Benetti committing another atrocious assault on Smith and again going unpunished. Rangers held on for a memorable triumph that restored the club's good name throughout Europe. Following the momentous defeat of Juventus the draw could hardly have been less kind to the Scots. PSV Eindhoven awaited in round two – the Dutch side were UEFA Cup holders and contained six of the Holland squad that had reached the World Cup final in Argentina, four of whom had played in the final itself: Rene and Willy van der Kerkhof, Ernie Brandts and Jan Poortvliet. Formidable opponents indeed.

Dutch coach Cees Rijvers opted for a deep defensive approach in the first leg in Glasgow looking to hit Rangers on the break before a full house of 44,000 spectators, yet within sixty seconds Tom Forsyth had sprung the offside trap only to send the ball wide of goal, a clear chance and one that the home side would live to regret. PSV began to grow in confidence as the game wore on, slowing the pace of the game but, in spite of this, Rangers almost snatched a winner at the death when a low twenty-yard volley from Robert Russell was well saved by Tony van Engelen. PSV were overjoyed at the result, and few could blame them, for their proud boast was of never having lost a European tie on their own ground. Although they acknowledged that the quality of Rangers' play had surprised them, it was surely unthinkable that the Light Blues could overcome such a record.

Twenty-nine thousand spectators packed the Philips Stadion two weeks later, with Rangers allocated a meagre 850 tickets, although many more were dotted throughout the ground, bringing the total number to perhaps as many as 1,500. The city of Eindhoven, close to the German border and dominated by the electrical giants Philips, was one more port of call for the Light Blue legions in the 'Rhine Triangle' – the industrial heartland straddling the borders of West Germany and Holland – to which Rangers seemed inexplicably drawn in the period from 1973 to 1982; one thinks of Mönchengladbach (1973), Enschede (1977), Eindhoven (1978), Köln (1979 and 1982), Dusseldorf (1979) and Dortmund (1982), all within perhaps two hours travel of each other. In 1978 the Philips Stadion must have been an eye-opener to the visiting Rangers fans, compact, covered, seated on three sides and with overhead heating at a time when the transformation of Ibrox from the traditional oval bowl to a modern ground with three new stands based on the 'goalpost' principle had just begun.

There were just thirty-four seconds on the clock when PSV struck – a devastating blow for the Light Blues – as Harry Lubse crashed a powerful shot past Peter McCloy from ten yards. Such an early blow left Rangers with no alternative but to attack and perhaps the goal imbued PSV with a feeling of complacency. The Ibrox men began to control play, pushing forward at every opportunity, but in a controlled, disciplined manner which John Greig had drilled into his side – possession football that the Dutch scarcely believed a Scottish club could master. The scoreline remained unchanged at the interval, but in the fifty-seventh minute Rangers turned the tie on its head when a delicate chip into the area from Tommy McLean was met by a magnificent diving header from Alex McDonald for the equaliser. Within three minutes, however, PSV had regained the ascendancy when Gerry Deijkers scored from twelve yards and many felt that the Dutch would now take full control. Rangers would not lie down and after Derek Parlane missed a clear chance the Scots struck again, Tommy McLean the creator, slipping a short free-kick to Kenny Watson whose left-foot drive from the edge of the area was deflected into the net by the head of Derek Johnstone. At 2-2 Rangers were through on the away goals rule, but PSV piled on the pressure, forcing the Ibrox men back into defence. Ernie

Brandts was thrown forward as the Dutch resorted to high balls into the danger area – something Scots clubs had been severely criticised for over the years – and Peter McCloy was forced into two fine saves from long-range shots until, with just three minutes remaining, came the moment which will live forever in the mind's eye of those fortunate enough to be present. Yet another high ball into the box was headed clear by captain Derek Johnstone – to the edge of the area where Gordon Smith swung a left-foot pass out to Tommy McLean, wide on the right just inside his own half. The break was on and McLean held the ball until the precise moment when he could release Robert Russell running through the PSV defence; Russell was through on goal courtesy of Tommy's precision pass and as Van Engelen advanced he had several options: he could chip the goalkeeper or go round him. He chose to do neither and curled the ball around the keeper and into the net – a superb goal in execution and timing that would deservedly win the Goal of the Season award.

Rangers had secured a magnificent victory and, with the scalps of both PSV and Juventus, now had every right to believe that they could go on to the ultimate glory of winning the European Champions' Cup, being paired in the quarter-finals with 1. FC Köln, a side certainly inferior to those they had already eliminated.

However, it would be March before the tournament came out of winter storage, by which time the Scottish Champions would be beset by an injury crisis and a fixture backlog created by a severe winter. Köln had won the West German League and Cup double in the previous season and were coached by the vastly experienced Hennes Weisweiler, described by John Greig as a 'wily old fox', an old protaginist of the Light Blues from Mönchengladbach 1973. He had already tasted European success with Borussia and wanted more. A rough-house of a Scottish Cup-tie at Kilmarnock eight days before the first leg cost Rangers dear, depriving them of the services of Davie Cooper, Derek Johnstone and Kenny Watson, and forcing John Greig, in his first season in charge, to include Billy Urquhart and (for his first game in two years!) Jim Denny. Köln may not have had the class of Juventus or PSV, but nevertheless they could count within their ranks five players who had been in the West German World Cup squad at Argentina: defenders Harold Kanopka and Herbert Zimmerman, midfielders Bernd Cullman and Heinz Flohe (who had played against Rangers eleven years earlier) and striker Dieter Muller. Bernd Schuster and Pierre Littbarski were also key players. Notwithstanding the quality of these players, the Bundesliga club had a very real respect for Rangers' outstanding results thus far in Europe. The Stadion Müngersdorfer was unrecognisable from the Scots' last visit; the old ground had been completely rebuilt and the 50,000 audience included a massive travelling support of 7,000 Rangers fans. As in Turin, John Greig sent his charges out with caution in mind, Sandy Jardine being detailed to shadow Flohe everywhere (a job he performed superbly). The real hero of the night was goalkeeper Peter McCloy who defied the Germans with several magnificent saves as the visitors' weakened

Müngersdorfer, 1979. Gordon Smith in action against 1. FC Köln.

side mounted a real backs-to-the-wall act of defiance. On one occasion when the keeper was beaten in the seventeenth minute, Ally Dawson cleared off the line from Neumann.

Gordon Smith had an outstanding chance to open the scoring late in the first half from a defence-splitting McLean pass only to shoot into the side-netting and the half ended goalless. Colin Jackson and Tom Forsyth were rock-solid at the heart of the visitors' defence as Köln pressed forward, until in the fifty-seventh minute Muller squeezed the ball home following a goalmouth scramble. Another goal-line clearance by Forsyth and a superlative last minute McCloy save from Flohe prevented further loss.

Rangers had no reason to be pessimistic about the return, but a freak snow-fall on the day of the game (21 March!) left Ibrox under six inches of snow, causing a twenty-four-hour delay. The pitch was cleared with the assistance of local schools, but no outside agency could help Rangers with their injury crisis. Derek Johnstone and Kenny Watson were still absent, and added to the list were Derek Parlane and reserve centre Chris Robertson, leaving Billy Urquhart as the sole available striker. In truth, the home side rarely looked capable of turning the tie around, with Köln dictating the flow of the game. One first-half chance arrived when goalkeeper Harold Schumacher parried a Davie Cooper free-kick, the rebound falling to Urquhart who hesitated, and the chance was lost. The goal, when it arrived, virtually sealed Rangers' fate; a low, driven free-kick from Kanopka was dummied by Flohe and turned into the net by Muller. Rangers now needed three goals and in a last desperate throw of the dice Greig sent on a half-fit Johnstone and Parlane to the fray. DJ almost made an immediate impact, creating an opening for Urquhart that was mis-kicked. A McLean free-kick after eighty-seven minutes levelled matters on the night, but Rangers were out. An outstanding opportunity to secure the Holy Grail had been lost. Köln were themselves defeated in the semi-finals by eventual winners Nottingham Forest (who had Rangers to thank for opening up the competition for them) 3-3, 0-1, but a Rangers team under a young and tactically aware (in European ties at least) manager had proved that they could compete at the highest level and great was the expectation for the next term's European campaign.

1978/79 European Champions' Cup, first round, first leg
Wednesday 15 September 1978, Stadio Communale, Torino
Juventus 1 (Virdis) Rangers 0
Attendance 70,000
McCloy; Jardine, A. Forsyth; T. Forsyth, Jackson, A. MacDonald; Miller, Russell, Parlane, Smith, Watson
First round, second leg
Wednesday 29 September 1978, Ibrox Stadium, Glasgow
Rangers 2 (A. MacDonald, Smith) Juventus 0
Attendance 44,000
McCloy; Jardine, A. Forsyth; T. Forsyth, Jackson, A. MacDonald; McLean, Russell, Parlane, Johnstone, Smith
Second round, first leg
Wednesday 18 October 1978, Ibrox Stadium, Glasgow
Rangers 0 PSV Eindhoven 0
Attendance 44,000
McCloy; Jardine, A. Forsyth; T. Forsyth, Jackson (Miller), A. MacDonald; McLean, Russell, Parlane (Cooper), Johnstone, Smith
Second round, second leg
Wednesday 1 November 1978, Philips Stadion, Eindhoven
PSV Eindhoven 2 (Lubse, Deijkers) Rangers 3 (A. McDonald, Johnstone, Russell)
Attendance 29,000
McCloy; Jardine, A. Forsyth; T. Forsyth, Johnstone, A. MacDonald; McLean, Russell, Parlane, Smith, Watson
Quarter-final, first leg
Tuesday 6 March 1979, Stadion Müngersdorfer, Köln
1. FC Köln 1 (Muller) Rangers 0
Attendance 50,000

McCloy; Jardine, Dawson; T. Forsyth, Jackson, A. MacDonald; McLean, Russell,
Parlane (Urquhart), Smith, Denny (Miller)

Quarter-final, second leg

Thursday 22 March 1979, Ibrox Stadium, Glasgow

Rangers 1 (McLean) 1. FC Köln 1 (Muller)

Attendance 44,000

McCloy; Jardine, Dawson (Johnstone); T. Forsyth, Jackson, A. MacDonald;
McLean, Russell, Urquhart (Parlane), Smith, Cooper

That next campaign would be in the European Cup-Winners' Cup, the League
Championship being thrown away on a crazy, inexplicable Monday night in the
East End of Glasgow, although in truth the fixture congestion and injury problems that had denied Rangers the European Cup also cost them the domestic
treble, and with it a golden chance for John Greig to make his first season in the
manager's chair an unsurpassable one.

It was very much a case of déjà vu two years later when Rangers yet again
found themselves involved in a preliminary round tie, this time against Lillestrom
of Norway. The Light Blues got off to the perfect start in the twelfth minute when
a left-wing move involving Kenny Watson, Davie Cooper and Alex McDonald
finished with Watson chipping the ball over the heads of the Norwegian defenders for Gordon Smith to flick the ball home via a post. The Copland Road Stand
had been opened just three days earlier, thus creating an infinitely improved
atmosphere despite the building site at the other end which would eventually
become the Broomloan Road Stand, but the enthusiasm of the 25,000 spectators
gradually faded as time went on with just that one goal to show for all Rangers'
attacking efforts. The home side, alas, fell into the age-old trap of the long speculative high ball for the head of Derek Johnstone, meat and drink to the Lillestrom
defensive barrier – all tall, athletic specimens.

A 1-0 home win is not exactly a disastrous result in European competition, but
after the glory of the preceding campaign many viewed it as a great disappointment and clearly there was a lot of work still to be done when Rangers travelled
to Oslo for the first time on official UEFA business. Indeed when the Ibrox men
had last visited the Norwegian capital it was in the days before the First World
War and it was still at that time named Christiana! Lillestrom had perceived that
interest in the tie was such that a move to the national stadium was necessary
– their own Arusen Stadion in Lillestrom held 15,000 whilst the Ulleval was the
greater capacity by some 10,000. In the event a meagre 6,175 spectators were
present (including one plane-load of Scots fans who missed the opening twenty
minutes!) to watch a professional performance by the Light Blues, who took the
sting out of the play in the opening fifteen minutes, reducing the Norwegians to
just the one chance when a Terje Holt header flashed just wide. Rangers controlled the pace of the game throughout the first half with Tommy McLean and Alex

McDonald running the midfield, and indeed it was 'Doddie' who secured the vital away goal in the forty-second minute with a superb fourteen-yard shot past Amundsen after Kenny Watson had headed on an Alex Miller cross. The tie was won and both teams knew it; indeed twice Lillestrom cleared the ball off their own goal line before Derek Johnstone wrapped things up with a second in the dying minutes.

There could be no doubting the pedigree of Rangers' next opponents Fortuna Dusseldorf, beaten finalists in the same competition the previous season when they lost a thrilling final 3–4 to Barcelona in Basle. Clearly a side of the highest quality with the Allofs brothers Klaus and Thomas in attack.

Ibrox was restricted to a capacity 36,000 crowd for the first leg, during which the Light Blues demonstrated the tactical awareness and patience instilled into them by their young manager. The game had an astounding start when Fortuna defender Heinz Baltes punched the ball away in mid-air for as clear a penalty as one could ever see – incredibly the French referee M. Anton Verbeke saw nothing amiss and waved play on. Rangers shrugged off this decision to press continuously with probing attacks that tested the German defences, but it was sixty-eight minutes before that strategy paid off when Ally Dawson's twenty-five-yard shot was parried by George Daniel only for Alex McDonald to turn the ball over the line. The dam had been breached and within seven minutes Tommy McLean astonishingly headed home a curling cross from Davie Cooper. The Gers had a great result in the bag and indeed both McDonald and Cooper came close to adding a third before a momentary loss of concentration in the eighty-first minute enabled Klaus Allofs to create an opening for Rudi Wenzel on the blind-side of the home defence from where he made no mistake.

In the twinkling of an eye the tie had been blown wide open, and Rangers were faced with a perilous trip to Dusseldorf and a return to the scene of one of their great triumphs in the competition, the Rheinstadion, now one of Europe's finest arenas following the 1974 World Cup. It was a siege from first minute to last, as the Germans blitzkrieged Peter McCloy's goal with a bombardment that was defied only by a disciplined and professional performance allied to raw courage. At the heart of the Ibrox defence was Sandy Jardine in his accustomed sweeper role, a tactic John Greig had perfected for European fixtures, but was also not averse to using in domestic fixtures. The night was full of drama, never more so than in the twenty-seventh minute when a netbound shot was blocked on the line by McCloy only for the ball to spin up into the air; as the Rangers goalkeeper scooped the ball clear Sandy Jardine came flying in, his knee coming into contact with Big Peter's cheekbone. McCloy had suffered a bad injury, one that left him blinded in one eye for the rest of the match, yet he would play perhaps his finest game in a Rangers jersey that night as he produced save after save to deny Fortuna. Indeed, Alex McDonald could even have snatched an unbelievable victory when his header was scooped off the line by Rudi Wenzel, but the game finished with the Germans besieging the Ibrox goal, Klaus Allofs coming closest, hitting the underside of the bar with a fierce shot. Rangers had survived and 47,000 onlookers (more than double Fortuna's average home crowd) rose at the final whistle to acclaim a courageous goalkeeper.

At the after-match press conference, Rangers' manager John Greig remarked: 'Peter played brilliantly for an hour although he could only see out of one eye. I'm thinking of buying him a patch to wear every Saturday!' For the first time in ten years Rangers would face a Spanish club in European competition, Valencia providing the barrier to Ibrox dreams of progressing to the last eight of a European trophy for the second successive year. Valencia were a club with a considerable pedigree: like Rangers they had reached three European finals, winning the Fairs Cities Cup in 1961/62 and 1962/63. Coach to the Spanish giants was the legendary Alfredo Di Stefano and if the Ibrox men were thankful that this wonderful player would no longer be facing them on the field of play, Valencia still had some formidable names in their ranks in the shape of old friend Rainer Bonhof and Mario Kempes who had become a household name following the 1978 World Cup.

In 1979, Valencia's home ground in the city of paella and oranges was known as the Estadio Luis Casanova – by the time Rangers returned in season 1999/2000 for the opening Champions' League fixture the stadium had reverted to its original name, Campo de Mestalla. Rangers did not have their troubles to seek for the first leg in Spain – Jackson, Forsyth and Russell were all absent through injury, while recent signing Gregor Stevens was ineligible. Sixty-one thousand spectators provided another red-hot atmosphere for the Light Blues, who were under pressure from the kick-off as Valencia's talented but temperamental stars threw off their stuttering League form to rise to the big occasion. Kempes it was who opened the scoring in the twenty-fourth minute with a stunning twenty-yard free-kick which he bent around a six-man defensive wall. The Ibrox men were up against it now, yet somehow survived intense pressure to stun the locals with an equaliser on the stroke of half-time when a low, dipping twenty-five-yard shot by McLean from a Cooper pass deceived goalkeeper Carlos Pereira to find the net. That score transformed the interval situation, yet the Scots still found themselves with their backs against the wall throughout much of the second half, with the Spanish Cup holders consistently striving to 'con' Austrian referee Erich Linemayer into awarding them a penalty – a tactic which finally paid off when Alex Forsyth was ludicrously adjudged to have fouled Kempes. Nevertheless, a penalty it was and Peter McCloy (the hero of Dusseldorf) produced the save of the night to block Rainer Bonhof's powerful spot-kick as Rangers held out for a fine 1-1 draw. Once again, John Greig's tactics had proven successful in an away European tie despite the problems faced by the Light Blues prior to the game; Rangers were in pole position for the Ibrox return but the tie was still to be won, and no one knew that better than John Greig. As to the match itself, a 36,000 capacity crowd inside Ibrox were witness to a world-class display from a truly gifted player – unfortunately he was wearing the white of Valencia. Rangers' away goal advantage disappeared in fifteen minutes when a Bonhof free-kick was deflected beyond McCloy by the head of Jardine. The Ibrox men did level matters within nine minutes when a McLean cross was headed home from eight yards by Johnstone, but undoubtedly the tie turned on the closing minutes of the half when a strong Urquhart penalty claim was denied, allowing Valencia to strike with a classic counter-punch when Kempes outpaced Watson to shoot home. The Light Blues were up against it now, and their fate was sealed on seventy-eight minutes with one of the most memorable goals seen at Ibrox when Kempes again took possession of a pass from Pablo. Kempes – one of the most direct players in the global game – was notoriously left-footed, a fact the Rangers players were certainly acquainted with, and when the Argentinian set off towards the Copland Road goal he was policed by Jardine, forced on to his right, making a diagonal run across the defence before suddenly stopping in mid-stride and thundering a thirty-yard shot into the top corner of the net with his right foot.

Rangers were out and Valencia would go on to the ultimate triumph – their third European crown – with a penalty decider win over Arsenal following a goalless draw at the Stade du Heysel, Bruxelles with a certain Liam Brady failing from the spot.

1979/80 European Cup-Winners' Cup, preliminary round, first leg
Tuesday 21 August 1979, Ibrox Stadium, Glasgow
Rangers 1 (Smith) Lillestrom 0
Attendance 25,000
McCloy; Jardine, Dawson; Smith, Jackson, Watson; McLean (J. McDonald), Russell, Johnstone (Robertson), A. MacDonald, Cooper
Preliminary round, second leg
Wednesday 5 September 1979, Ulleval Stadion, Oslo
Lillestrom 0 Rangers 2 (A. MacDonald, Johnstone)
Attendance 6,175
McCloy; Miller, Dawson; Jardine, Jackson, Watson; McLean (Cooper), Russell, Johnstone, A. McDonald, Smith
Second round, first leg
Wednesday 19 September 1979, Ibrox Stadium, Glasgow
Rangers 2 (A. MacDonald, McLean) Fortuna Dusseldorf 1 (Wenzel)
Attendance 36,000
McCloy; Miller, Dawson; Jardine, Jackson, A. MacDonald; McLean, Russell (Watson), Johnstone, Smith, Cooper
Second round, second leg
Wednesday 3 October 1979, Rheinstadion, Dusseldorf
Fortuna Dusseldorf 0 Rangers 0
Attendance 47,000

McCloy; Miller (A. Forsyth), Dawson; Jardine, Jackson, Watson, McLean,

A. MacDonald, Johnstone, Smith (Cooper), Parlane

Second round, first leg

Wednesday 24 October 1979, Estadio Luis Casanova, Valencia

Valencia 1 (Kempes) Rangers 1 (McLean)

Attendance 61,000

McCloy; Miller, A. Forsyth; Jardine, Johnstone, Watson; McLean (Parlane),

A. MacDonald, Urquhart, Smith, Cooper (Dawson)

Second round, second leg

Wednesday 7 November 1979, Ibrox Stadium, Glasgow

Rangers 1 (Johnstone) Valencia 3 (Kempes 2, Jardine o.g.)

Attendance 36,000

McCloy; Jardine, A. Forsyth; Miller, Watson, A. McDonald; McLean, Smith,

Johnstone, Urquhart (Parlane), Cooper (Mackay)

SIX

A Club in Turmoil

Season 1979/80 was such a cataclysmic one for the Light Blues that defeat in the Scottish Cup final 0-1 to Celtic meant that there would be no European football in the coming season. The following season was an improvement – if still unacceptable – and the annexation of the Scottish Cup with a fine 4-1 replay win over Dundee United meant that Rangers would once again compete in their favourite European tournament in 1981/82.

The rain poured down incessantly throughout Rangers' visit to Prague – the club's first in European competition to the city built on seven hills; indeed, it was remarkably the Ibrox club's first trip behind the Iron Curtain for twelve years (a period which by contrast had encompassed no fewer than five trips to West Germany and three to the Netherlands), and would end with a shambolic performance in a drab, grey, colourless city enslaved by a foreign power. The miserable weather would match the mood of the visitors, struggling at home, and the bleak surroundings.

Dukla Prague were the club of the Czechoslovakian Army, named after a Carpathian mountain pass which was the scene of an historic victory for the combined Czech and Soviet forces during the Second World War. The venue for the first leg – the Stadion Juliska – was one of the most extraordinary locations ever to host a Rangers European tie, built into a hill with one massive stand seating almost 12,000 spectators that towered over the rest of the ground. Above the stadium, looking down approvingly on the arena, were the homes of famous Czech sportsmen – Olympian athlete Emil Zatopek and Wimbledon champion Jan Kodes – and below Juliska, running down towards the River Vltava, stood a massive edifice of Stalinist Gothic design – the International Hotel where both team and followers were staying during their brief visit to Prague.

John Greig had studied Dukla in action in a four-club tournament in Rotterdam (hosted by Feyenoord), and quickly identified Zdenek Nehoda as their top player – a world-class forward capped 77 times for his country. Indeed, four of the army side had won European Championship Winners' medals with Czechoslovakia in 1976, and six had achieved Olympic gold in Moscow 1980. Clearly, this was a side of some quality yet Dukla were not a popular club amongst the good citizens of Prague, Sparta and Slavia being the traditional favourites, whilst the army club, for all their success over the past twenty years, had won few friends. Indeed the 22,500 attendance on a dreadful day weather-wise was massive by Dukla standards, and a tribute to the reputation of the visitors.

Yet the Light Blues could not have got off to a worse start when Petr Rada swept upfield in the fourth minute and tried a speculative shot from twenty-five yards which skidded along the sodden pitch and splashed underneath the diving McCloy. The Czechs were in command and Rangers were up against it. The interval arrived without further damage but within ten minutes of the restart another goalkeeping error cost Rangers dear when McCloy failed to hold a Ladislav Vizek shot, allowing Frantisek Stambacher to net the rebound. A 2-0 scoreline was bad enough, but in the seventy-fifth minute a near-post Nehoda header left the Scots with a mountain to climb for the return, and the dark skies overhead reflected the gloom of the visitors when McLean was sent off with just eight minutes remaining, on the word of a linesman, for retaliation against Stanislav Pelc. An away goal would have transformed the outcome, and remarkably one almost materialised in the final minute when a Stevens shot was cleared off the line, Colin McAdam's effort from the rebound producing a fine save from Netolicka.

The new North Stand (now of course the Govan Stand) was in use for just the second time and an early goal was essential if Rangers were to have any hope whatsoever of overturning the tie before 35,000 spectators at Ibrox. The frantic opening twenty minutes saw several clear-cut openings created as the Light Blues laid siege to the Czech goal, and just as many spurned. One almighty scramble in front of the Dukla goal was somehow resisted before, almost inevitably, Stambacher shot low past Jim Stewart for the opening goal after twenty-three minutes, with the goalkeeper found wanting. The tie appeared won, yet Rangers came storming back with two goals in the dying minutes of the half, both created by Cooper, Jim Bett converting his pass with an angled shot, then McDonald following up after Coop's shot had struck the crossbar at the culmination of a fine move involving Jardine and Bett. Hope was renewed and the home side again laid siege to the army goal throughout the second half – a McAdam header hit the post in the fifty-third minute, Netolicka produced one superb save from McDonald and both Forsyth and Ian Redford had shots blocked inside the six-yard box, but there was to be no further scoring and Rangers would exit the competition in the opening round for the only occasion in the history of their involvement with the tournament.

Dukla meanwhile would only progress as far as the next round, being eliminated by eventual winners Barcelona (1-0, 0-4), and Rangers were left to contemplate the loss of revenue that a visit to Glasgow by the Catalan giants would have generated.

1981/82 European Cup-Winners' Cup, first round, first leg
Wednesday 16 September 1981, Stadion Juliska, Praha
Dukla Praha 3 (Rada, Stambacher, Nehoda) Rangers 0
Attendance 22,500
McCloy; Jardine, Dawson; Forsyth, Jackson (Stevens), McClelland; McLean,
Russell, McAdam, Bett, Johnstone (Redford)
First round, second leg
Wednesday 30 September 1981, Ibrox Stadium, Glasgow
Rangers 2 (Bett, McDonald) Dukla Praha 1 (Stambacher)
Attendance 35,000
Stewart; McClelland (Redford), Dawson; Jardine, Forsyth, Bett; Cooper, Russell,
McAdam (Johnstone), McDonald, Johnston

For the very first time the UEFA Cup beckoned for Rangers in season 1982/83,
but certainly not for the first (or last) time the Ibrox men found themselves paired
with old adversaries Borussia Dortmund. The Westfalen Stadion had been built for
the 1974 World Cup, and was the model selected by Willie Waddell in the redevel-
opment of Ibrox Stadium. Rangers and their fans must have felt at home when
they travelled to Westfalia for the first leg, a 54,000 sell-out in a magnificent ground
(semi-final venue in the 2006 World Cup) that lay adjacent to the Rote Erde Stadion
where the Light Blue class of 1966 had performed so heroically. The Rangers of
1982 did their predecessors proud against formidable opposition who at the time
led the Bundesliga. Central defenders Craig Paterson (in fine form following his
recent record transfer from Hibernian) and John McClelland (newly returned
from a memorable World Cup with Northern Ireland in Spain) were outstanding as the visitors survived a battering in the opening fifteen minutes. Eventually
Rangers began to turn the tide, with the midfield skills of Russell, Robert Prytz (a
European Cup finalist with Malmö in 1979), Bett and Redford beginning to dictate the play, neutralising Romanian World Cup star Marcel Radacanu. The visitors
were as likely to score as the hosts and, indeed, Derek Johnstone struck the crossbar
with a powerful drive, then later saw a header cleared off the line. Nevertheless, the
night ended goalless thanks to a crucial Paterson tackle in the dying minutes that
saved a certain goal but unfortunately resulted in the centre half sustaining an ankle
injury that would seriously compromise his Rangers career.

The Ibrox return was by no means a foregone conclusion; West German clubs
were notoriously dangerous in away ties and Borussia were fully aware that a
score draw would be enough in Glasgow.

A near-capacity crowd witnessed a fascinating tussle – John Greig had urged
caution, patience and discipline, and the visitors twice threatened Stewart's goal in
the opening minutes. But it was Rangers who finally broke the deadlock on the
cusp of the interval when Cooper diverted a Russell drive over the line from close
range. The Light Blues controlled the second half with Swedish international Prytz

outstanding, and victory was sealed in the eighty-fourth minute when Johnstone headed home a right-wing Cooper cross.

It was an outstanding victory for the Ibrox men, yet the second-round draw would send them back once again to the 'Rhine Triangle' – to Dortmund's near-neighbour 1. FC Köln.

For once under John Greig's leadership domestic form was impressive, even including a win at Aberdeen (the club's first for all of eight years), yet although Köln trailed Dortmund in the Bundesliga their playing strength was as impressive as ever – goalkeeper Harold Schumacher, midfielder Rainer Bonhof and forwards Pierre Littbarski, Klaus Allofs, Stefan Engels and Klaus Fischer were all international stars of world renown, coached moreover by Dutchman Rinus Michels of Ajax and Barcelona fame.

Rangers produced a truly superb display of football at Ibrox – a performance that rekindled memories (if only fleeting ones) of the great team of the early '60s – opening the scoring after nine minutes when a throw-in by Prytz had been flicked on by an overhead kick from Cooper to be met on the volley by Johnstone from eight yards before Schumacher could move. Rangers attacked relentlessly throughout the first half; Kanopka cleared a Paterson header off the line and Prytz missed an open goal from twelve yards. The Light Blues were dominating the game, yet disaster struck on the hour when Littbarski clearly played the ball twice at a free-kick some thirty yards out before Allofs caught Stewart by surprise with a low shot. Only the referee was unaware of the infringement, but the goal stood, and suddenly Rangers were right up against it. An eighty-fifth minute Cooper free-kick was met by McClelland at the near post, leaving Schumacher helpless. Two minutes later the German goalkeeper produced a superb save to turn wide Dave McKinnon's twenty-yard piledriver. A 2-1 scoreline from the first leg at Ibrox did scant justice to a Rangers side who had played superbly well. For no apparent reason Michels and his players whipped up a campaign of hate before the return, claiming that Glasgow had been a roughhouse – yet if anything it had been the Germans who had mixed it when they were being comprehensively outplayed. The propaganda even extended to the visitors' training session in the Stadion Müngersdorfer on the eve of the game, the floodlights being switched off after just twenty minutes due to an 'electrical fault'.

The outcome of the game itself would produce Rangers' worst European result in nineteen years, yet the opening minutes were full of promise with Johnstone going agonisingly close after just six minutes with a header from a Cooper corner. One minute later, however, Littbarski played a one-two with Allofs before netting via a post. Jim Bett came close immediately theraftr, yet in the eleventh minute a deep Fischer cross was met on the volley by Engels, his strike coming off the underside of the crossbar and rebounding off Stewart's back into the net.

Eight minutes later an Allofs cross was met by Littbarski, his shot being blocked by Stewart only for Fischer to swivel and sweep the ball home. Engels added a penalty in the twenty-first minute and incredibly Rangers had lost four goals in fifteen minutes. In truth, the scoreline was a travesty of justice. The Germans had scored with almost every attack and Rangers had hardly played badly, but in reality the tie was over.

The visitors regained their composure and closed ranks to ensure the loss of just one more goal, an Allofs header in the fifty-second minute, but the second half was more noteworthy for the Köln player who was ordered off and the one who certainly should have been but was not. Willmer was dismissed late in the game for retaliation on substitute McAdam, yet the infamous Schumacher escaped scot-free when he committed an abominable assault on Bett reminiscent of the goalkeeper's attack on Patrick Battison in the 1982 World Cup. The Ibrox man was poised to head the ball into the net after it had come off the underside of the crossbar, only to be felled by a karate kick to the chest from the German. Once again, as in Spain, the arrogant goalkeeper walked away unpunished.

Rainer Bonhof had thus completed a hat-trick of European successes against Rangers with three different clubs, but Köln would be eliminated in the very next round by Roma (1-0, 0-2). Meanwhile, for Rangers, a season of considerable promise would go downhill from now on and John Greig's side would never be the same again.

1982/83 UEFA Cup, first round, first leg
Wednesday 15 September 1982, Westfalen Stadion, Dortmund
Borussia Dortmund 0 Rangers 0
Attendance 54,000
Stewart; McKinnon, Dawson; McClelland, Paterson, Bett; Cooper, Prytz (Miller), Johnstone, Russell, Redford
First round, second leg
Wednesday 29 September 1982, Ibrox Stadium, Glasgow
Rangers 2 (Cooper, Johnstone) Borussia Dortmund 0
Attendance 44,500
Stewart; McKinnon, Dawson; McClelland, Paterson, Bett; Cooper, Prytz, Johnstone, Russell (Redford), McDonald
Second round, first leg
Wednesday 20 October 1982, Ibrox Stadium, Glasgow
Rangers 2 (Johnstone, McClelland) 1. FC Köln 1 (K. Allofs)
Attendance 30,420
Stewart; McKinnon, Dawson (McDonald); McClelland, Paterson (Stevens), Bett; Cooper, Prytz , Johnstone, Russell, Redford
Second round, second leg
Wednesday 3 November 1982, Stadion Müngersdorfer, Köln
1. FC Köln 5 (Engels 2, Littbarski, Fischer, K. Allofs) Rangers 0

Attendance 61,000

Stewart; McKinnon, Dawson; McClelland, Stevens, Bett; Cooper (McDonald), Prytz Johnstone, Russell, Redford (McAdam)

When the 1983/84 European Cup-Winners' Cup tournament got underway, no one could have anticipated that this would be not just manager John Greig's final campaign as Rangers boss, but also the club's last sojourn in the competition.

The holiday island of Malta would be the club's destination in the opening round, a first ever visit to the George Cross Island, to face Valletta as the first part of a Maltese-Scottish double act, with Hamrun Spartans taking on Dundee United in the Champions' Cup immediately afterwards.

The main problems for the Scots lay not in the standard of the opposition but that of the pitch and the intense heat – baked earth, bare in patches, weeds and deep rutting were just some of the problems at the national stadium, Ta'Qali, but it had been passed as playable by UEFA.

Any pre-match worries were soon dispelled when Paterson headed home the opening goal in seven minutes from a Cooper free-kick, and the same combination created a second goal nine minutes later when Coop's corner was headed down by the centre-half for Dave McPherson to net. Rangers were well in command – and three goals in as many minutes just after the half-hour mark totally destroyed the home side with Ally McCoist creating all three – scored by McPherson, again, McDonald and Prytz. The first-half rout was complete when McPherson joyfully completed his hat-trick from close range from a McDonald cross. It had been a long time since any Rangers team had scored 6 goals in 45 minutes, but three minutes after the restart 'Slim' wrote himself into the history books with a wicked curling chip from the edge of the box to become the only Ranger in the club's European campaigns to notch four goals in a single match – a record that stands to this day.

Rangers coasted throughout the second half with only a Prytz penalty on the hour worthy of note, and Dundee United made it a Scottish double with a 3-0 win to ensure that the sun-drenched Scots in the 18,213 crowd had been well entertained. Eight goals had been scored and not a single one from a certain Ally McCoist!

The Ibrox return was of academic interest only, reflected in the attendance of 11,500 – Rangers' lowest home crowd for a European tie. David Mitchell netted in the first minute, Ian Redford for goal number ten in the last and in between Billy McKay's twenty-five-yard shot for number six had the distinction of being the club's 200th in European competition.

After that stroll in the sunshine, the Ibrox men faced the daunting prospect of overcoming Porto to reach the last eight. The Portuguese side led their championship race ahead of the Lisbon giants Benfica and Sporting, while Rangers were struggling at home with a meagre 7 points from the opening 8 League fixtures, trailing Dundee United, Celtic and Hearts by five points at this early stage. The John Greig era was in its dying days as Rangers faced one of Europe's most underrated teams. Having already eliminated Dinamo Zagreb, Porto were clearly formidable opponents as would be amply illustrated at Ibrox. The Portuguese side defended in depth throughout the first period, masters of the offside trap and of maintaining possession. One McPherson shot forced Ze Beto into a fine save, before the youngster was released on the overlap by a precision pass from Russell, his cross from the right spinning from the grasp of the Porto goalkeeper, presenting Sandy Clark with the chance to head home after thirty-five minutes. The visitors took command of the game in the second half, overwhelming Rangers with their possession play. McCloy stood defiant as the pressure built up around him. To be blunt, Porto played Rangers off the park for much of the game, yet with the minutes ticking away the score remained 1-0, perhaps underlining the lack of punch in the visitors' ranks. In an instant, the game was transformed as a long through-ball from Sandy Clark saw substitute David Mitchell chasing an apparently lost cause as Ze Beto advanced from his goal to effect an easy clearance. Astonishingly, the Portuguese custodian – under very little pressure – completely missed his kick, presenting the Aussie with the simple task of turning the ball into an empty net. With just seven minutes left, Rangers had a 2-0 lead to take to Porto, an acceptable scoreline by any reckoning and yet the tie had one more twist in the tale when a high ball thrown forward into the home goalmouth produced an abominable error by the experienced McCloy, mispunching right to the feet of Jacques Pereira who slotted the ball home. McCloy's gross misjudgement would cost Rangers dear and the tragedy was that he had performed so heroically throughout the preceding eighty-seven minutes.

Before the trip to Portugal, manager John Greig finally succumbed to the intolerable pressures which had been swirling around him and resigned. The Aer Lingus charter flight which carried Rangers to Porto found Tommy McLean in temporary charge of the squad as speculation mounted that Alex Ferguson was about to quit Aberdeen to return to his former club. In the event, Fergie signed a new contract with the 'Dons' on the eve of the match (and also of course the eve of Aberdeen's European Cup-tie with Belgian side Beveren).

The Estadio Das Antas was one of the most intimidating in Europe – a towering oval bowl of a stadium with precious little cover. Sixty-three thousand spectators gathered on a night of sweeping rain to inspire their team into the quarter finals. The 631 travelling Rangers supporters would endure a night of discomfort and, at times, downright terror as, located in the one area of the ground, a wire mesh cage surrounded by 12ft-high fencing, they were subject to a continuous barrage of missiles from opposition fans as the local police simply stood by and watched. It would, in all honesty, have been little consolation to them were they to have known that elsewhere in Das Antas the official Rangers party and Press were being shabbily treated; offered no hospitality by the Porto Officials, they were left to mind for themselves as they searched for seats and strived to watch the game from an eyrie atop the stadium.

The game itself was a story of unrelenting pressure from the home side, with the Scots defending intelligently, well-marshalled by McLean's tactics; a central defensive partnership of Paterson and McClelland, with McPherson patrolling the area in front, stood firm throughout the first forty-five minutes as wave after wave of attacks poured down on them. Twice McCloy defied Fernando Gomes with superb saves, but was, alas, helpless to deny Porto the single goal they needed when Gomes – Europe's Golden Boot winner the previous season – bundled the ball home from five yards after Antonio Frasco's run down the left had been blocked by McKinnon. Rangers fought back, with McPherson, Redford and Prytz all coming close but the end was nigh and the Ibrox men – at a time of crisis for the club – had been eliminated.

Everyone knew that Porto were a fine side, but just how good they were was emphasised when they went all the way to that year's final in Basle before going down 1-2 to Juventus and within three years they had won the European Champions' Cup, defeating Bayern München 2-1 in Vienna. For Rangers, Jock Wallace would succeed John Greig as manager, and later that season would win the League Cup to qualify for another European campaign, this time in the UEFA Cup.

1983/84 European Cup-Winners' Cup, first round, first leg
Wednesday 14 September 1983, National Stadium, Ta'Qali
Valletta 0 Rangers 8 (McPherson 4, Prytz 2, 1 pen, Paterson, McDonald)
Attendance 18,213
McCloy; Dawson, McClelland; McPherson, Paterson, McKinnon; Prytz, McCoist (Davies), Clark (D. Ferguson), McDonald, Cooper
First round, second leg
Wednesday 28 September 1983, Ibrox Stadium, Glasgow
Rangers 10 (McDonald 3, Mitchell 2, Redford 2, Dawson, Mackay, Davies)
Valletta 0
Attendance 11,500
Stewart; Dawson, McClelland; McPherson, Paterson (D. Ferguson), Redford; Prytz (Mackay), Davies, Mitchell, McDonald, Cooper
Second round, first leg
Wednesday 19 October 1983, Ibrox Stadium, Glasgow
Rangers 2 (Clark, Mitchell) Porto 1 (Jacques)
Attendance 27,800
McCloy; Dawson, McClelland; McPherson, Paterson, Redford; Prytz (Mitchell), McCoist, Clark, Russell, Cooper (McDonald)

Second round, second leg
Wednesday 2 November 1983, Estadio Das Antas, Oporto
Porto 1 (Gomes) Rangers 0
Attendance 63,000
McCloy; McKinnon, Dawson; McClelland, Paterson, McPherson; Prytz
(McCoist), Russell, Clark (Mitchell), Redford, Cooper

So it was farewell then European Cup-Winners' Cup – a tournament which provided Rangers with much success, memorable games and of course the club's greatest triumph. An adventure that started in 1960 with the welcoming of Ferencvaros to Ibrox had ended somewhat unsatisfactorily on a night of torrential rain in the Estadio Das Antas, Oporto.

In 1984, Dublin may well still have been the city of 'Molly Malone' and of 'Cockles and Mussels' but it was no longer the 'Fair City' of legend which had given Rangers such a warm welcome in the days leading up to the First World War. Instead, a hostile, alien city of grinding and abject poverty (in the days before EU handouts amounting to billions of pounds sterling funded by UK taxpayers) awaited Rangers and their fans. The background to this tie was that of the terrorist activity in Northern Ireland being at its height, and a threatening, intimidatory atmosphere awaited Rangers and the Light Blue followers. The Unionist traditions of the Ibrox club and their legions were clearly perceived by certain sections of the Republican movement as being 'fair game' for attack, and Rangers' fans found themselves under threat from the moment of their arrival at Dalymount by elements. It should be stressed, however, that this was totally unconnected with either Bohemians Football Club, or football, with the GARDA making no effort whatsoever to protect the visiting fans. Indeed, at the end of the game, Rangers fans exiting the ground were deliberately ambushed by the Irish Police.

Inside the ground, while play raged on around him, Rangers' goalkeeper Nicky Walker found himself under constant bombardment from the Irish spectators during the first half, as a variety of missiles rained down on him: golf balls, bottles, darts, cans, and tumblers were amongst the projectiles aimed at Walker, who was forced to stand some thirty yards from goal throughout the first half. No intervention by the GARDA occurred, and a Union flag was burned on the terraces. In such circumstances, the loss of three goals was perhaps understandable, although many felt that Nicky should have brought the missile attacks to the attention of the referee, but in hindsight such an action would surely have led to the abandonment of the game, and it is doubtful in the extreme if the safety of either Rangers or their supporters could have been assured.

As to the game itself, Bohemians had lost just once at home (to Hamburg) in their previous seven European campaigns, and thus were no easy victims for the Scots, who nevertheless opened the scoring in seven minutes when McCoist guided a Cooper cross into the net, but, with mayhem all around him, Walker failed to reach a pass-back from Paterson, allowing Rocky O'Brien to net. Rangers, however, regained the lead when McPherson headed home a Cooper corner past Irish goalkeeper Dermot O'Neil, only for Walker to lose a second when he failed to hold a cross, allowing O'Brien to scramble the ball home.

Trouble again broke out during the interval, when a single spectator wearing a Celtic shirt scaled the fencing at the home end of the ground, ran the full length of the field to where the Rangers fans stood and began hurling missiles into the visitors' end, incredibly without any intervention by the police. Not unnaturally, the Ibrox fans could no longer suffer such provocation and intimidation and someone broke onto the field from the away end, whereupon the brave Irish neanderthal took fright and fled. Suddenly, as if at a hidden signal, the GARDA were reinforced by riot police, and started forcing their way onto the terracing occupied by the Rangers fans who had clearly had enough, confronted as they were by elements who had no interest at all in the football, rightly perceiving a hostile force in the Irish police, whose conduct that night should have led to an independent judicial inquiry, and retaliatory fights broke out on the terraces despite appeals from Jock Wallace for calm. Rangers slumped in the second half, perhaps understandably so, and a long-range shot from local postman Gino Lawless deceived Walker for the winning goal after fifty-one minutes.

Rangers, therefore, suffered their first defeat of the season and a defence which had conceded just 2 goals in 9 domestic fixtures had suddenly suffered the loss of three in one night, but perhaps that was more due to events surrounding the fixture than to any fault of the players. Thankfully, UEFA took no action against Rangers or their supporters, perhaps recognising that they had been the victims of a deliberate campaign of violence and intimidation totally unconnected with either football or Bohemians Football Club. For Rangers fans who had travelled by car or bus, the journey north was one of terror, being subject to missile attack at every town and village on the road north, commencing almost at the instant the convoy was escorted out of Dublin by the GARDA, a clearly pre-planned operation by nationalist thugs who perceived Rangers and their followers as the Unionist enemy. It was only when the supporters reached safe haven in Belfast that they could breathe easily.

Bohemians had nevertheless proved that they were worthy opponents and Jock Wallace warned that only the very best would do for Rangers in the Ibrox return, which attracted an amazing 31,000 attendance, a figure bettered only by Celtic that season. Ludicrously, Rangers allocated the entire Broomloan Road Stand to Bohemian fans – all twenty of them!

The story of that second leg was one of incessant Rangers pressure against a solid Irish defence, with some incredible misses frustrating the Ibrox men, both Redford and Mitchell striking the woodwork. An ignimonious exit stared Rangers in the face until a roar of relief split the heavens with just six minuters remaining when a Cooper free-kick was headed home by captain Paterson (who had recently replaced the sadly soon-to-depart McClelland), the ball only just finding the corner of the net low down at the far post. A second headed goal by Redford from another Cooper free-kick in the dying seconds clinched victory for the Light Blues, but it had been too close for comfort by some considerable way.

Rangers would now face the might of Internazionale Milano in the next round – one of the great names of world football, and a side containing world-class players in the form of Walter Zenga, Franco Baresi, Sandro Altobelli, Karl Heinz Rummenigge and Liam Brady. The Stadio Giuseppe Meazza (or San Siro) is one of the most intimidating in Europe, an arena that generates an incredible atmosphere, and Rangers must have felt like Christians about to encounter the lions in the Colosseum in ancient Rome as they lined up in a defensive forma-tion with McPherson included as sweeper behind two central defenders and five in midfield. Wallace's plans received an early setback when Rummenigge eluded his marker (McClelland) down the right flank, crossing a magnificent ball to the far post where Altobelli headed across goal for Antonio Sabato to bullet home a header after seventeen minutes, and within two minutes only a superb McCloy stop from Rummenigge prevented a second. Rangers restricted Inter to just that one goal until midway through the second half when Altobelli again was the crea-tor for substitute Franco Causio (making his 700th appearance in Italian football) to notch a second, yet within minutes McCoist was presented with a gilt-edged opportunity to snatch a priceless away goal when a thunderous thirty-yard shot by Ian Redford struck the underside of the bar with Zenga helpless. The striker was entirely on his own as the ball descended with the goal gaping wide open; from no more than three yards the young Ally stood motionless, as if rooted to the spot, allowing the ball to hit the top of his head and bounce clear when a sim-ple nod of the head would have assuredly led to a goal. It was a miss difficult to comprehend even today, a miss on a par with that of Willie Johnston in the 1971 Scottish Cup final and Peter van Vossen at Celtic Park in November 1996.

A score of 2-0 was bad enough, but in the dying minutes Altobelli burst through again, his cross being headed home by Rummenigge to present Inter with a 3-0 first-leg lead. 'We'll go for their jugular', proclaimed Jock Wallace of the Ibrox return, promising a blood-and-thunder affair that would rock Inter, but few believed that the Light Blues had an earthly chance, least of all the wealthy Italians who strutted around their hotel as if they owned all of Glasgow. Charter flights that had been arranged to bring their fans to Glasgow had been cancelled as most supporters planned ahead for the next round. Rangers had won the League Cup in the interim, but Inter would surely be a different story.

What a night was witnessed at Ibrox, however, as Rangers followed the Wallace instructions to the letter, with Mitchell introduced at centre forward to unsettle the Italian defence. Defender John McClelland (making his final appearance in

Light Blue) – moved up front to lend height and weight to the attack – stunned Inter with an early goal after just five minutes when the Ulsterman headed down for Cammy Fraser to strike a ferocious shot that Zenga could only parry, enabling Mitchell to net with a diving header. Ibrox erupted and the Scots poured forward in search of a second only to be caught with a sucker punch ten minutes later when Brady released Altobelli to score. The tie took another twist within sixty seconds after Iain Ferguson had hammered home a twenty-yard shot. Remarkably, the host club were dominating proceedings and when Iain Ferguson added a third ten minutes after the interval from an opening created by Robert Prytz, the fat was well and truly in the fire. Rangers still needed two more goals, however, and the loss of Ferguson – a player who always relished the European arena – through injury perhaps proved crucial. The Light Blues laid siege to Zenga's goal in the closing stages only for a panic-stricken defence to hang on desperately.

Rangers had restored their pride, whilst their aristocratic opponents went home to widespread criticism although they would eventually reach the semi-finals before succumbing to Real Madrid (2-0, 0-3).

1984/85 UEFA Cup, first round, first leg
Tuesday 18 September 1984, Dalymount Park, Dublin
Bohemians 3 (O'Brien 2, Lawless) Rangers 2 (McCoist, McPherson)
Attendance 10,000
Walker; McKinnon, Dawson; McClelland, Paterson, Redford; McPherson, Fraser, Clark (I. Ferguson), McCoist (McDonald), Cooper
First round, second leg
Wednesday 3 October 1984, Ibrox Stadium, Glasgow
Rangers 2 (Paterson, Redford) Bohemians 0
Attendance 31,000
McCloy; McKinnon, Dawson; McClelland, Paterson, Redford; Russell, McPherson, I. Ferguson (Mitchell), McCoist (C. Fraser), Cooper
Second round, first leg
Wednesday 24 October 1984, Stadio Giuseppe Meazza, Milano
Internazionale Milano 3 (Sabato, Causio, Rummenigge) Rangers 0
Attendance 65,591
McCloy; Dawson, McClelland; McPherson, Paterson, Redford; Russell (I. Ferguson), Fraser, McCoist (Fleck), Prytz, Cooper.
Second round, second leg
Wednesday 7 November 1984, Ibrox Stadium, Glasgow
Rangers 3 (I. Ferguson 2, Mitchell) Internazionale Milano 1 (Altobelli)
Attendance 30,594
McCloy; Dawson, McClelland; McPherson, Paterson, Redford; McKinnon, Fraser, Mitchell, I. Ferguson (McCoist), Prytz (Munro)

When Rangers returned to the Basque region to face Atletico Osasuna in the 1985/86 UEFA Cup first round, controversy raged around the tie, the debate centring on Rangers' demand that their loyal travelling support did not travel to the city of Pamplona in the wake of the Heysel Stadium disaster in Brussels some four months earlier. English clubs and fans were now banned from Europe and Rangers arbitrarily decreed that they would accept no tickets from Osasuna for the second leg in Spain, even going to the extreme of pressurising bus companies into cancelling supporters' clubs bookings to convey their members across Europe. Twenty years ago, in the days before budget airlines, the majority of fans would travel to games in Western Europe by coach. In the event, several hundred fans did 'Follow Follow' to Pamplona, including one bus – the Nithsdale Loyal Rangers Supporters' Club and friends.

The Light Blues had started the domestic season well and led the title race when Osasuna arrived in Glasgow. Torrrential rain greeted the Spaniards, on their inaugural European venture, when they visited Ibrox for the first leg, turning the pitch into something of a quagmire and severely restricting Rangers' attacking options.

Conditions were farcical, with only the referee believing the pitch to be playable. The Light Blues' game was a fast and skilful close-passing one, totally unsuited to a waterlogged surface. Osasuna defended in depth, and it took the Ibrox men all of fifty-four minutes to break the deadlock, Paterson's courageous diving header from a Hugh Burns free-kick doing the trick.

Gers' manager Jock Wallace threw on substitutes Derek Johnstone and Ted McMinn, sensing the Spaniards' vulnerability to an aerial assault. So it proved, for DJ would create havoc in the visitors' defence seeing one header strike an upright. The match finshed at 1-0, however, and Rangers had every reason to believe they could progress into round two as they travelled to Pamplona, famous for the running of bulls through the streets of the city during the annual festival.

The season had started to turn sour for Wallace's Rangers since the first leg, as they lost three consecutive domestic fixtures without notching even a solitary goal. A certain Ian Durrant made his European debut in Northern Spain, with Johnstone in the starting line-up, having so troubled Osasuna in the first leg.

There was a capacity crowd of 25,600 in Estadio El Sadar on a warm Spanish evening and Rangers got off to the worst possible start after twelve minutes when a Martin cross somehow eluded both Paterson and McPherson in the centre of defence, enabling home skipper Ripodas to head home.

Cooper, identified before the tie by Osasuna's Yugoslav coach Ivan Brzic as the main threat, was being marked out of the game by the suffocating home defence and up front the Spaniards had their own wing wizard in the shape of Martin who was a constant torment to the Scots defence, adding a second in the fortieth minute when he converted a Benito cross. Rangers were up against it, but worked their way back into the game in the last half-hour in search of the crucial away goal that would turn the tie in their favour. It almost came too – when Paterson's header was cleared off the line by Castenedo.

Regrettably, that was the Scots' best chance and when the final whistle blew it was Atletico Osasuna who progressed to round two where they would be eliminated by Belgian side SV Waregem (0-2, 2-1). For Jock Wallace, the visit to Pamplona would be his final European tie as Ibrox Boss but he would return to Spain to coach Seville Club De Futbol. Defeat in Estadio El Sadar was a bitter disappointment for all friends of Rangers, including director Jack Gillespie, for whom this defeat was undoubtedly a factor in his decision to sell his shareholding to the Lawrence group, thus giving that company control of the club, eventually leading to the Souness revolution.

1985/86 UEFA Cup, first round, first leg
Wednesday 18 September 1985, Ibrox Stadium, Glasgow
Rangers 1 (Paterson) Atletico Osasuna 0
Attendance 29,479
Walker; Burns, Munro; McPherson, Paterson, Bell; McCoist, Russell, Williamson (Johnstone), Fraser, Cooper (McMinn)
First round, second leg
Wednesday 2 October 1985, Estadio El Sadar, Pamplona
Atletico Osasuna 2 (Ripodas, Martin) Rangers 0
Attendance 25,600
Walker; Burns, Munro; McPherson, Paterson, Bell; McCoist, Russell (McMinn), Johnstone, Durrant, Cooper (Williamson)

SEVEN

The Souness Revolution

The arrival of Graeme Souness as player-manager revolutionised the club and Scottish football. Suddenly Rangers were signing international footballers in big-money transfers, including England international Terry Butcher, Chris Woods and Graham Roberts. Ilves Tampere of Finland it was who provided the opposition in the Light Blues' first European tie of the Graeme Souness era, in the UEFA Cup. Coincidentally it was also the club's first visit to the Scandinavian country.

Ibrox staged the first leg before 27,436 spectators on 17 September 1986 – a night which many to this day recall as being Davie Cooper's finest in Light Blue. The Finns were no pushovers, although many friends of Rangers did fear that complacency could be a danger to the home side. Souness for one would surely brook no thoughts on that score however; three times he had played in Finland with Liverpool on European Champions' Cup business, resulting in a 1-0 win and 1-1 draw against Oulon Tyovaen Palloilliat and a 0-1 defeat at the hands of HJK Helsinki. Whilst Liverpool had progressed each time on the aggregate score, it was hardly impressive by the Anfield club's exceptionally high standards of the time.

Ilves were out to prove from the start that they were more than capable of holding their own, attempting to stem the home attacks with a callous and ruthless approach that enraged the crowd. Mikko Korhanen was booked before, after just twenty-one minutes, a vicious tackle on Ally McCoist resulted in the dismissal of Pekka Heino – a decision which would ultimately have a profound effect on the outcome of the tie. Rangers opened the scoring on the half-hour mark when a Cooper corner was nodded on by Butcher allowing Robert Fleck to net with a bullet header past Mika Malinen. The interval loomed when 'Fleckie' added a second, scrambling a loose ball home when Malinen parried Cooper's shot, Ian Durrant having whipped the ball back across goal. Six minutes into the second half a piece of sheer magic from Cooper when he waltzed past five Finnish defenders created the opportunity for Fleck to complete his hat-trick, enabling the chunky twenty-one-year-old striker to become the first Rangers player since Colin Stein (1968/69) to net three in consecutive competitive games (Robert having notched a hat-trick in a 4-0 win over Clydebank the previous Saturday). McCoist added a fourth after seventy minutes when he drove a right-foot shot high into the net from a Cammy Fraser opening and Rangers had, by any standard, a healthy lead to take to Tampere.

One year after Heysel, the relatively small number of Light Blue followers who wanted to travel to Finland found their best efforts obstructed by the club, with Chief Executive David Holmes and his sidekick the former Mars bar salesman Freddie Fletcher regarding supporters as an intrusion and an incumberance rather than customers! Nevertheless, the loyal band did travel, some the long and tiring way round by ferry whilst others flew. One Gers fan from Edinburgh who perhaps had cause to regret his trip flew in to Helsinki with this correspondent from London where he worked during the week. Upon arrival, flush with the excitement of travelling and imbued with more than a few drinks from the in-flight bar, he rushed off to telephone his wife, back at the family home in Edinburgh, to advise of his safe arrival, unfortunately forgetting that she knew nothing of his planned trip, believing him to be working in London all that week.

Graeme Souness, meanwhile, ensured that the club followed Liverpool's tried and trusted methodical outlook for European ties by chartering their own aircraft to fly out the day before the game, returning home immediately afterwards. Tampere was a picturesque textile town, home to 200,000 inhabitants and situated between two of Finland's many lakes, surrounded by forest greenery. A meagre 2,109 attendance in the 25,000-capacity Rasina Stadion hardly represented a big-match atmosphere, and that perhaps contributed to what was undoubtedly a languid performance from a Rangers side without the injured Graeme Souness, Cammy Fraser, Ted McMinn and Derek Ferguson, resulting in rare appearances (for the Souness era) for Colin Miller and Robert Russell. A nondescript first half was enlivened after twenty-six minutes with a spectacular McCoist effort that hit the post after a run that eluded three tackles. A goalless first forty-five minutes was nothing to write home about, but at least Rangers seemed comfortably on course for the next round until, nine minutes into the second half, a soft penalty award brought Ilves to life when Aro Hjelm fell to the ground in a challenge with David McPherson following a Michael Belfield (late of Wimbledon) cross. Hjelm converted the resulting spot-kick and the 'Lynxs' were suddenly in great heart, adding a spectacular second twenty minutes later when Arto Uimonen beat Woods with a diving header from a Lemivaara cross. There was never any realistic prospect of Ilves taking the tie into extra time, but a 0-2 defeat for Rangers was less than impressive, to say the least. Without question it had been the team's worst performance under Souness, and the Rangers manager did not mince his words: 'We played like a pub team!'

That game in Tampere also marked the arrival on the scene of Phil Boersma as physiotherapist – a controversial appointment not so much because of Boersma's religion (he wasted no time in telling all who cared to listen that he was Souness' first Roman Catholic signing for Rangers) but because of his complete lack of qualifications for the crucial role he now held within the club. Graeme Souness had imported to Ibrox many excellent habits from both Liverpool and Italy – the appointment of an unqualified physio was not one of them.

Rangers returned to Porto in round two, to face not their conquerors of three years earlier (they were en route to annexing their first European Cup), but city rivals Boavista. The first leg was at Ibrox and there was ill feeling on the eve of battle when the Portuguese were refused permission to train at Ibrox, due to the heavy rain. Souness brought all his experience gained with Liverpool (whom he had captained to the 1984 Champions' Cup) and Sampdoria to stress the importance of avoiding the loss of an away goal. Despite this, however, that is precisely what happened after half an hour when Nelson streaked past Stuart Munro wide on the right before whipping over a cross that Tonanho converted. The Light Blue legions were stunned, but within three minutes the scores were level when a Cooper corner was headed home by McPherson. Rangers suffered a severe injury blow when Souness limped off with a calf muscle injury, to be replaced by McMinn, but the home side struck again on the cusp of the interval when a long, raking pass from Butcher released McCoist, who raced away to round goalkeeper Hubert and stroke the ball into an unguarded net. However, consistent pressure throughout the second half failed to yield a third goal despite an outstanding display from McMinn, who was denied a stonewall penalty in the dying minutes when he was scythed down – incredibly, Swedish referee Bo Helen awarded an indirect free-kick.

Rangers had more than Europe in mind before the return clash with the Portuguese: two games with Celtic, to be precise, the first of which was won 2-1 at Hampden in the League Cup final, the second (a League fixture at Parkhead) ending in a 1-1 draw. A 2-1 lead is a precarious one at the best of times, and Boavista coach Joao Alves cranked up the pressure before the return by accusing Rangers of roughhouse tactics in Glasgow, stating rather ludicrously that Butcher should have been ordered off not once, but twice. All his words meant nothing, however, once play commenced in the Estadio Dos Bessa. Boavista had eliminated Fiorentina in the previous round and required just one goal to add another noteworthy scalp. The visitors' performance was professional and disciplined, however, as they controlled the pace of the game. One Chris Woods save from Jose Augusto early in the second half was world-class as he bent backwards in mid-air to tip the ball over the bar. Progress was assured after seventy minutes when Cooper's run and lay-off allowed Derek Ferguson (older brother of Barry) to send a twenty-yard drive into the roof of the net and, for only the second time since Barcelona, the Ibrox men were through to round three.

Chris Woods' wonder save against Boavista.

The third-round ballot paired the Ibrox club with old friends in the form of Bundesliga giants Borussia Mönchengladbach. The new Rangers management were under no illusions as to the enormity of their task – it was no coincidence that Rangers had played five pre-season games against West German opposition.

Both teams had injury worries – Souness himself was out, and Borussia's coach, the legendary Jupp Heynckes, was forced to field twenty-two-year-old goal-keeper Uwe Kamps, believing that the out-of-form Erik Thorstvedt did not have the nerve to play at Ibrox! The stadium hosted a fiercely competitive game with the tough-tackling Borussia defenders taking no prisoners, but Rangers opened the scoring in the fourteenth minute when Ian Durrant raced into the box to fin-ish off a six-man move involving Jimmy Nicholl, Davie Cooper, Cammy Fraser, Stuart Munro and Ally McCoist with a swift shot that went in off the underside of the crossbar. Rangers were on top, and McCoist, Butcher and Durrant again all came close before a moment's loss of concentration on the stroke of half-time cost the Light Blues dear, when full-back Andre Winkhold broke clear of Stuart Munro, outpaced the left flank of the Ibrox defence and swung over a cross that eluded Chris Woods, allowing Uwe Rahn to head home.

A crucial away goal had been lost, and despite incessant home pressure the Blues were unable to breach the massed German defence, with Kamps sav-ing at the death from both McCoist and McMinn to secure a 1-1 draw. That loss of concentration at Ibrox would have serious long-term conequences for Rangers – Graeme Souness resolved to address the perceived weakness in defence with the capture of Graham Roberts from Tottenham Hotspur and that goal by Uwe Rahn would be the last conceded by Chris Woods for a full eleven games.

Graham Roberts would not, of course, be signed in time for the return in Mönchengladbach, but Souness was back and he dominated the midfield on a night of frustration for the Light Blues which frankly left a bad taste in the mouth.

Rangers attacked from the whistle in the Bokelberg, with wingers Cooper and McMinn consistently upsetting the Borussia defence. McCoist hit the bar with a long-range shot after eight minutes and a strong penalty claim, when Butcher was pulled down by Hans-Jorg Criens, was denied by an erratic Belgian referee who would play a central role in the night's proceedings. Alex Ponnet persistently took no action against the brutal tactics of the home defenders with a display of officiating that would lead to his being downgraded by the Belgian FA. Ponnet had a nightmare of a game that night, his interventions proving critical. In the seventy-fourth minute, as Rangers pressed for the crucial opening goal, he ordered off Munro after a clash with Andre Winkhold – a harsh decision to say the least. Subsequently, with three minutes remaining, he ludicrously booked Cooper for comments made as he was about to take a free-kick, not realising he had already cautioned the Ranger. Inevitably, the red card was again produced.

The Light Blues finished the game on the attack, but a goalless draw meant elimination, and amidst memorable scenes at the end with Terry Butcher in tears as the players paid tribute to the 3,500 travelling support, the greatest frustration of all was the realisation that Rangers were a better team than their opponents, who nevertheless progressed to the semi-finals before being eliminated by Dundee United (0-0, 0-2).

1986/87 UEFA Cup, first round, first leg
Wednesday 17 September 1986, Ibrox Stadium, Glasgow
Rangers 4 (Fleck 3, McCoist) Ilves Tampere 0
Attendance 27,436
Woods; Nicholl, Munro; Souness (McMinn), McPherson, Butcher; Fraser, Fleck, McCoist, Durrant, Cooper
First round, second leg
Wednesday 1 October 1986, Rasina Stadion, Tampere
Ilves Tampere 2 (Hjelm pen, Uimonen) Rangers 0
Attendance 2,109
Woods; Nicholl, Munro; Miller, McPherson, Butcher; Russell, Fleck, McCoist, Durrant (Bell), Cooper (Nisbet)
Second round, first leg
Thursday 23 October 1986, Ibrox Stadium, Glasgow
Rangers 2 (McPherson, McCoist) Boavista 1 (Tonanho)
Attendance 38,772

Woods; Nicholl, Munro; Souness (McMinn), D. McPherson, Butcher; Fleck
(Nisbet), D. Ferguson, McCoist, Durrant, Cooper

Second round, second leg

Tuesday 4 November 1986, Estadio Dos Bessa, Porto

Boavista 0 Rangers 1 (D. Ferguson)

Attendance 23,000

Woods; Nicholl, Munro; D. Ferguson, D. McPherson, Butcher; Fraser, McMinn,
McCoist (Fleck), Durrant, Cooper

Third round, first leg

Wednesday 26 November 1986, Ibrox Stadium, Glasgow

Rangers 1 (Durrant) Borussia Mönchengladbach 1 (Rahn)

Attendance 44,500

Woods; Nicholl, Munro; D. Ferguson, McPherson, Butcher; Fraser (West),
McMinn, McCoist, Durrant, Cooper

Third round, second leg

Wednesday 10 December 1986, Bokelberg Stadion, Mönchengladbach

Borussia Mönchengladbach 0 Rangers 0

Attendance 36,000

Woods; Dawson, Munro; Souness, McPherson, Butcher; Bell (West),
D. Ferguson, McCoist, McMinn, Cooper

The championship secured in Graeme Souness' first season as player-manager,
Rangers entered the European Champions' Cup for the first time in nine years.
The first-round draw could not have been any tougher – Dinamo Kiev, Champions
of the USSR. It would be the club's first visit to the Soviet Union in competitive
European football, although they had undertaken a memorable, unbeaten tour in
1962.

Kiev were a side of the highest quality; the vast majority of their squad
formed the national side of the USSR that would go on to win Olympic gold
in Seoul the following year, as well as being runners-up in the 1988 European
Championships, held in West Germany. Two of their stars, Oleg Kuznetsov and
Alexei Mikhailichenko, would in later years join Rangers. Travel difficulties
were momentous for those Gers fans willing and able to travel – in the wake of
Heysel the club were still positively discouraging fans from travelling to European
away games, and on top of that there were very real obstacles to be overcome in
respect of the Soviet Tourist Agency, Intourist, who were bluntly dismissing all
enquiries with the advice that visas could not be issued on the requested dates
due to a lack of available accomodation in Kiev. Wherever the truth of the matter lay, eventually a limited number were able to travel, including the author,
courtesy of a tour operator who specialised in trade union visits to Warsaw Pact
countries. However, one myth that has grown arms and legs over this tie is that
those who travelled were able to do so because they had become members of the

Communist Party. Not so – this is a complete fabrication that should be wholly dismissed.

As to the game itself, Rangers, without the suspended Cooper and Munro, gave a superbly disciplined and professional defensive display in the Republic Stadium before a 100,000 audience (the largest ever attendance at a Rangers' European tie) denying the Ukranians space and time to create any openings. Avi Cohen, an experienced Israeli international, was utilised as sweeper behind a central defensive partnership of Graham Roberts and Terry Butcher. Kiev's breakthrough, when it arrived, came via the penalty spot, Mikhailichenko converting the spot-kick after seventy-two minutes.

A 1-0 defeat left all to play for at Ibrox and controversy swirled around the stadium two weeks later when, with the Soviet Champions having trained the previous evening (as per UEFA regulations) on the normal-sized Ibrox pitch, the touchlines were brought in on both wings in a bid to negate the width and pace of Kiev wingers Vasily Rats and Oleg Blokhin. No matter the ethics of such a tactic, and it was certainly within the laws of the game as Kiev found out when they checked it out post-match, Rangers could never within their wildest dreams have imagined that they would receive the gift that the visitors presented to them after twenty-four minutes. An attack had broken down with the ball safely in the hands of goalkeeeper Victor Chanov. His clearance from hand produced an error of schoolboy proportions: striking Sergei Baltacha on the backside, it fell perfectly for Ally McCoist who slipped the ball into the path of Mark Falco who coolly stroked the ball into the net.

The aggregate scores were now level and, as Rangers controlled the game, the capacity crowd began to dream of an outstanding European scalp, the second goal arriving five minutes into the second half when a Trevor Francis cross was headed on by Falco to McCoist who guided his header into the corner of the net.

Teams of the quality of Dinamo Kiev are not prone to accepting defeat readily and this night was no different as the Ukranians piled on the pressure in the closing stages, using their pace to maximum effect in an effort to turn the home defence. The closing quarter appeared to last forever for the Light Blue legions, with the visitors motoring. This was to no avail, however, for a solid defence held out for one of the great Ibrox nights. Next up were old friends, again from Eastern Europe, in the shape of Gornik Zabrze. There could be no denying that the Polish Champions would be formidable opponents, with the first leg in Glasgow. Rangers had broken the £1 million transfer barrier soon after the defeat of Kiev with the signing of Richard Gough from Tottenham Hotspur, who would be ineligible to play in Europe until the quarter-finals.

The Light Blues were in superb form during the opening forty-five minutes, opening the scoring as early as the sixth minute when Jimmy Nicholl played a one-two with Falco before crossing to the near post where McCoist netted with a half-volley past goalkeeper Josef Wandzik. It was all Rangers with Souness controlling the midfield, ably abetted by Ian Durrant and Derek Ferguson. A second goal was inevitable and duly arrived in the twenty-third minute when Durrant netted after a Francis cross was only half-cleared by defender Jacek Grembocki. The half ended with the 41,366 crowd in ecstasy as Rangers went 3-0 up when Souness released Durrant who, being forced wide by Joachim Klemenz, chipped the ball across goal to Falco who coolly headed home.

The second half would be a different story and Rangers lost a potentially crucial goal when Jan Urban shrugged off challenges from both Butcher and Roberts to net after fifty-six minutes. There was no further scoring and the Scottish Champions had to travel to southern Poland with a good 3-1 lead, but one that was by no means insurmountable. Stadion Gornik in Zabrze was the venue for Rangers' visit in 1987, although visiting press and supporters all stayed in nearby Katowice. Conditions in the Silesian heartland were basic and poverty-stricken to say the least; Poland was still a Communist state in 1987 despite the growth of the Solidarity movement under Lech Waleska.

Gornik, as a club, was formed in 1948 as a miners' club, but the stadium itself had a previous history, opened in September 1934 and named the 'Adolf Hitler Kampfbahn'. Indeed, under German occupation the town of Zabrze was renamed Hindenburg.

To the game itself; Rangers soaked up early Gornik pressure in front of 23,250 spectators before silencing the home crowd when a mazy run by Cooper saw him elude three defenders before threading a fine pass to McCoist who was hauled to the ground as he rounded Jozef Wandzik and duly converted the resultant penalty himself.

The home side levelled the scoreline in the sixty-third minute when substitute Andrzej Orzeszek powered home an eighteen-yard shot into the top corner of the net. The Rangers defence had been dominant throughout with Roberts and Butcher at its heart, but that goal had lifted Gornik and six minutes later Ryszard Cyron hit the bar with a rising shot. Luckily, the storm was weathered and the Ibrox men held out comfortably in the closing stages to progress to the quarter-finals.

Into the very heart of the tournament, the last eight, Rangers found themselves travelling behind the Iron Curtain for the third consecutive round, to the impoverished country of Romania under the dictatorship of Nicholae Ceaucescu – to face Steaua Bucharest, another old acquaintance.

Having already eliminated sides of the calibre of Dinamo Kiev and Gornik Zabrze, there were many who believed that this could at last be Rangers' year in the European Cup. However, the inexplicable transfer of both Mark Falco and Robert Fleck before the quarter-finals, leaving just one experienced striker at Ibrox (Ally McCoist), who promptly got injured, was rank bad management on the part of Graeme Souness. The player-manager had strengthened the squad with the signings of, amongst others, Ray Wilkins, Mark Walters and John Brown – but only Wilkins could play in Europe. The grim reality of Ceaucescu's Romania awaited Rangers, with power cuts an everyday occurrence due to a shortage of energy in a country gripped by freezing temperatures. Shops were devoid of even the basic necessities of life, the people hungry and poverty-stricken, but what they did have was a strong football team in Steaua, a team that incorporated the class of Gheorghe Hagi and Marius Lacatus. Champions' Cup winners just two years earlier, they were unbeaten in domestic football over the previous two seasons.

A capacity 33,000 packed the Stadion Steaua for the tie, scheduled for an afternoon kick-off due to the power shortages and including vast numbers of uniformed soldiers, depicting the home side's status as the army club. Early goals in both legs would prove to be too great a handicap for a Rangers team missing the injured Butcher, who had suffered a broken leg in a home League fixture against Aberdeen the previous December. The loss of Cohen through injury would be another severe blow.

Steaua opened the scoring in just two minutes through Victor Piturca and dominated the entire match, adding a second midway through the second half through a deflected free-kick from Stefan Iovan. The goal may have been fortuitous, but not the final score of 2-0.

If Rangers were not already chasing a lost cause, then they certainly were after the opening two minutes of the Ibrox return when Lacatus took advantage of a square defence to collect a long forward pass and lob the ball over Chris Woods. Steaua threatened to repeat the act with several counter-attacks, yet somehow by the half-hour mark the home side had scored twice through a Gough header and a McCoist penalty. The Romanians closed the game down in the second half, however, leaving Rangers to ponder a golden opportunity lost.

Steaua lost 0-0, 0-2 to Benfica in the semi-finals, and less than two years after Rangers' visit Nicholae Ceaucescu was overthrown.

1987/88 European Champions' Cup, first round, first leg
Wednesday 16 September 1987, Republic Stadium, Kiev
Dinamo Kiev 1 (Mikhailichenko pen) Rangers 0
Attendance 100,000
C. Woods; Nicholl, Phillips; Roberts, Souness, Butcher; D. Ferguson, Cohen (Kirkwood), McCoist, Durrant, McGregor
First round, second leg
Wednesday 30 September 1987, Ibrox Stadium, Glasgow
Rangers 2 (Falco, McCoist) Dinamo Kiev 0
Attendance 44,500
C. Woods; Nicholl, Phillips; McGregor, Souness, Butcher; Francis (Fleck), Falco, McCoist, Durrant, Cohen (Kirkwood)
Second round, first leg
Wednesday 21 October 1987, Ibrox Stadium, Glasgow
Rangers 3 (McCoist, Durrant, Falco) Gornik Zabrze 1 (Urban)
Attendance 41,366

Woods; Nicholl. Phillips; Roberts, D. Ferguson (Cohen), Butcher; Francis (Fleck),
Falco, McCoist, Durrant, Souness

Second round, second leg

Wednesday 2 November 1987, Stadion Gornik, Zabrze

Gornik Zabrze 1 (Orzeszek) Rangers 1 (McCoist pen)

Attendance 23,250

Woods; Nicholl. Phillips; Roberts, D. Ferguson (Cohen), Butcher; McGregor,
Cooper, McCoist (Fleck), Durrant, Souness

Quarter-final, first leg

Wednesday 2 March 1988, Stadion Steaua, Bucharest

Steaua Bucharest 2 (Piturca, Iovan) Rangers 0

Attendance 33,000

C. Woods; Gough, Munro; Roberts, Wilkins, Nisbet (D. Ferguson); Nicholl,
Souness, McCoist (Francis), Durrant, D. Cooper

Quarter-final, second leg

Wednesday 16 March 1988, Ibrox Stadium, Glasgow

Rangers 2 (Gough, McCoist pen) Steaua Bucharest 1 (Lacatus)

Attendance 44,000

C. Woods; Nisbet (Francis), Munro; Roberts, Wilkins, Gough; D. Ferguson,
Souness, McCoist, Durrant, D. Cooper

That broken leg suffered by Terry Butcher was instrumental in Rangers failing
to annexe the 1987/88 League Championship and consequently the Ibrox men
had to settle for the UEFA Cup in the following campaign. Nevertheless, international signings continued to arrive for record transfer fees.

Remarkably, having visited Poland for the first time in eighteen years some
eleven months earlier, Rangers found themselves embarking upon the selfsame
journey in the opening round of the 1988/89 UEFA Cup – to the coalfields of
Silesia. The official Rangers party had taken time out of their schedule to visit
nearby Auschwitz during their visit, as did the author some eleven months later
when the Ibrox men returned to Katowice – on this occasion to play GKS
Katowice in the opening round of the UEFA Cup. It was the fourth successive European tie in which the Light Blues would face opponents from Eastern
Europe – a sequence of fixtures that had many friends of Rangers asking whether
the then board had specifically requested such pairings in order to discourage
travelling fans in the aftermath of the 1985 Heysel Stadium disaster. Wherever
the truth lay, GKS (Coalminers' Sports Club) Katowice were welcomed to Ibrox
on 7 September and had much the better of a first half notable for one bizarre
incident that saw John Brown, playing in his first European game, receive a yellow card for throwing the Polish trainer's bag off the pitch. 'Bomber' was rightly
incensed by the infuriating time-wasting tactics of the Polish players, but would
receive a harsh two-match ban from UEFA for the incident. The second half

would be a different story as Rangers took control with Brown twice coming close in the opening minutes with headers – the first being held by visiting goalkeeper Janusz Jojko, the second striking the crossbar. The breakthrough finally came after seventy-three minutes when a Davie Cooper corner was head-flicked on by Terry Butcher, the ball eventually falling to Mark Walters who drilled it home.

GKS were not yet out of the game, but Rangers finished on top with Kevin Drinkell twice coming close, firstly in the seventy-eighth minute when his header from a Brown cross was inches wide, then five minutes later his close-range shot produced an instinctive save from Jojko.

Four weeks later, Rangers returned to the Slaski Stadion, Chorzow (scene of their defeat to Gornik in 1969), for the second leg, the 18,000-capacity Stadion GKS (or Ulica Bukowa – Beech Street) undergoing major reconstruction to its quaint ground at the time. In any case, the 40,000 crowd present at the Slaski fully justified the switch. There was a real shock for the Light Blues in just four minutes when Jan Furtok opened the scoring with a curling twenty-yard free-kick, but Rangers responded immediately, coming close three times before Terry Butcher equalised with a header from a Walters corner after thirteen minutes. The Ibrox captain made it a double four minutes later when a Ray Wilkins free-kick was headed home.

The tie was effectively over, but GKS rallied after the interval when a Miroslaw Kubisztal shot and a Krzysztof Walczak header produced superb saves from Woods, the equaliser finally arriving in the sixty-third minute when a Jerzy Kapias cross, partially cleared by Ian Durrant, fell to Kubisztal whose low right-foot shot beat the unsighted Woods. Rangers regained the lead eight minutes later when Durrant steered a Walters corner home from ten yards, and an Ian Ferguson piledriver from an Ally McCoist cutback sealed the victory after seventy-eight minutes. Old friends awaited Rangers in the next round – 1. FC Köln, for the third time in eleven years and the fourth time overall.

It was to the familiar territory of the Stadion Müngersdorfer that the Light Blues travelled for the first leg but the demands of the domestic calendar would cost Rangers dear, with a League Cup final against Aberdeen having been played just three days earlier. Controlling play for seventy-five minutes in a disciplined performance, during which time golden opportunities were spurned by both Butcher and McCoist, the roof fell in on the visitors in the closing fifteen minutes through goals by Olaf Janssen and old adversary Thomas Allofs. The harsh ordering-off of McCoist following a clash with Paul Steiner in the dying seconds was the final nail in the coffin.

A 0-2 deficit left Rangers with a mountain to climb in the return match, their slim hopes dissipating even further by the loss of the suspended McCoist and Wilkins, and the injured Durrant and Brown. Just as in 1979, Köln faced a weak-ened opposition.

In truth, although Rangers pressed consistently, luck was never with them; Mark Walters struck the crossbar with a forty-fourth minute free-kick, and Richard Gough the post with a sixty-fifth minute header. The deadlock was finally broken with fifteen minutes remaining by Kevin Drinkell with a powerful header, but just when it appeared that extra time might be forced, a late goal by Janssen sent the Germans through to face Real Sociedad, going under 0-1, 2-2.

1988/89 UEFA Cup, first round, first leg
Wednesday 7 September 1988, Ibrox Stadium, Glasgow
Rangers 1 (Walters) GKS Katowice 0
Attendance 41,120
Woods; Stevens, Brown; Gough, Wilkins, Butcher; Drinkell, I. Ferguson, Cooper, Durrant (D. Ferguson), Walters
First round, second leg
Wednesday 5 October 1988, Slaski Stadian, Chorzow
GKS Katowice 2 (Furtok, Kubisztal) Rangers 4 (Butcher 2, Durrant, I. Ferguson);
Attendance 40,000
Woods; Stevens, Munro; Gough, Wilkins, Butcher; Cooper, I. Ferguson, McCoist, Durrant (McGregor), Walters
Second round, first leg
Wednesday 26 October 1988, Stadion Müngersdorfer, Köln
1. FC Köln 2 (Janssen, T. Allofs) Rangers 0
Attendance 42,000
Woods; Stevens, Munro; Gough, Wilkins, Butcher; Drinkell, I. Ferguson, McCoist, D. Ferguson, Walters (Nisbet)
Second round, second leg
Wednesday 9 November 1988, Ibrox Stadium, Glasgow
Rangers 1 (Drinkell) 1. FC Köln 1 (Janssen)
Attendance 42,204
Woods; Stevens, Munro; Gough, Nicholl (McCall), Butcher; D. Cooper (Nisbet), I. Ferguson, Drinkell, D. Ferguson, Walters

The League Championship had been secured in 1988/89, and although no one could have forseen the years to come, this would be the first of nine successive titles. Transfer activity surpassed even the high-profile signings of recent years with the £1.6 million capture of England international Trevor Steven from Everton and, the most sensational of them all, the £1.5 million signing of former Celtic striker Maurice Johnston from French club Nantes, snatched from under the very noses of the Parkhead club.

Such major signings had many friends of Rangers anticipating a prolonged run in the Champions' Cup, perhaps even the ultimate triumph – only for the first-round ballot to throw up an old and dangerous foe, namely West German

Champions Bayern München. The Bavarian club were as formidable as ever and Rangers were weakened by the loss of Richard Gough through injury; despite Mark Walters opening the scoring from the penalty spot the scores were rapidly levelled by Kogl on the half-hour. The visitors struck swiftly at the start of the second half through Olaf Thon, then with a wonder goal from Klaus Augenthaler who unleashed a swerving, long shot from out wide. Bayern were in command thereafter, running out 3-1 winners to effectively kill the tie stone dead.

The delights of München's 'Oktoberfest' awaited 12,000 Light Blue followers who travelled for the return match, which was just as well for the game was nothing to write home about, ending in a goalless draw. Rangers never looked likely, without the suspended Ally McCoist and with Israeli international Bonni Ginzburg in goal, to reduce the deficit.

Bayern went as far as the semi-finals before going out to the holders (and eventual winners) AC Milan on away goals (1-0, 1-2).

1989/90 European Champions' Cup, first round, first leg
Wednesday 13 September 1989, Ibrox Stadium, Glasgow
Rangers 1 (Walters pen) Bayern München 3 (Kogl, Thon, Augenthaler)
Attendance 40,253
Woods; Stevens, Munro; Nisbet, Wilkins, Butcher; Steven, I. Ferguson,
D. Ferguson, Johnston, Walters
First round, second leg
Wednesday 27 September 1989
Olympic Stadium, München
Bayern München 0 Rangers 0
Attendance 40,000
Ginzburg; Stevens, Munro; Gough, Wilkins, Butcher; Steven, I. Ferguson,
Cowan (Drinkell), Johnston, Walters

The sun-kissed island of Malta awaited Rangers in the opening round of the 1990/91 European Champions' Cup – to face old friends Valletta. The Scottish Champions won with ease in both games, although not quite as emphatically as in 1983. Maurice Johnston scored five of the goals in the 10-0 aggregate win (4-0, 6-0), the Ibrox return being remembered more for goalkeeper Chris Woods' miss from the penalty spot than for any individual goal. Mark Hateley had been signed from Monaco in a £1 million transfer, but the arrival of such an experienced English international striker was offset somehow by the departure of Terry Butcher following a fall-out with Graeme Souness. Butcher's loss was significant, given that he had been such an iconic figure for the past four years. The next round would be a different matter entirely with Crevna Zvezda Beograd (Red Star Belgrade) the opponents. The opposition was as formidable as any left in the competition. Red Star were a team of the highest class. It is reported that

Ibrox assistant manager Walter Smith, when he returned to Glasgow following a spying mission, uttered just one word, of the four-letter variety, to manager Graeme Souness.

Smith's feelings of foreboding were well founded – in the first leg Red Star tore the visitors apart with their class and pace, watched by 82,500 packing the sprawling bowl that is their very own 'Maracana' Stadium. Souness' team selection puzzled many onlookers, two wingers having been included, namely Mark Walters and Pieter Huistra, in the absence of Mark Hateley. The nightmare began in just the eighth minute when the pace of Dusko Radinovic tore the left flank of Rangers' defence asunder, his low cross being diverted into his own net by John Brown. The Light Blues were being overrun by the Slavs, with the class and speed of Robert Prosinecki, Dragisa Binic, and Darko Pancev showing them to be a class apart. Somehow, by dint of good fortune and outstanding goalkeeping on the part of Chris Woods, Rangers survived without further loss as the clock ticked past the hour mark. Indeed, Rangers seemed to be gaining a foothold in the game when a superb free-kick by Prosinecki found the net via an upright after sixty-five minutes with serious questions being asked about the discipline of the wall and the positioning of the goalkeeper. Seven minutes later, Huistra should have secured a priceless away goal, heading wide when it seemed easier to score. In their very next attack, Red Star surged up the park for Pancev to take clinical advantage of hesitation on the part of Gough.

'How can I possibly win the European Cup with eleven Scots in the team?' Souness lamented to the Scottish Press at Belgrade Airport on the way home after the match. If any one single result convinced Graeme Souness that he would never achieve the ultimate glory at Ibrox then this surely was it. Rangers had been comprehensively torn apart in the Red Star Stadium, and with UEFA's restrictive 'non-national' ruling about to be imposed across Europe, restricting the number of non-Scots the club could field to four initially, then one year later to three, Ibrox dreams of the European Cup were slowly dissipating; the manager would depart for Liverpool within five months. The Ibrox return was almost incidental, with an abysmal attendance of just 23,821 spectators reflecting both the hopelessness of the task facing Rangers and the absurdly high admission prices. In the event, Red Star controlled the pace of the game, both with their skill and their wholly unnecessary spoiling tactics. A fine Pancev volley opened the scoring after fifty-one minute, but McCoist's looping header from a Nigel Spackman cross salvaged some pride on the night.

The Slavs, meanwhile, went on to annexe the trophy on penalties after an apology of a final against Marseille. Ironically, two of the most attractive, attacking sides in Europe produced one of the worst ever finals.

For Red Star, the break up of Yugoslavia, and the subsequent Balkans War in which the region tore itself apart, meant that they were unable to build upon their success or even defend the trophy. 'The lamps went out' on the state of

Yugoslavia and, as civil war tore Belgrade apart, it was clear that Rangers had visited the city just in time.

1990/91 European Champions' Cup, first round, first leg
Wednesday 19 September 1990, National Stadium, Ta'Qali
Valletta 0 Rangers 4 (Johnston 2, McCoist (pen), Hateley)
Attendance 8,000
Woods; Stevens, Munro (Brown); Gough, Spackman, Butcher; Steven, McCoist, Hateley, Johnston, Walters
First round, second leg
Tuesday 2 October 1990, Ibrox Stadium, Glasgow
Rangers 6 (Johnston 3 [1 pen], Dodds, Spencer, McCoist) Valletta 0; Attendance 20,627
Woods; Stevens, Munro; Cowan (A. Robertson), Dodds, Brown; Steven, Walters, Spencer, Johnston, Huistra
Second round, first leg
Wednesday 24 October 1990, Stadion Crevna Zvezda, Beograd
Crevna Zvezda Beograd 3 (Prosinecki,Pancev, Brown o.g.) Rangers 0
Attendance 82,500
Woods; Stevens, Munro; Gough, Spackman, Brown; Steven, Ferguson, Walters, Johnston, Huistra (McCoist)
Second round, second leg
Wednesday 7 November 1990, Ibrox Stadium, Glasgow
Rangers 1 (McCoist) Crevna Zvezda Beograd 1 (Pancev)
Attendance 23,821
Woods; Stevens, Munro; Gough (Nisbet), Spackman, Brown; Steven, Dodds (A. Robertson), McCoist, Hateley, Walters

A third consecutive League Championship (for the first time since the war) meant a third successive entry to the European Champions' Cup in 1991/92 under new manager Walter Smith. For the first time since its inception, the basic format would change with the last eight being formed into two groups of four. Rangers' director/secretary Campbell Ogilvie, a much respected figure in football circles, was instrumental in the conception of the idea.

The medieval city of Prague was enjoying a second spring and, now free at last from the yoke of socialist repression, was the venue for Walter Smith's Rangers' first European tie as manager. Prague was now at the heart of Europe – a thriving, vibrant place full of colour, laughter and warmth, with the cafes and restaurants of Wenceslas Square full of the joys of life, whereas when the Scottish Champions had last visited the city a decade earlier it had been dull, drab, lifeless and unwelcoming. Walter Smith, recognising the realities of UEFA's non-national ruling, had sought to alter the make-up of his squad. Departures included Chris Woods,

Trevor Steven and Mark Walters; amongst the arrivals were Scottish international Andy Goram and Stuart McCall. For other reasons, Maurice Johnston also
departed and one high-profile international arrival was Alexei Mikhailichenko
from Sampdoria, a midfielder of the highest class who joined the club with a CV
second to none. Prague may have changed beyond all recognition, but the Light
Blues' performance was almost as abysmal as that against Dukla exactly ten years
earlier. In truth, Sparta's 1-0 win, courtesy of Jiri Nemec's dipping cross (misjudged
by Goram) flattered Rangers. The home side were denied three strong penalty
claims. Rangers seemed to have won the day in the Ibrox return thanks to two
Stuart McCall goals at Ibrox, but a defensive blunder eight minutes into extra time
allowed Sparta to qualify on away goals, Goram fumbling a deflected Horst Siegl
backheel. No one, least of all the author, would dispute that 'The Goalie' went on
to become an Ibrox legend – but his culpability was clear against the Czechs.

Few had rated the Czechs highly, indeed the feeling amongst many close to the
club was that Sparta had been underestimated, despite the obvious quality in their
ranks with the likes of Vaclav Nemecec, Jiri Nemec and Jiri Novotny. Wherever
the truth lay, they went on to eliminate Olympique Marseille (Trevor Steven
et al.), and, under the new league format, effectively were semi-finalists, finishing second behind eventual winners Barcelona. Indeed, had the two games with
Barça been a two-legged tie, Sparta would have won (1-0, 2-3).

1991/92 European Champions' Cup, first round, first leg
Wednesday 18 September 1991, Stadion Letna, Praha
Sparta Praha 1 (Nemec) Rangers 0
Attendance 11,053
Goram; Stevens, D. Robertson; Gough, Spackman, Nisbet; McCall, Ferguson
(Durrant), Hateley, McCoist (Brown), Huistra
First round, second leg
Wednesday 2 October 1991, Ibrox Stadium, Glasgow
Rangers 2 (McCall 2) Sparta Praga 1 (Siegl)
Attendance 34,260
Goram; Stevens, D. Robertson; Brown (Durrant), Spackman, Nisbet; Kuznetsov,
McCall, McCoist (Spencer), Johnston, Mikhailichenko

EIGHT

The Champions' League

Season 1992/93 would go down in the record books as one of the greatest in the club's history (if not the greatest), Walter Smith's men securing a fifth Treble for the Ibrox men, but if anything it is the European exploits that many to this day recall with pride.

Summer transfer activity centred around the return of the prodigal sons Trevor Steven and Dave McPherson from Olympique Marseille and Hearts respectively. Denmark was a country long visited by Rangers on summer tours – as early as 1911 the club had played in Kobenhavn, and frequent sojourns there ever since had endeared the city of the Little Mermaid and the Tivoli Gardens to the club and its supporters. The meeting with unfashionable Danish Champions Lyngby would, however, be the Light Blues' first encounter in a European competition.

The opening tie at Ibrox produced a comfortable enough 2-0 victory with goals from Mark Hateley and Pieter Huistra after thirty-nine and sixty-seven minutes respecively, although Ian Durrant very nearly added a third in the dying minutes with as spectacular an effort as has ever been seen at Ibrox, his dipping volley from the halfway line being cleared off the goal-line by a Danish defender. The return two weeks later was switched from the small Lyngby Stadion to the newly refurbished national stadium, the Parkenstadion (formerly the Kobenhavn Idraettspark). It was to prove to be 'Wonderful, Wonderful Kobenhavn' for the vast Light Blue travelling support as Rangers completed the double with a disciplined performance that was capped by Durrant's eighty-fifth minute winner. For one group of fans, however, the long trip by coach was memorable for all the wrong reasons – delayed en route, they witnessed only the last four minutes of the game.

There were certainly no travel difficulties for the next round when Rangers were paired with English Champions Leeds United. The Yorkshire club were more than fortunate to still be in the tournament – defeated on away goals by VfB Stuttgart (0-3, 4-1) they suddenly found themselves reinstated by UEFA when the realisation dawned that the Germans had breached the regulation decreeing that clubs were barred from using more than three non-nationals in any one game. The result of the second leg was amended to one of 3-0, necessitating a one-off third match in Barcelona which Leeds won 2-1.

Controversy raged around the tie when both clubs refused to countenance the allocation of tickets for away supporters, a ban that the two sets of fans got around by supplying briefs to each other. Leeds were formidable opponents; included in their squad was old friend Gordon Strachan (formerly of Aberdeen and Manchester United), currently, of course, manager of Celtic. The mercurial Eric Cantona was there, as was Scottish international midfielder Gary McAllister and future Ranger Rod Wallace.

The tie was inevitably dubbed 'The Battle of Britain' by the media – and within sixty seconds of the start Ibrox was silenced by a quite stunning eighteen-yard strike from McAllister after a Strachan corner had been partially cleared. For twenty minutes Leeds dominated play, but Rangers had perceived a weakness in visiting goalkeeper John Lukic, in that he was susceptible to the cross ball. A succession of corners finally paid dividend when he fisted Durrant's inswinger into his own net after twenty-one minutes. Before the interval the Light Blues had the lead when another Durrant corner saw Lukic parry McPherson's effort only for McCoist, ever the predator, to convert the rebound. The noise and tension was unbearable, with the atmosphere on one of the great European nights electric. The second half produced no more goals, and Rangers had a narrow 2-1 lead to take to Elland Road. With one side of the ground under reconstruction, the capacity of the Leeds ground was restricted to just 25,000 and just as at Ibrox the crowd was silenced in the opening minutes when Hateley, on the turn from all of twenty-five yards, volleyed the ball over Lukic into the roof of the net. With their away goal now negated, the home side piled on the pressure without success, the Ibrox defence holding firm with Messrs Goram, Gough and Brown outstanding. In a swift counter-attack on the hour, Rangers struck a decisive blow with a quite superbly executed goal, Durrant's perfectly weighted ball down the left releasing Hateley in full flow. His cross on the run to McCoist at the far post produced a header back across goal that found the corner of the net.

Rangers were through, with not even a late Cantona goal taking the shine off a magnificent success and in three Scotland-England clashes in the European Cup the Scottish Champions had emerged victorious twice. 'We haven't heard much from our English colleagues this evening', mused one Scottish journalist in the Elland Road press box as the game drew to a close, and at the end of the game Rangers received a standing ovation from the Leeds United fans – thus illustrating just how absurd had been the non-allocation of tickets to away fans.

The last eight, as in the previous season, would be divided into two groups of four, but on this occasion a new concept would be introduced – i.e. the Champions' League, run by TEAM Marketing, whose task was to generate the

Ally McCoist heads home Rangers' second goal at Elland Road in 1992.

maximum possible advertising, sponsorship and television revenue. From now on, European football would never be the same again – all commercial revenue would be directed into a central pool with clubs no longer having control over the raising of gate income, nor from advertising or television sources. A bonus system was introduced, with clubs receiving the incentive of financial reward, firstly for qualifying for the Champions' League then for each point secured. For better or for worse, from now on the rich would get richer and richer; television market share would be a key factor in how the tournament was run from here on in, with the original eight within seven years being expanded to thirty-two, not all of them champion clubs within their own country. The draw placed Rangers in the same group as Club Brugge, CSKA Moscow and Olympique Marseille with the French giants, beaten finalists two years earlier, first to visit Ibrox on a night of torrential rain on 25 November 1992. Manager Walter Smith was not without his problems prior to the match, his team selection in the first place being restricted due to UEFA's non-national policy, and as if that was not bad enough, Ally McCoist and Ian Ferguson (both Scots) were out through injury and suspension respectively, and captain Richard Gough would last only forty-five minutes before succumbing to injury, forcing the inclusion of youngsters Neil Murray, Steven Pressley and Gary McSwegan, all participating in their first European ties. For seventy-five minutes Marseille played Rangers off the park on a pitch barely playable. The home side were being comprehensively outclassed,

0-2 down through goals by Alain Boksic and Rudi Voller after thirty-one and fifty-five minutes respectively, with Goram keeping the score respectable with two breathtaking saves. Suddenly, out of the blue, substitute McSwegan scored with a spectacular header in the seventy-eighth minute with his first touch of the ball to secure his first competitive goal for the club. Three minutes later Hateley headed a Durrant cross into the net and, quite unbelievably, Rangers had stolen a 2-2 draw.

Because of the severity of the Russian winter, CSKA Moscow were obliged to play all of their home games in Germany – one against Rangers in Bochum, the other two in Berlin. The Ibrox men had once won 5-0 in the Ruhr city, in 1933, but almost sixty years later it was a much more serious matter. The Russian Champions had eliminated cup holders Barcelona in the previous round, coming from 0-2 down in the Nou Camp to win 3-2. A massive 8,500 Gers fans were present in the Ruhrstadion and there was very nearly a nightmare start inside the first minute when three CSKA forwards converged on a loose ball inside the six-yard box with the net gaping, only for David Robertson to materialise from nowhere and sweep the ball clear. Ferguson's deflected shot after thirteen minutes gave Rangers a 1-0 win in a dour game where the Light Blues were worthy winners.

The Champions' League now went into a three-month winter hibernation and when the spring thaw arrived Rangers were visiting the medieval Belgian city of Brugge. The Olympiastadion was a fortress for the home side, compact and atmospheric, and incidentally named after the district of Brugge in which it was located – not an Olympic Stadium as so many mistakenly reported. Rangers' performance in Brugge was at times as fine a display as any for many a year in Europe; the home side made a better fist of the first half and led at the interval through a Tomasz Dziubinski goal a minute before the break. However, it was the Light Blues who commanded the second half, and finally gained a deserved equaliser through Pieter Huistra in the seventy-third minute. On the same night in Berlin Marseille similarly drew 1-1 with CSKA Moscow, meaning that Rangers were still on level terms with the French. Yet the game had not been without cost, Goram suffering a serious knee injury following an accidental clash with team-mate McPherson that would severely hinder him in the months ahead, although not to his total exclusion. Two weeks later Club Brugge arrived in a Glasgow once again under leaden skies and a blanket of torrential rain. This was a game in which victory was essential for both sides if any hopes of progress to the final were to be realised. Rangers started well, taking the lead through a Durrant goal in the thirty-ninth minute only to suffer a severe blow when Hateley was harshly red-carded. The Belgians equalised through Lorenzo Staelens early in the second half, and the tie appeared to be slipping away from the home side until, with a quarter of an hour remaining, Scott Nisbet scored one of the most incredible goals witnessed at the stadium when, from wide on the right, he hit a swerving

Ian Ferguson scores against CSKA Moscow in Bochum, 1992.

cross that took one bounce and flew at a crazy angle past Danny Verlinden into the net. It was an absolute fluke but it gave Rangers a priceless win. Sadly three days later Nisbet would suffer an injury at Celtic Park that would force him to quit football altogether.

On the same evening, meanwhile, Marseille swamped CSKA Moscow 6-0, a result that raised many eyebrows, with accusations and suspicions being aimed at both clubs, but in fact the real scandal lay ahead.

The Stade Velodrome in the seaport of Marseille is one of Europe's most intimidating arenas – and ill feeling between Marseille and Rangers was generated pre-match when the French Champions reneged on an agreement to supply Rangers' fans with 4,000 tickets, limiting the eventual quantity to one quarter of that due to the importance of the fixture, effectively a European Cup semi-final with the award for victory to either side being a place in the final at München's Olympic Stadion.

Marseille were certainly one of the two finest sides in Europe, packed with international stars from across the globe. Their owner, Bernard Tapie, had spent millions in an attempt to conquer Europe – a dream he had yet to realise. Rangers' performance in the Stade Velodrome was a momentous one that would take them to the very brink of the European Cup final. A Franck Sauzee goal following a Robertson error gave the home side the first-half advantage but Durrant's equaliser levelled the scoreline and the visitors held out in the closing stages despite intense Marseille pressure; the game might even have been won when in a swift breakaway substitute McSwegan's shot flashed inches wide. Walter Smith would afterwards ponder the cost of the absence of the suspended Hateley.

So now it was down to the final matchday with Rangers and Marseille level on points, but with the French holding the slightest but most vital of advantages in that, in the two games between the clubs, they had come out on top, albeit only on away goals. The task facing the Scottish Champions was therefore a simple one: gain at least one more point than Marseille on matchday six or face elimination. With Rangers at home to CSKA Moscow and Marseille away to Club Brugge it was all to play for.

There was ill feeling between Club Brugge and Olympique Marseille – the Belgian club and their fans felt that they had been badly treated at the Stade Velodrome on matchday two. The visiting fans had been the subject of shocking abuse from the Marseille crowd, whilst home coach Raymond Goethals had insulted the opposition with disparaging remarks about Brugge following his side's 3-0 win. The Belgians had sworn revenge, promising that they would defeat Marseille in their home ground, where they had remained unbeaten for so long. They had made that very promise to Rangers following the two games in March: 'keep the group alive until matchday six and we will defeat the French'. The group was indeed alive on matchday six, but something had changed in the last few days. The Belgians all along had sworn that they would avenge their honour against the French for their shameful treatment in the Velodrome, yet on the eve of battle mysteriously changed their tune. Three key players were supposedly injured, the next weekend's league game was much more important, and Brugge meekly surrendered an unbeaten home record they were extremely proud of, going down to an early Boksic goal in two minutes. Meanwhile, at Ibrox intense home pressure failed to achieve the breakthrough, perhaps a dozen chances being squandered with, again, the suspended Hateley being sorely missed.

Marseille were through to the final where they would defeat favourites AC Milan 1-0 in Munich courtesy of a Basile Boli (a Ranger one year later) goal. However, the French club would within a matter of weeks become embroiled in a scandal that eventually saw their president Bernard Tapie found guilty of bribery and corruption and imprisoned for four years whilst his club were relegated and stripped of the French Championship they had won that season. The story had broken that Tapie had bribed players from 'Le Championat' club Valenciennes to throw a vital League game prior to Munich. Marseille had clinched the title with a 1-0 win. Amongst the evidence to come out in the French Court was a list of games that Tapie had bribed opponents to throw and included amongst that list was the game in Brugge, the game that had denied Rangers. The Ibrox men had come so agonisingly close to the European Cup final in a season that, without question, was Walter Smith's finest hour. Ten games unbeaten in Europe's premier club competition is a record to be proud of. With the benefit of hindsight, we can perhaps judge that the squad of players peaked that term, achieving the only domestic treble of the Souness/Smith era, and who is to say that but for the bribery and corruption of M. Tapie, Rangers would have secured the Holy Grail. The

French courts and UEFA have already convicted Tapie of corruption in French domestic football. When, one may ask, will Rangers get justice?

1992/93 European Champions' Cup, first round, first leg
Wednesday 16 September 1992, Ibrox Stadium, Glasgow
Rangers 2 (Hateley, Huistra) Lynbgy 0
Attendance 40,036
Goram; Durrant, D. Robertson; Gough, McPherson, Brown; Mikhailichenko,
I. Ferguson, McCoist, Hateley, Huistra
First round, second leg
Wednesday 30 September 1992, Parkenstadion, Kobenhavn
Lyngby 0 Rangers 1 (Durrant)
Attendance 4,273
Goram; McCall, D. Robertson; Durrant, McPherson, Brown; Steven, I. Ferguson,
McCoist, Hateley, Huistra
Second round, first leg
Wednesday 21 October 1992, Ibrox Stadium, Glasgow
Rangers 2 (McCoist, Lukic o.g.) Leeds United 1 (McAllister)
Attendance 44,000
Goram; McCall, D. Robertson; Gough, McPherson, Brown; Steven (Huistra),
I. Ferguson, McCoist, Hateley, Durrant
Second round, second leg
Wednesday 4 November 1992, Elland Road, Leeds
Leeds United 1 (Cantona) Rangers 2 (Hateley, McCoist)
Attendance 25,118
Goram; McCall, D. Robertson; Gough, McPherson, Brown; Gordon
(Mikhailichenko), I. Ferguson, McCoist, Hateley, Durrant
Champions' League Group A
Matchday one
Wednesday 25 November 1992, Ibrox Stadium, Glasgow
Rangers 2 (McSwegan, Hateley) Olympique Marseille 2 (Boksic, Voller);
Attendance 41,624
Goram; Murray, D. Robertson; Gough (Pressley), McPherson, Brown; Steven
(McSwegan), McCall, Durrant, Hateley, Mikhailichenko
Matchday two
Wednesday 9 December 1992, Ruhrstadion, Bochum
CSKA Moscow 0 Rangers 1 (I. Ferguson)
Attendance 9,000
Goram; McCall, D. Robertson; Durrant, McPherson, Brown; Steven, I. Ferguson,
McCoist, Hateley, Mikhailichenko
Matchday three
Wednesday 3 March 1993, Olympiastadion, Brugge

Club Brugge 1 (Dziubinski) Rangers 1 (Huistra)

Attendance 19,000

Goram; Nisbet (Pressley), D. Robertson; Murray, McPherson, Brown;

Mikhailichenko, McCall, McCoist, Hateley, Huistra

Matchday four

Wednesday 17 March 1993, Ibrox Stadium, Glasgow

Rangers 2 (Durrant, Nisbet) Club Brugge 1 (Staelens)

Attendance 42,731

Goram; Nisbet, Murray; Gough, McPherson, Brown; Steven, McCall, McCoist,

Hateley, Durrant (Hagen)

Matchday five

Wednesday 7 April, 1993, Stade Velodrome, Marseille

Olympique Marseille 1 (Sauzee) Rangers 1 (Durrant)

Attendance 44,000

Goram; McCall, D. Robertson (Murray); Gough, McPherson, Brown; Steven,

I. Ferguson, McCoist, Durrant, Huistra (McSwegan)

Matchday six

Wednesday 21 April 1993, Ibrox Stadium, Glasgow

Rangers 0 CSKA Moscow 0

Attendance 43,142

Goram; McCall, D. Robertson; Gough, McPherson, Brown; Steven, I. Ferguson,

McCoist, Durrant, Huistra (McSwegan)

After the glory of 1992/93, it was perhaps too much to expect another unbeaten campaign, but defeat in the opening round to Levski Sofia was a dreadful disappointment for the Light Blues, particularly as it was mainly self-inflicted. Summer investment had been limited in the main to just the one player, namely Duncan Ferguson for £3.75 million from Dundee United. The signing did not meet with universal approval from all friends of Rangers, many believing that a more balanced strengthening of the squad might have paid a better dividend, particularly as Ferguson played in exactly the same position as Mark Hateley, an Ibrox icon. There was no Goram, Gough, Brown or McCoist at Ibrox (a knock-on effect of the 64-game campaign of 1992/93) and the choice of the three non-Scots raised many eyebrows, as this was one tie surely ideal for Alexei Mikhailichenko, but that was still no reason to play Duncan Ferguson wide on the left. Rangers created numerous chances during the first half, all spurned until, on the stroke of half-time, David McPherson opened the scoring following an Ian Durrant corner. A Hateley header in the fifty-sixth minute made it 2-0, and a satisfactory scoreline seemed assured until the seventy-seventh minute when a Hateley clearance was intercepted by Levski substitute Georgi Ivanov, his centre being headed goalwards by Daniel Borimirov, squirming home through goalkeeper Ally Maxwell's hands. Rangers responded immediately with another Hateley header making it 3-1, but an appalling error by Duncan Ferguson after eighty-two minutes allowed Nikolai Todorov to head home from an Emil Kremenilev cross. Defensive errors had gifted the Bulgarians two goals, and Rangers had a precarious 3-2 lead, which should still have been enough in the hostile atmosphere of the Stadion Vasilij Levski, where they had performed so competently twenty-six years earlier.

An evening kick-off and torrential rain provided a bonus compared to the climate of 1967 and the visitors controlled most of the early play only to lose a bad goal after thirty-six minutes when Richard Gough failed to clear a Levski attack and captain Nasko Sirakov shot on the turn to open the scoring. Level pegging was restored on the stroke of half-time when Durrant ghosted in at the far post to head home a Gary Stevens cross. A 1-1 scoreline at the interval saw Rangers well in control, but unaccountably falling back into defence the longer the game went on. Maxwell produced several fine saves although the tie could have been killed stone dead after seventy-five minutes when McPherson's header from a Trevor Steven free-kick produced a superb save from goalkeeper Nikola Nikolov.

Catastrophe struck with sixty seconds remaining; a corner to the Light Blues was inexplicably taken long and quickly, when surely time should have been wasted, both substitutes sent on, and play delayed. Instead, Levski broke upfield and Nikolai Todorov's powerful shot from thirty yards exploded behind Ally Maxwell. It was the Light Blues' first defeat in thirteen Champions' Cup matches – a record for a Scottish club. The home crowd celebrated long and noisily into the night but for Rangers the post-mortem began. It was clear that serious errors of judgement in terms of team selection and tactics had been made and that, although Levski were eliminated by Werder Bremen in round two (2-2, 0-1) they had been underrated, as was demonstrated when Bulgaria, with seven Levski players in their squad, reached the 1994 World Cup semi-finals.

1993/94 European Champions' Cup, first round, first leg
Wednesday 15 September 1993, Ibrox Stadium, Glasgow
Rangers 3 (Hateley 2, McPherson) Levski Sofia 2 (Borimov, Todorov)
Attendance 37,013
Maxwell; Stevens, D. Robertson; McCall, McPherson, Pressley: Steven,
I. Ferguson, Durrant (Morrow), Hateley, D. Ferguson
First round, second leg
Wednesday 29 September 1993, Stadion Vasilij Levski, Sofia
Levski Sofia 2 (Sirakov, Todorov) Rangers 1 (Durrant)
Attendance 50,000
Maxwell; Stevens, Wishart; Gough, McPherson, McCall; Steven, I. Ferguson,
Durrant, Hateley, Hagen

UEFA moved the Champions' League goalposts for season 1994/95, restricting access to the competition to the champion clubs of just the leading twenty-four nations under the governing body's complicated co-efficient system. The reasons were twofold, firstly reflecting that following the collapse of Communist dictatorships in Eastern Europe, the break-up of the Soviet Union and other satellite states meant that there were now around fifty independent members of UEFA, and secondly to ensure that competing clubs in the Champions' League would be drawn from the major European nations, those who could provide the greatest market share in terms of commercial and television revenue. This had not always been ensured even in such an elite field; for example, in the initial season of 1992/93 England, Germany and Spain were not represented. Now they were virtually assured of automatic qualification, as were the champion clubs of France and Italy, with eight now gaining outright qualification. There had been little commercial advantage in Dinamo Kiev playing Spartak Moscow; the fixtures UEFA envisaged when the Champions' League was created were the likes of AC Milan against Barcelona.

It was elitism at its worst, but all clubs, including Rangers, simply had to accept the situation and get on with it. There had been two major summer signings, central defender Basile Boli from Marseille and Brian Laudrup from Fiorentina, and with such substantial investment qualification for the Champions' League was not just expected but demanded. The opposition in the qualifying round would be AEK Athens – the Light Blues' first ever visit to Greece.

The heat and humidity of the historic city of Athens, home to the Parthenon and the Acropoulis, meant that Rangers had a plethora of logistical problems to cope with. Greek football fans are amongst the most volatile anywhere in the world, and those of AEK were no different. It would be four days in hell for the visitors; left to stew in intense heat in their chartered aircraft for two hours upon arrival at Athens Airport, the Scottish Champions were under armed police guard throughout their stay, being provided with an armoured coach to take them to training and to the match itself, all too necessary as was demonstrated by the hail of missiles that greeted their arrival at the Nikos Goumas ground on the night of the game. Inside the ground, the atmosphere was intimidating with visiting Gers fans pelted throughout by missiles. Nottingham Forest players, due to play a friendly against Olympiakos Piraeus the next night (2-2), were present amongst the Light Blue followers but left before kick-off due to the hate and hostility of the AEK fanatics.

This litany is by no means meant to provide excuses for what was a truly lamentable display as Rangers were blitzed in Nea Filadelphia, being extremely lucky to lose by only 0-2. A first-half bombardment had been survived more by good fortune and the goalkeeping of Andy Goram than by anything else, only for AEK debutant Dimitris Saravakos to open the scoring on the stroke of half-time. The same player, signed that summer from bitter rivals Panathinaikos (on a free transfer) underlined his value with a second goal after seventy minutes to leave the visitors with a mountain to climb in Glasgow.

Searching questions were asked of Walter Smith's team selection and tactics in Athens. Pre-season preparations had consisted of a three-game tour of Denmark and Germany, followed by two tournament fixtures at Ibrox, yet the defensive line-up against AEK was an unfamiliar one, consisting of three players who had never played together in that formation (Gough, Pressley, Stevens). Rangers frankly never looked like recovering at Ibrox, where the solitary tactic was the long, high ball to Mark Hateley and Duncan Ferguson. Boli, suspended in Athens, was inexplicably fielded out of position at right-back, and a single second-half goal from Toni Savevski killed the tie stone dead.

The defeat was both a financial and footballing disaster for the Ibrox men whilst AEK performed abysmally in their Champions' League group, amassing a meagre two points from six games, albeit in a section that included both eventual finalists Ajax and Milan.

1994/95 European Champions' Cup, qualifying round, first leg
Wednesday 10 August 1994, Nikos Goumas Stadium, Athinai
AEK 2 (Saravakos 2) Rangers 0
Attendance 35,000
Goram; Stevens, D. Robertson; Gough, Pressley, McCall; Laudrup, I. Ferguson, Durie (Durrant), Hateley, Murray
Qualifying round, second leg
Wednesday 24 August 1994, Ibrox Stadium, Glasgow
Rangers 0 AEK 1 (Savevski)
Attendance 44,789
Goram; McCall, D. Robertson; Gough, Boli, McPherson; Durie (Durrant), I. Ferguson, D. Ferguson, Hateley, Laudrup

The arrival of Paul Gascoigne from Lazio, Oleg Salenko from Atletico Madrid, Gordan Petric from Dundee United and Stephen Wright from Aberdeen represented an injection of quality that made a third consecutive failure to qualify for the Champions' League utterly unthinkable. The arrival of Gascoigne, England's one player of true world class at the time, underlined once again the pulling power of Rangers at the time when it came to signing players of the highest class. Salenko too came with international credentials of the highest order, having once scored no fewer than five goals in a World Cup finals match for Russia against Cameroon at USA 1994. Petric too was a key signing, manager Walter Smith having firmly set his mind on playing three central defenders behind two wing-backs; the Serbian would be joined by Scots Richard Gough and Alan McLaren (signed the previous season from Hearts).

For once, the preliminary round draw favoured Rangers, pairing them with Anorthosis Famagusta from Cyprus (the club's first visit to the divided island). Initial concern that the Cypriot club's home of Famagusta lay in the Turkish

Republic of Northern Cyprus soon dissipated when it was learned that, since the invasion of the island, the club had in fact been based in Larnaca in the southern part of Cyprus recognised by Britain.

Manager Walter Smith would in retrospect concede that Rangers underestimated Anorthosis and the Scottish Champions could consider themselves most fortunate to finish the first leg with a 1-0 lead. It was a laboured performance to say the least, with the visitors including in their ranks a certain Nikolai Todorov of Levski Sofia infamy together with two other Bulgarians – Ilian Kiriakov and Valentin Ignatov. Kiriakov would dominate the midfield, totally overshadowing £4.3 million signing Gascoigne. It took a goal from substitute Gordon Durie midway through the second half to give the Light Blues a slender lead, that would surely have been non-existent were it not for the goalkeeping of Andy Goram. Larnaca would be a different matter, however, the visitors giving a professional, disciplined performance to gain a goalless draw, securing qualification for Europe's premier club competition. The game ended on a comical note when, with Ally McCoist poised to come on as a substitute, a pulled hamstring suffered by Ian Durrant meant instead the introduction of Neil Murray, thus denying McCoist inclusion in the lucrative bonus scheme for all players who had played in either or both of the ties against the Cypriots, should qualification be achieved. It was, McCoist later commented, the most expensive hamstring in history. The Champions' League revisited, but the draw would place Rangers in the 'Group of Death' with Borussia Dortmund, Juventus and Steaua Bucharest. It could scarcely have been any tougher, and when Rangers visited post-revolution Bucharest for the opening fixture the comments of Steaua Coach Dimitriu Dimitru ('It is to our advantage that we play our opening fixture at home against the weakest team in the group') perhaps hinted at the Ibrox men's rating on the Continent. Dimitru's comments were perhaps a surprise, given that the Romanians had suffered a 0-4 defeat at Ibrox just six weeks earlier in a pre-season friendly. The Champions' League would be a different story, however.

Rangers gave a resolute, defensive performance in Bucharest, shrugging off the ordering-off of McLaren (together with Damian Militaru) for an obscure off-the-ball incident that was spotted, alone of the 26,000 spectators present in Stadion Steaua, by a linesman. Perhaps undeservedly, however, the Scottish Champions were sunk by a stunning eighty-fourth minute twenty-yard left-foot volley from Daniel Prodan (later to sign for the Light Blues), from a corner, that screamed past Goram.

It was the Ibrox club's first ever defeat in the Champions' League. Criticised (mainly by stay-at-home television viewers) for their negative approach in Bucharest, the Light Blues held their own in a 2-2 draw with Borussia Dortmund at Ibrox next time up, thanks to goals from Richard Gough and Ian Ferguson. It was a game the home side might have won, despite the absence of the suspended McLaren and the injured David Robertson. Rangers, of course, were already

Paul Gascoigne in action against Borussia Dortmund at Ibrox in 1995.

handicapped by UEFA's non-national ruling, and just to make matters worse the iconic figure of Brian Laudrup exited at the interval with an injury that would mark him absent for the next dozen games.

If the Light Blues were to have any realistic hope of being one of the two clubs to qualify from the group (unlike 1992/93 when only one team qualified) then they faced the daunting prospect of securing at least one win in the back-to-back matches with Italian giants Juventus – the Juventus of Gianlucci Vialli, Fabrizio Ravanelli and Alessandro del Piero. Reality, however, dawned on match-day three when Rangers were comprehensively and overwhelmingly outclassed in the Stadio Delle Alpi by Juventus, the 1-4 scoreline scarcely even beginning to reflect the 'Old Lady's' superiority. Within the opening fifteen minutes the home side had netted three times, and even though the interval arrived with the score-line unchanged the blunt truth was that, at that stage, the Italians looked more than capable of inflicting as great a humiliation on the Light Blues as that of Real Madrid (0-6) or Eintracht Frankfurt (1-6, 3-6). Thankfully, Juve relaxed their play during the second half, content with their lot, and the home fans even cheered Richard Gough's late consolation goal, perhaps more appreciative of the loyalty of the Gers fans than of their team's football. Alex Cleland, tormented throughout

Stadio Delle Alpi, 1995. Rangers are 3-0 down at half-time against Juventus and a grim-faced Walter Smith and Archie Knox trudge towards the dressing-room.

by Del Piero, was red-carded after taking a wild swipe at the Italian youngster, thankfully not connecting. There was sympathy for the full-back from several Juve players as he left the field, Ravanelli in particular consoling the Ranger.

Criticism once again focused on the tactics employed by the Ibrox management, the team being set out to play in much the same way as they would were the venue Firhill or Fir Park rather than the Stadio Delle Alpi. On and off the field, all friends of Rangers felt the team were out of their depth, and one observer, viewing the style and class of life along the Via Roma in the Piedmont capital, the stylish designer boutiques, cafes and restaurants, offered the comment that Rangers, on and off the field of play, were perhaps 'closer to Armenia than Armani'. The Ibrox club may have been Scottish Champions, prepared to spend millions on international talent from around the globe, but they were not, certainly at the present time, in the same league as Juventus.

The Ibrox return would result in an even greater drubbing, although on this occasion Rangers deserved better. After losing an early Del Piero goal, the home side pressed consistently, forcing Juventus back into defence. A blatantly off-side strike by Ravanelli midway through the second half ended home hopes of securing an honourable result, but what the Scottish Champions certainly did not deserve was the loss of two more goals in injury time. One must, however, qualify any unstinted praise for the Turin giants with the addendum that, after a lengthy criminal investigation and trial, the then Juventus club doctor Riccardo Agricola received a suspended twenty-two-month prison sentence for supplying performance-enhancing drugs to the Juve players between 1994 and 1998. One is tempted to ask, no matter how comprehensive the reversal, were the reasons for Rangers' two defeats sporting or otherwise?

The 0-4 final scoreline was an injustice – but if the home fans felt hard done by imagine the feelings of one onlooker, a member of the German media covering the game. In Glasgow for four days, he had put his entire expenses allowance (some £80 per day) on the Italians to win by an exact score of 3-0. Juve's fourth goal came in ninety-five minutes.

Incredibly, after two such heavy losses the Light Blues still had an outside chance of qualification provided they won their two remaining fixtures, but all faint hopes of progress were finally extinguished when Steaua secured a 1-1 draw at Ibrox on matchday five, despite a wonder goal from Gascoigne when he ran fifty yards through the Romanian defence before scoring. Some semblance of pride was restored in Dortmund in the final group fixture when Rangers, in all truth, deserved better than a 2-2 draw through goals from Brian Laudrup and Gordon Durie. The game could have been won in the opening fifteen minutes as the Light Blues played their finest football of the season, opening up the German defence at will and scorning several chances on a treacherous surface. The game was to an extent marred by the grossly unjust ordering-off of Gascoigne for two yellow-card offences. A strong penalty appeal by Gazza was waved away by the Spanish referee, the action quickly switching to the other end where Borussia came close to scoring. The referee approached the Ranger to explain his decision, words were exchanged, and a second yellow card produced. The official later admitted that he had not realised that Gascoigne was already on a yellow card when the second was produced, and there can be no doubt that had he not approached the Englishman nothing would have come of it.

The campaign had been something of a reality check for the Ibrox men; after the glory and heroics of 1992/93 it had always been presumed that another Champions' League campaign would produce similar, if not better, results. After 1995/96 no one was under any such illusions.

Juventus went on to defeat Ajax on penalties after a 1-1 draw in the Rome final.

1995/96 European Champions' Cup, qualifying round, first leg

Wednesday 9 August 1995, Ibrox Stadium, Glasgow

Rangers 1 (Durie) Anorthosis Famagusta 0

Attendance 43,519

Goram; Wright, D. Robertson; Gough, McLaren, Reid (Durie); McCall,
Gascoigne, I. Ferguson (Miller), Hateley, Laudrup

Qualifying round, second leg

Wednesday 23 August 1995 Antonis Papadopolous Stadium, Larnaca

Anorthosis Famagusta 0 Rangers 0

Attendance 9,500

Goram; Wright, D. Robertson; Gough, McLaren, Petric; McCall, Gascoigne
(Durrant [Murray]), Miller, Hateley, Durie

Champions' League Group C

Matchday one

Wednesday 13 September 1995, Stadion Steaua, Bucharest

Steaua Bucharest 1 (Prodan) Rangers 0

Attendance 26,000

Goram; Wright, Cleland; Gough, McLaren, Petric; Miller (Durie), Gascoigne,
McCoist, Durrant (Murray), Laudrup

Matchday two

Wednesday 27 September 1995, Ibrox Stadium, Glasgow

Rangers 2 (Gough, Ferguson) Borussia Dortmund 2 (Herrlich, Kree)

Attendance 33,209

Goram; Wright, Cleland; Gough, McCall, Petric; Miller, Gascoigne, McCoist,
Durie (Durrant), Laudrup (I. Ferguson)

Matchday three

Wednesday 18 October 1995, Stadio Delle Alpi, Torino

Juventus 4 (Ravanelli 2, Conte, Del Piero) Rangers 1 (Gough)

Attendance 50,000

Goram; Wright (Brown), D. Robertson; Gough, Moore, Petric; Durie, McCall
(Murray), McCoist, Salenko, Cleland

Matchday four

Wednesday 1 November 1995, Ibrox Stadium, Glasgow

Rangers 0 Juventus 4 (Del Piero, Torricelli, Ravanelli, Marocchi)

Attendance 42,523

Goram (Thomson); Wright (Durrant), Bollan; Gough, Brown, Petric; I. Ferguson,
Gascoigne, Miller (McCoist), Salenko, McCall

Matchday five

Wednesday 22 November 1995, Ibrox Stadium, Glasgow

Rangers 1 (Gascoigne) Steaua Bucharest 1 (A. Ilie)

Attendance 30,882

Goram; Brown (Bollan), D. Robertson; Gough, McLaren, Petric; Durrant (Miller),

Gascoigne, McCoist, McCall (Murray), Laudrup

Matchday six

Wednesday 6 December 1995, Westfalenstadion, Dortmund

Borussia Dortmund 2 (Moller, Riedle) Rangers 2 (Laudrup, Durie)

Attendance 35,800

Goram; Cleland (Durrant), D. Robertson; Gough, McLaren, Bollan; Miller

(McCoist), Gascoigne, Durie, McCall, Laudrup

If the 1995/96 Champions' League qualifying round draw had been kind to Rangers, then the same could certainly not be said of the following year when the Light Blues were paired with Alania Vladikavkaz. The Russian Champions were clearly a formidable side, one of the few clubs in the post-Soviet era to break the Moscow domination of the League Championship. Spartak Moscow had reached the Champions' League proper in each of the previous three years, and the new, if unfashionable, title holders expected nothing less. Alania led 1-0 at half-time in the first leg at Ibrox through Igor Yanovskyi on the half-hour, and Rangers' prospects looked bleak in the extreme. However, they fought back to win 3-1 with goals from Derek McInnes, Gordon Petric and Ally McCoist. A 3-1 lead to take to Vladikavkaz was hardly perfect, but it could have been much worse, for the Russians missed a penalty in the dying minutes at Ibrox. The trip to southern Russia was always going to be a daunting one in terms of travel and football. Based in the Republic of Northern Ossieta, Vladikavkaz was the furthest point in the Caucasus reached by the German Army in the Second World War. A city of 300,000, it was not the sort of place you would want to visit or which might have some future as a tourist attraction. Close to the border with Georgia and also a mere 100km from Grozny and a war zone, it was rather less than accessible to the West. A group of Rangers fans got there by way of Glasgow–Copenhagen–Stockholm–Moscow–Vladikavkaz, a five-day sojourn. In such an alien environment, Rangers were to stagger the Russians, perhaps astonishing themselves and certainly the rest of Europe with a quite stunning 7-2 win. They had the stimulus of a goal after thirty-three seconds, by McCoist, who went on to score a hat-trick. The result, one of Rangers' most impressive in Europe, meant a 10-3 aggregate, achieved after having trailed 0-1 after forty-five minutes at Ibrox. Alania could scarcely be described as 'one-season wonders' – they would only narrowly fail to retain their title, losing 1-2 to Spartak Moscow in a play-off staged in St Petersburg. The victory gave many friends of Rangers the hope that this would be a breakthrough season in the Champions' League campaign, particularly when the draw put Rangers in a not-too-strenuous Section A including Auxerre from France, Swiss Champions Grasshoppers from Zurich and Ajax. Just to underline the point, those Gers fans en route from Moscow learned of the draw in-flight, one optimistic soul enquiring as to the make-up of Group B in an effort to ascertain who might provide the opposition in the last eight. However, the European campaign turned into an absolute nightmare, almost certainly Rangers' worst ever. The elimination of the Russian Champions had led many friends of the club to believe that at last the Light Blues had a team capable of the ultimate success, but such dreams quickly turned to dust in the opening fixture in Zurich's Stadion Hardturm, as a shambolic performance led to a 0-3 defeat at the hands of Grasshoppers, prompting the infamous, but wholly justified, jibe by the Grasshoppers coach, Christian Gross, when he said they had come to Switzerland as 'holiday makers'. This was the same Monsieur Gross who later became manager of Tottenham Hotspur for a few months. If he meant that Rangers had grossly underestimated the Swiss team, it was an opinion with which many Light Blue followers agreed. An early goal from Murat Yakin was followed by two from Kubilay Turkyilmaz. The Swiss could scarcely believe their luck. Rangers' performance was lamentable, appalling defensive errors typifying a pathetic opening to the Champions' League campaign and leaving many to seriously question the tactical awareness of the coaching staff at Ibrox. Rangers, probable favourites to win the game, and just possibly favourites to win the group given their results against the Russians, were rightly criticised, and scathingly, and from then on were always struggling to maintain any kind of impact, particularly in the next game, at home to Auxerre. Although playing well, Rangers lost a close, hard-fought encounter, by 2-1, with Thomas Deniaud the marksman, twice heading home from Bernard Diomede crosses. In goal for the French was a certain Lionel Charbonnier.

Beaten in the two opening games, the third was always going to be make or break, but given that it meant a trip to Amsterdam, Ajax and the lately opened Amsterdam Arena, it was surely going to be difficult. A massive travelling support was present in the old city, but this was the Ajax of Frank and Ronald De Boer, both to join Rangers in later years, of Patrick Kluivert and Marc Overmars. In the event, it proved impossible. Rangers were beaten 4-1, at times outclassed, just as they had been a year earlier by Juventus in Turin. As in the two previous group games, defensive weaknesses in the air were exposed with Portuguese midfielder Dani heading two goals. Rangers were certainly not helped on this occasion by the pointless action of Paul Gascoigne, troubled by demons in his private life, midway through the first half, which saw him quite properly ordered off the field. Gazza went down in the Ajax goal area, reaching for a cross, and then took a childish swing with his foot at Winston Bogarde. In the return against Ajax, the Ibrox side, shorn of no fewer than a staggering twelve players (eight through injury, four suspended) were desperately unlucky to lose 1-0, but Arnold Scholten's goal meant a fourth successive defeat and all hopes of qualifying for the later stages of the competition were well gone. All that was left was a salvage job; they managed to achieve a 2-1 win at Ibrox against Grasshoppers, courtesy of a McCoist double. The final game, away to Auxerre, produced a similar scoreline, this one in favour of Auxerre. Europe had turned its back on Rangers for an unimpressive group performance in what was becoming a more and more prestigious tournament. This season, Rangers had been in racy company – Auxerre had been coached, for thirty years, by the evergreen Guy Roux, who had taken them from the regional leagues to Le Championnat, to the last eight of the Champions' League, whilst Ajax had won the tournament two years earlier.

1996/97 European Champions' Cup, qualifying round, first leg
Wednesday 7 August 1996, Ibrox Stadium, Glasgow
Rangers 3 (McInnes, McCoist, Petric) Alania Vladikavkaz 1 (Yanovskyi)
Attendance 44,799
Goram; Cleland, Albertz; Gough, Petric, Bjorklund; McCall, I. Ferguson (McInnes), McCoist (Van Vossen), Durie, Laudrup
Qualifying round, second leg
Wednesday 21 August 1996, Spartak Stadium, Vladikavkaz
Alania Vladikavkaz 2 (Yanovskyi, Suleimanov) Rangers 7 (McCoist 3, Laudrup 2, Van Vossen, Miller)
Attendance 32,000
Goram; Cleland, Albertz; Gough, Petric, Bjorklund; McCall, McInnes (Durrant), McCoist (Durie), Van Vossen (Miller), Laudrup
Champions' League Group A
Matchday one
Wednesday 11 September 1996, Stadion Hardturn, Zurich
Grasshopper-Club Zurich 3 (Turkyilmaz 2, Yakin) Rangers 0
Attendance 20,030
Goram; Cleland (McInnes), Albertz; Gough, Petric, Bjorklund; McCall, Gascoigne, McCoist (Van Vossen), Durie (Miller), Laudrup
Matchday two
Wednesday 25 September 1996, Ibrox Stadium, Glasgow
Rangers 1 (Gascoigne) AJ Auxerre 2 (Deniaud 2)
Attendance 37,344
Goram; Cleland, Albertz; Gough, Moore (Andersen), Bjorklund; Van Vossen, Gascoigne, McInnes, Durie (I. Ferguson), Laudrup
Matchday three
Wednesday 16 October 1996, Amsterdam Arena
Ajax 4 (Dani 2, Babangida, Wooter) Rangers 1 (Durrant)
Attendance 47,000
Snelders; Cleland, Albertz; Gough, Moore, Bjorklund; McCall, Gascoigne, McInnes (Miller), I. Ferguson (Durrant), Laudrup (Van Vossen)
Matchday four
Wednesday 30 October 1996, Ibrox Stadium, Glasgow
Rangers 0 Ajax 1 (Scholten)
Attendance 42,265

Snelders; Shields, Robertson; Petric, Wilson (Andersen), Bjorklund; Durrant, Miller (Van Vossen), McInnes (McCoist), Albertz, Laudrup

Matchday five

Wednesday 20 November 1996, Ibrox Stadium, Glasgow

Rangers 2 (McCoist 2, 1 pen), Grasshopper-Club Zurich 1 (Berger)

Attendance 34,192

Goram; Cleland, Robertson; Gough, Wilson, Petric; Moore, Miller, McCoist, Albertz, Van Vossen (Andersen)

Matchday six

Wednesday 4 December 1996, Stade Abbe-Deschamps, Auxerre

AJ Auxerre 2 (Laslandes, Marlet) Rangers 1 (Gough)

Attendance 21,300

Goram; Shields, Robertson; Gough, Petric (Wilson), Moore; Steven, McInnes, Andersen, I. Ferguson, Van Vossen (McCoist)

For the following season, Rangers had in effect a new team after their successful 'nine in a row' in the Scottish League. Walter Smith had signed several Italian players, namely Lorenzo Amoruso from Fiorentina, Sergio Porrini from Juventus, Marco Negri and Rino Gattuso from Perugia, as well as Swedish World Cup midfielder Jonas Thern, ex-Napoli and Roma, and more recently Benfica in Portugal. Did Rangers at last have a team with the know-how and acumen as well as the skills, to make an impact in Europe? Porrini for one had a considerable pedigree having been a Champions' League finalist with Juve in 1997. The new signings had come at a considerable cost, some £14 million, leading many to query the wisdom of such expenditure in what was effectively the first full summer of Bosman.

The Champions' League format had been changed. It was regrettably no longer a tournament exclusively for champion clubs. There were now two qualifying rounds to be negotiated. The opener took Rangers for the very first time to the Faroe Islands to play Gotu and to overwhelm them 5-0 in front of 2,500 spectators – the largest ever attendance at a football match on the islands. It was an intriguing experience. The Faroes are a group of islands in the far Atlantic, which gained independence from Denmark, although there are still strong cultural ties. The population is 43,000. Torshaven is the capital, the airport is on another island and the football ground on yet another, on a clifftop overlooking the sea. It was all an island-hopping business. The home leg was a 6-0 victory, and Rangers at least had two wins behind them. Their opposition in the second qualifier was somewhat different – IFK Goteborg, Swedish champions. The first leg was played in the Stadion Ullevi in Goteborg and saw Rangers hold their own, with the tie goalless at half-time and the Swedes, if anything, somewhat apprehensive of their hugely talented multi-national opponents. It was not too much to suppose that Rangers might win this match, but two goals conceded in as many minutes early in the second half through Stefan Pettersson and Par Karlsson set Rangers a mammoth task and a third late in the game from substitute Peter Eriksson meant an overwhelming deficit for the second leg. The absence of Brian Laudrup, injured in the Faroe Islands, had scarcely helped. This defeat, more than others, left many questioning the tactical insight of manager Walter Smith, demonstrating an inability to alter tactics to cope with the flow of play, struggling as the game developed and, although IFK were a good side, it should not have been an insurmountable task for Rangers to progress. The second match produced a 1–1 draw with Rangers never looking likely to make much of an impact.

Under the convoluted rules of European football, Rangers, having been eliminated from the Champions' League, were now eligible to compete in the UEFA Cup. For the first time, the Light Blues would compete in two European competitions in the one season. Drawn against the French club Racing Club de Strasbourg, this tie should have been relatively straightforward for Rangers. Strasbourg were near the bottom of the French League, yet somehow the Light Blues contrived to lose, both home and away, to the French team by identical scores, 2–1. The first leg, played in the Stade de la Meinau, was remarkable for all three goals coming from the penalty spot and also, if for nothing else, the appeal by Brian Laudrup to Walter Smith midway through the first half for a change in approach due to the poverty of the opposition. No change was forthcoming, and yet another lamentable European defeat was the result. One prominent Scottish broadcaster, at the time working in France, had described Strasbourg to the author as the 'worst team in France'. Quoting the same man – 'not even Walter Smith could fail to beat such a poor side'. Where, then, did that leave Rangers?

This defeat came to be seen as a watershed because afterwards, given the growing influence of ENIC, the financial house that had invested £40 million in the club the previous year, changes had to be made. Walter Smith, by the end of the season, was gone and was replaced for the first time in the club's history by a foreign coach, namely Dick Advocaat from the Netherlands. Strasbourg, to be fair to them, rather belied their domestic league position by going on to eliminate Liverpool and then coming the width of a crossbar from dumping out eventual winners Internazionale – they lost to the Italians only after extra time.

1997/98 European Champions' Cup, qualifying round, first leg
Wednesday 23 July 1997, Svangaskard, Toftir
Gotu IF 0 Rangers 5 (Durie 2, McCoist 2, Negri)
Attendance 2,500
Niemi; Cleland, Vidmar; Moore (Wright), I. Ferguson, Bjorklund; Thern, Durie, Negri, Albertz, Laudrup (McCoist)
Qualifying round, second leg
Wednesday 30 July 1997, Ibrox Stadium, Glasgow
Rangers 6 (Negri 2, Durie, McCoist, Albertz, I. Ferguson) Gotu IF 0
Attendance 44,433

Niemi; Moore, Vidmar; Porrini (Cleland), I. Ferguson, Bjorklund; Thern, Gascoigne (Albertz), Negri, McCoist, Durie (Durrant)

Qualifying round one

Wednesday 13 August 1997, Ullevi Stadion, Goteborg

IFK Goteborg 3 (Pettersson, Karlsson, Eriksson) Rangers 0

Attendance 20,000

Goram; Cleland, Stensaas; Porrini, Vidmar, Bjorklund; Thern, Gascoigne, Negri (McCoist), Albertz (I. Ferguson), Durie

Qualifying round two

Wednesday 27 August 1997 Ibrox Stadium, Glasgow

Rangers 1 (Miller) IFK Goteborg 1 (R. Andersson)

Attendance 45,585

Goram; Moore, Stensaas; Porrini, I. Ferguson (Laudrup), Bjorklund; Thern, Gascoigne, Negri, McCoist (Durie), Miller (Albertz)

UEFA Cup, first round, first leg

Tuesday 16 September 1997, Stade De La Meinau, Strasbourg

RC Strasbourg 2 (Baticle 2 pens) Rangers 1 (Albertz pen)

Attendance 12,450

Snelders; McCall, Vidmar (Andersen); Porrini, Petric, Bjorklund; Gattuso (Miller), Gascoigne, Durie, Albertz, Laudrup

First round, second leg

Tuesday 30 September 1997, Ibrox Stadium, Glasgow

Rangers 1 (Gattuso) RC Strasbourg 2 (Baticle, Zitelli)

Attendance 40,145

Goram; Cleland, Stensaas; Porrini, McCall, Bjorklund (Miller); Gattuso, Gascoigne, Negri, Durie (Johansson), Laudrup (Andersen)

NINE

The Little General

Season 1998/99 saw a new era for Rangers under the guidance of Dutch coach Dick Advocaat. He had been brought to Ibrox as much as anything to make a mark in Europe. New signings aplenty arrived in his wake – Arthur Numan from PSV Eindhoven, Giovanni van Bronckhorst from Feyenoord, and Andrei Kanchelskis from Fiorentina to name just three. Given that Rangers had failed for the first time in ten years to win the Scottish League Championship, they were competing in the UEFA Cup. It almost brought complete and utter disaster in the opening round. They were faced with Irish minnows Shelbourne of Dublin, a semi-professional side. Due to fear of potential trouble in the Republic of Ireland, the game was switched from Dublin to Tranmere on Merseyside and saw a vast number of Rangers supporters travelling for the game. Rangers started well enough, but by half-time, they found themselves incredibly two goals down, goals conceded to breakaways. And with an hour gone, Rangers were 3-0 down. Goals had come from Sergio Porrini, an own goal, Mark Rutherford and Pat Morley. Rangers were staring at their worst defeat in European competition, not to mention one of the worst ever. Fortune smiled on them in the shape of two penalties given for needless but clear handballs by Tony McCarthey, each converted by Jorg Albertz to get them back into the match. New signing Gabriel Amato also notched a brace, with fellow newcomer Giovanni van Bronckhorst scoring one. Rangers eventually won 5-3; it was a remarkable comeback from a very serious fright for the Light Blue legions.

Rangers won the Ibrox leg of the tie comfortably 2-0, through two goals from Finnish international Jonaton Johansson, then had to ponder much more substantial, to say the least, opposition in the shape of PAOK of Greece, who had in the previous season dumped Arsenal out of the competition. The Glasgow team were certainly helped in the first leg at Ibrox by the ordering-off of Triandafinou Maheridis for a quite horrendous tackle on Gordon Durie. Durie went off on a stretcher and was to miss almost all of the rest of the season. The referee showed only a yellow card but, apparently realising what he had done, the next time the Greek player went into a tackle – this one an innocuous foul – he was shown a red card. Rough justice was done. Rangers won 2-0 with second-half goals coming from Andrei Kanchelskis and Rod Wallace.

The Thessaloniki stadium, known as 'The Tomb', was a frightening venue for visiting teams, one of the most daunting in Europe. Rangers, however, displayed great discipline and composure in attaining a goalless draw to send them into the first round of the competition proper, where they seemed to be favoured by a straightforward draw against Beitar with the first game in historic Jerusalem. Rangers trailed to a first-half Yossi Abuksis penalty – a very soft award – but made it 1-1 with a late goal from Albertz. The second leg at Ibrox was probably more comfortably won than the 4-2 scoreline would suggest. More serious opposition awaited in Bayer Leverkusen of Germany, one of the top Bundesliga sides, formidable opposition by any standards. Many of the more pessimistic Rangers fans prophesied that this would mean the end of the campaign for another season, but one of Rangers' finest European performances, in the Bay Arena in Leverkusen, resulted in a 2-1 win, goals coming from Van Bronckhorst and Johansson. Thus they had built an impressive platform for the return at Ibrox, where a 1-1 draw saw them through to the last sixteen of the competition. Johansson once again gave the Light Blues the lead, but when a bad Barry Ferguson miss was followed soon afterwards by an Ulf Kirsten strike a nervous closing ten minutes ensued. Sadly, on the night Rangers lost their French goalkeeper, Lionel Charbonnier, when he crashed into a post and suffered ligament damage that kept him out for the rest of season; Antti Niemi of Finland substituted.

There they were to face Parma of Italy, a dazzling prospect as they were one of the leading teams in Serie A and a club that had already won European trophies. The Rangers victory over Bayer Leverkusen in Germany suggested that Dick Advocaat had justified his presence at Ibrox by producing a notable European scalp. Under Walter Smith, Rangers had struggled in recent years, often against quite modest European opposition, but that surely had changed. Parma would establish just how good this 'New Rangers' could be. Against players of the calibre of Gianluigi Buffon, Dino Baggio, Hernan Crespo, Juan Sebastian Veron, Fabio Cannavaro and Lilian Thuram, they would find out. Parma, in truth, seemed in easy control for much of the first half at Ibrox, showing all the best qualities of Italian football, and Abel Balbo gave them the lead. Wallace equalised late in the game and Rangers might have won the match in the dying seconds when Durie headed over with the goal at his mercy. The return game in Parma saw Rangers take the lead after twenty-eight minutes, a low and powerful drive from twenty-five yards from Jorg Albertz striking home, effectively cancelling Parma's away goal at Ibrox. Rangers then were in a strong position, but the turning point of the game came with Sergio Porrini's sending off, having collected a second yellow card. The decision appeared harsh but Rangers were up against it, having to play the entire second half with ten men. Two minutes after the interval, slack defending and lack of concentration in defence allowed Balbo to score from close range. Parma took the lead in the sixty-third minute, with a fierce shot from Stefano Fiori. Rangers were still in the game, but a moment of madness from Lorenzo Amoruso – a handball with no opponent nearby – no danger apparent, let Enrico Chiesa score from the resulting penalty and it was all over, 3-1 to Parma.

If the manner of Rangers' second-half collapse in the Estadio Ennio Tardini left a little to be desired, there can be no question that Parma were a team of the highest quality. In fact, they went on to win the UEFA Cup that season, beating Olympique Marseille 3-0 in the Moscow final. They had already won two other European trophies – the Cup-Winners' Cup in 1993 and the UEFA Cup of 1995. For good measure in between, they added the Super Cup of 1994.

1998/99 UEFA Cup, first qualifying round, first leg
Wednesday 22 July 1998, Prenton Park, Tranmere
Shelbourne 3 (Rutherford, Morley, Porrini o.g.) Rangers 5 (Albertz 2 pens, Amato 2, Van Bronckhorst)
Attendance 6,047
Niemi; Porrini, Van Bronckhorst; Petric, Amoruso, Thern (I. Ferguson); Gattuso (Amato), B. Ferguson, Durie, Graham (Johansson), Albertz
First qualifying round, second leg
Wednesday 29 July 1998; Ibrox Stadium, Glasgow
Rangers 2 (Johansson 2) Shelbourne 0
Attendance 46,906
Niemi; Porrini, Numan; Amoruso, Moore, Van Bronckhorst (I. Ferguson); Kanchelskis (Amato), B. Ferguson, Durie (Gattuso), Johansson, Albertz
Second qualifying round, first leg
Tuesday 11 August 1998, Ibrox Stadium, Glasgow
Rangers 2 (Kanchelskis, Wallace) PAOK 0
Attendance 35,392
Niemi; Porrini, Numan; Amoruso, Moore, B. Ferguson (Albertz); Kanchelskis, I. Ferguson, Durie (Amato), Wallace, Van Bronckhorst (Gattuso)
Second qualifying round, second leg
Tuesday 25 August 1998, Toumbas Stadium, Thessaloniki
PAOK 0 Rangers 0
Attendance 30,388
Charbonnier; Porrini, Numan; Amoruso (Petric), Moore, B. Ferguson; Kanchelskis (Gattuso), I. Ferguson, Wallace, Van Bronckhorst, Albertz (Amato)
First round, first leg
Tuesday 15 September 1998, 'Teddi', Malcha Stadium, Jerusalem
Beitar Jerusalem 1 (Abuksis pen) Rangers 1 (Albertz)
Attendance 15,000

Charbonnier; Porrini, Vidmar (Stensaas); Amoruso, Moore, B. Ferguson; Kanchelskis, I. Ferguson, Johansson (Albertz), Wallace (Graham), Van Bronckhorst

First round, second leg

Thursday 1 October 1998, Ibrox Stadium, Glasgow

Rangers 4 (Gattuso, Porrini, Johansson, Wallace) Beitar Jerusalem 2 (Salloi, Ohana pen)

Attendance 45,610

Charbonnier; Porrini, Vidmar; Amoruso, Moore (Hendry), Van Brockhorst; Gattuso, B. Ferguson, Johansson (Miller), Wallace, Albertz

Second round, first leg

Thursday 22 October 1998, Bay Arena, Leverkusen

Bayer Leverkusen 1 (Reichenberger) Rangers 2 (Van Bronckhorst, Johansson)

Attendance 22,500

Charbonnier; Porrini, Vidmar; Wilson, Hendry, Van Bronckhorst; Kanchelskis, B. Ferguson, Johansson (I. Ferguson), Wallace (Durie), Albertz

Second round, second leg

Thursday 5 November 1998, Ibrox Stadium, Glasgow

Rangers 1 (Johansson) Bayer Leverkusen 1 (Kirsten)

Attendance 50,012

Charbonnier (Niemi); Porrini, Numan; Amoruso, Hendry, Van Bronckhorst; Kanchelskis (I. Ferguson), B. Ferguson (Wilson), Johansson, Wallace, Albertz

Third round, first leg

Tuesday 24 November 1998, Ibrox Stadium, Glasgow

Rangers 1 (Wallace) Parma 1 (Balbo)

Attendance 49,514

Niemi; Porrini (Durie), Numan; Amoruso, Hendry, B. Ferguson; Kanchelskis, I. Ferguson, Johansson (Amato), Wallace, Albertz

Third round, second leg

Tuesday 8 December 1998, Estadio Ennio Tardini, Parma

Parma 3 (Balbo, Fiori, Chiesa pen) Rangers 1 (Albertz)

Attendance 16,437

Niemi; Porrini, Numan; Amoruso, Hendry, Van Bronckhorst; B. Ferguson (Miller), I. Ferguson, Durie (Vidmar), Wallace (Amato), Albertz

Having reclaimed the Scottish League title in Dick Advocaat's first year at the club, Rangers found themselves once again in the Champions' Cup, with two qualifying rounds to be tackled if they were to qualify for the Champions' League itself. In the second round the opponents were FC Haka of Valkeakoski in Finland. The outcome was far from a formality. The previous season the then Finnish Champions HJK Helsinki had reached the Champions' League, accumulating five points along the way (a total that Rangers have failed to achieve in three of their sojourns in Europe's premier club competition) in a campaign that included a 2-0 home win over Benfica. Nevertheless, Rangers would progress comfortably, winning the first match, away, 4-1, followed with a 3-0 success at Ibrox. Advancing to the third qualifying round, Rangers were obliged to face Parma of Italy for the second time in eight months. The prospect was as frightening as ever, Parma retaining a star-studded cast, but this time it was to prove different and become perhaps Dick Advocaat's finest hour. To general astonishment, Rangers defeated the Italians 2-0 at Ibrox with goals from Tony Vidmar and Claudio Reyna. Indeed, Giovanni van Bronckhorst had an outstanding chance late in the game to make the first game lead even more formidable, but blazed his shot over the bar, deep into the Copland Road stand. Parma had been certainly handicapped by being reduced to ten men in the first half when two yellow cards saw Fabio Cannavaro take the walk of shame.

The tie still had to be won and Parma were certainly capable of beating anyone by three goals on their own ground. Rangers' performance in the second leg was again superbly disciplined. They conceded only one goal from an error by Lionel Charbonnier, from a Johan Walem free-kick in the sixty-seventh minute. This heaped enormous pressure on Rangers as the Italians went flat out to at least even the score. Yet, during the course of the game, Rangers twice struck Italian woodwork, so the result could have been more impressive. Rangers had achieved what many thought to be impossible in eliminating Parma and qualifying for the Champions' League. There, they would not have their sorrows to seek – into the hat they went and out came opponents Bayern Munich, PSV Eindhoven and Valencia.

Parma, it should be said, had lost Veron and Enrico Chiesa to Lazio and Fiorentina respectively but had been strengthened by the arrival of Argentine international midfielder Ariel Ortega. Under UEFA's 'co-efficient' system, which rates all clubs and nations, Parma, when Rangers played them, had the highest co-efficient of any team in Europe, underlining the quality of the achievement.

The Champions' League had been expanded to thirty-two teams playing eight groups of four, no doubt to maximise television and other commercial income. The European Cup, founded in 1955/56, after four decades was unrecognisable. Those nations with the greatest market share of commercial and television revenue now had the potential to have no fewer than four teams apiece in the group stages. Once upon a time Europe's premier club competition had been restricted to the champion clubs only but this was no longer the case. Indeed the 1999 final in Barcelona had been contested between Manchester United and Bayern Munich, neither of whom were reigning champions of their domestic league.

Many regarded Valencia as the whipping boys of the group that Rangers now entered, given that, at the time of the opening game, they were struggling in the Spanish League. Preposterously, one Scottish journalist described them as the 'Aberdeen of Spain', the 'Dons' being at the very bottom of the Scottish League

Rangers manager Dick Advocaat at the scene of one of his greatest triumphs: the Philips Stadion, Eindhoven, where he had previously coached.

at the time. Valencia, however, proved to be outstanding opponents, with former Light Blue Joachim Bjorklund included in their ranks as well as quality players of the ilk of Claudio Lopez and Gaizka Mendieta. A strong, purposeful side, they won the opening game by 2-0 in the Campo de Mestella, through counters from 'Kily' Gonzalez and a Craig Moore own goal.

Having lost their first game in the group, Rangers needed, beyond any doubt, to take at least something from the next fixture – Bayern München at Ibrox. Playing very well, Rangers should certainly have won this game. They led from early in the match – another Jorg Albertz goal – only to be defied in the dying seconds, a ninetieth-minute goal from Michael Tarnat, deflected, leaving a 1-1 draw.

With only one point from the two opening games, Rangers clearly needed total success in the next game against PSV Eindhoven, at the stadium where the Scottish Champions had enjoyed one of their greatest successes. Rangers repeated that victory with an outstanding display in the Philips Stadion, a late Jorg Albertz goal giving them the 1-0 win. 'We should play all our games here', remarked one Light Blue follower in the wake of a remarkable double against a club with such a proud home record in European ties. Those Gers fans who had travelled to Eindhoven faced all sorts of problems: a restrictive Dutch membership card scheme and local by-laws that directly conflict with EU law e.g. the requirement for foreign visitors (even those resident in Holland) to carry one's passport at all times, and the illegality of the selling-on of match tickets, even at face value, as opposed to the use of soft drugs which are legal! Perhaps the Dutch had never heard of the European Union.

One of the great European nights.

In the return at Ibrox, Rangers overwhelmed the Dutchmen 4-1 with an exceptional performance from Michel Mols, including two goals. That meant that Rangers now led the group and victory from the next game, at home to Valencia, would guarantee progress into the next round. Sadly, once again the Spaniards proved too strong, winning 2-1. They were two up at half-time before Moore reduced the deficit.

Nevertheless, Rangers needed only a draw from their final group game to qualify for the second group stage. That game was against Bayern München – in Germany.

In the Olympic Stadion, Rangers produced an exceptional performance despite going down 1-0 to a disputed penalty award, the goal coming from Thomas Strunz. During the game, Rangers hit German woodwork no fewer than three times but the most distressing event of the evening was the serious knee injury sustained by Mols in a quite unnecessary clash with Oliver Kahn, the Bayern goalkeeper. The Dutch striker, a £4 million signing from Utrecht, had been in sparkling form in his first three months with the club, but having suffered a cruciate knee ligament injury he would never be the same player again.

Finishing third in the group put Rangers once again into the UEFA Cup where they were to face old foes Borussia Dortmund. A 2-0 first-leg lead at Ibrox should have been enough to take them through, but in the return leg in the Westfalenstadion in Dortmund, an injury time equaliser from Freddi Bobic confounded them, an absolute fluke in that, with almost the last kick of the ball, Dortmund had won a free-kick. Goalkeeper Jens Lehmann charged up the field to spread confusion in the Rangers defence. The ball came over, and fell at his

Disaster strikes in Munich, 1999, as Michael Mols is helped off with a cruciate knee ligament injury. The Dutch forward would never be the same player again.

feet. He took a wild swing at it, missing completely only for the ball to hit his standing leg, breaking perfectly for Bobic to hook into the net. Rangers had squandered numerous chances to score on the counter-attack, and late in extra time Barry Ferguson and Neil McCann combined to miss an absolute sitter. It would certainly have taken Rangers through on away goals. Instead, it meant a penalty shoot-out, and against any German team in penalty shoot-outs you lose.

1999/2000 European Champions' Cup, second qualifying round, first leg
Wednesday 28 July 1999, Stadion Tehtaankentta, Valkeakoski
Haka 1 (Niemi) Rangers 4 (Mols 2, Amoruso, Johansson)
Attendance 3,341
Klos; Adamczuk, Numan; Amoruso, Moore, B. Ferguson; Reyna (Nicholson), Wallace (Johansson), Mols, Van Bronckhorst (Albertz), McCann
Second qualifying round, second leg
Wednesday 4 August 1999, Ibrox Stadium, Glasgow
Rangers 3 (Wallace, Johansson, Amato) Haka 0
Attendance 46,443
Klos; Adamczuk, Numan (Vidmar); Amoruso, Moore, B. Ferguson (Nicholson); Johansson, Wallace, Mols (Amato), Albertz, Van Bronckhorst

Third qualifying round, first leg

Wednesday 11 August 1999, Ibrox Stadium, Glasgow

Rangers 2 (Vidmar, Reyna) Parma 0

Attendance 49, 263

Klos; Porrini, Vidmar (Albertz); Amoruso, Moore, B. Ferguson; Reyna, Wallace, Mols, Van Bronckhorst, McCann

Third qualifying round, second leg

Wednesday 25 August 1999, Estadio Ennio Tardini, Parma

Parma 1 (Walem) Rangers 0

Attendance 24,087

Charbonnier; Porrini, Vidmar; Amoruso, Moore, B. Ferguson (Albertz); Reyna, Adamczuk (Hendry), Mols, Wallace (McCann), Van Bronckhorst

Champions' League Group F

Matchday one

Wednesday 15 September 1999, Campo de Mestalla, Valencia

Valencia 2 (Kily Gonzalez, Moore o.g.) Rangers 0

Attendance 54,971

Charbonnier; Porrini (Kanchelskis), Vidmar; Amoruso, Moore, B. Ferguson; Reyna, Amato, Mols, Van Bronckhorst (Johansson), McCann (Albertz)

Matchday two

Tuesday 21 September 1999, Ibrox Stadium, Glasgow

Rangers 1 (Albertz) Bayern München 1 (Tarnat)

Attendance 49,960

Charbonnier; Porrini, Numan; Amoruso, Moore, B. Ferguson; Reyna, Johansson (McCann), Mols (Hendry), Albertz, Van Bronckhorst

Matchday three

Tuesday 28 September 1999, Phillips Stadion, Eindhoven

PSV Eindhoven 0 Rangers 1 (Albertz)

Attendance 30,000

Charbonnier; Porrini, Numan; Amoruso, Moore, B. Ferguson; Reyna (Albertz), Wallace, Mols, Van Bronckhorst, McCann

Matchday four

Wednesday 20 October 1999, Ibrox Stadium, Glasgow

Rangers 4 (Mols 2, Amoruso, McCann) PSV Eindhoven 1 (Van Nistelrooy pen);

Attendance 50,083

Klos; Porrini, Vidmar; Amoruso, Moore, B. Ferguson; McInnes, Wallace (Kanchelskis), Mols (Johansson), Van Bronckhorst, McCann (Albertz)

Matchday five

Tuesday 26 October 1999, Ibrox Stadium, Glasgow

Rangers 1 (Moore) Valencia 2 (Mendieta, Lopez)

Attendance 50,063

Klos; Porrini, Vidmar (Albertz); Amoruso, Moore, B. Ferguson; McInnes
(Kanchelskis), Wallace (Johansson), Mols, Van Bronckhorst, McCann

Matchday six

Wednesday 3 November 1999, Olympic Stadion, München

Bayern München 1 (Strunz pen) Rangers 0

Attendance 54,000

Klos; Porrini, Numan (McCann); Amoruso, Moore, B. Ferguson; Reyna, Wallace
(Amato), Mols (Johansson), Albertz, Van Bronckhorst

UEFA Cup, third round, first leg

Thursday 25 November 1999, Ibrox Stadium, Glasgow

Rangers 2 (Wallace, Kohler o.g.) Borussia Dortmund 0

Attendance 49,268

Myhre; Adamczuk, Numan; B. Ferguson, Moore, Vidmar; Reyna (Kanchelskis),
Wallace (McCann), Amato (Johansson), Albertz, Van Bronckhorst

Third round, second leg

Tuesday 7 December 1999, Westfalenstadion, Dortmund

Borussia Dortmund 2 (Ikpeba, Bobic) Rangers 0

Attendance 38,000

Borussia Dortmund won 3-1 on penalties

Myhre; Adamczuk (Vidmar), Numan; Amoruso, Moore, Albertz (Durie); Reyna,
B. Ferguson, Wallace (Kanchelskis), Van Bronckhorst, McCann

Season 2000/01 saw Rangers again in Europe as Scottish Champions, faced with two qualifying ties to get entry to the Champions' League. This time the opposition was much less daunting. FBK Kaunus of Lithuania should not have given Rangers much difficulty, yet it took two late goals from Billy Dodds in injury time to confirm a 4-1 win at Ibrox in the first match. A goalless draw in Kaunus meant that Rangers were through to the third round, where they faced an apparently straightforward task in coping with Herfolge of Denmark. They did, with the score 3-0 home and away. Their Champions' League group this time around was to be Monaco, Galatasaray and Sturm Graz.

The opening match of the group saw Rangers entertain the Austrians and a 5-0 win was the resounding result. It was one of Rangers' most impressive Champions' League performances, distinguished by the play of Ronald de Boer, a player of the highest quality who had already sampled Champions' League success with Ajax and who joined Rangers from Barcelona. His twin brother, Frank, was also to join the club four years on. De Boer was one of three big-money signings from the Netherlands – Fernando Ricksen from AZ Alkmaar and Bert Konterman from Feyenoord being the others, neither of whom, it is fair to say, had the pedigree of De Boer.

The 5-0 win over Sturm Graz was one of the great European nights at Ibrox. Rangers missed a penalty and struck the Graz woodwork twice, but saw goals

Giovanni van Bronckhorst's winning goal against Monaco in 2000.

from Michael Mols, Ronald de Boer (his first for the club), Jorg Albertz, Giovanni van Bronckhorst and Billy Dodds. It was the first time that Rangers had won their opening match in a Champions' League group. The second match was to be in Monaco, a second visit to the principality – the first had been back in 1961 and had featured one of the great exhibitions from the legendary Jim Baxter.

There was a massive travelling support amongst the 11,161 crowd in the Stade Louis II, with Rangers again producing a superlative result, winning 1-0 with a Van Bronckhorst goal scored in the seventh minute, a low, swerving shot from some twenty-five yards. Inevitably, protecting that precious lead, Rangers were under the most severe pressure from the home team for the rest of the match, with Italian forward Marco Simone outstanding, but Dick Advocaat showed his tactical nous by introducing Turkish midfielder Tugay in a sweeping role that proved most effective. Rangers held out for the 1-0 win, and were now in a strong position in the group, all the more so when news filtered through that Sturm Graz had incredibly overwhelmed Galatasaray 3-0 in Austria.

As in the previous season (1999/2000), the six Champions' League games were divided into two lots of three, played in successive midweeks and thus just seven days later Rangers found themselves away from home once again, travelling to the Ali Sami Yen in Istanbul, home of Galatasaray. Included in the Turkish ranks was old friend Georghi Hagi, the veteran midfielder who had played against Rangers for Steaua Bucharest some twelve years earlier. The Scottish Champions were quite concerned about this tie, more so for events off the field of play than anything that might await them on it. The Ali Sami Yen ground was very much within an inner-city conurbation, a motorway flying over one end of the ground. It was small

Mario Jardel, once a Rangers target, scores the winning goal for Galatasaray in Istanbul.

and cramped with tightly packed contours and an atmosphere both intimidating and wonderful, the home fans singing in harmony from all parts of the ground. Rangers, in fact, were seriously concerned about security since the previous season, at a UEFA Cup semi-final match, two Leeds United fans had been murdered in the city. Thankfully, there was no trouble. The Rangers fans who travelled were made very welcome and enjoyed Turkish hospitality.

The Ibrox men had travelled to Istanbul as group leaders, with two wins out of two and every chance of winning the group, despite the fact that Galatasaray were UEFA Cup holders. After forty-five minutes, with no score, that impression remained. Tugay, playing at his old club, had received a hero's welcome and again operated most effectively as a sweeper. However, a lack of concentration in defence led to two quick goals after the interval from Bulent Akin and Hakan Unsal, turning the tide for the Turks with the visitors handicapped by the presence in goal of a barely fit Stefan Klos. A third goal after seventy minutes from former Rangers target Brazilian Mario Jardel seemed to put an end to it all. Rangers, however, came back with late goals from Andrei Kanchelskis and finally, with the last kick of the game, a thundering free-kick from twenty yards by Van Bronckhorst, making the Dutch midfielder the first Ranger to score in three consecutive Champions' League games.

Galatasaray's 3-2 win put them in control of the group before they came to Ibrox. Here was a game that Rangers should have won, but missed chances, particularly one by McCann whose header, unchallenged, went straight to the goalkeeper, proved costly. The game ended goalless. With two games to play, Rangers were still in a reasonably comfortable position, but they were no longer in control of the group. The penultimate game saw Rangers visit the Arnold Schwarzenegger Stadium in Graz, knowing that a win would assure their qualification for the next group stage of the Champions' League, which no Scottish club had ever managed to do – a great incentive. The home club had rather a mixed story to tell as they had beaten Monaco and Galatasary in their own stadium, but had lost away matches to Rangers and Monaco. Before the game, Rangers had something of an injury problem, losing goalkeeper Stefan Klos and having to hurry back Van Bronckhorst, who had sustained a groin injury playing for Holland in Cyprus in October in a World Cup qualifying match (4-0 to the Dutch). He was patently unfit and indeed would not play for the club again until the following March. During the summer of 2001, he would be transferred to Arsenal.

The injury to Klos meant that Rangers had to make an emergency signing. Danish goalkeeper Jesper Christiansen came from Odense in Denmark for a fee quoted as £1.2 million. He played in the Graz game which the home side won 2-0 through goals from Sergei Yuran and Gilbert Prilasnig, Rangers being handicapped by the preposterous ordering-off of Arthur Numan. It was a case of mistaken identity with a first yellow card. The player later won an appeal against his ordering-off for two yellow cards. Since the second Graz goal came in the final minutes of the game, Rangers were unlucky, but they still had the chance to qualify from the group if they won against Monaco in Glasgow.

With an early goal from Kenny Miller, they made a perfect start, but Monaco were level by half-time, Francisco da Costa equalising after thirty-eight minutes. Seven minutes into the second half, Michael Mols put Rangers ahead again with a low shot under the advancing goalkeeper and the home team certainly seemed to be in command, only for carelessness in defence – Amoruso losing possession – allowing Simone to equalise. Incidentally, playing for Monaco in both games was none other than Dado Prso, the Croatian forward who was to join Rangers in 2004.

The draw at Ibrox did not of itself eliminate Rangers from the competition. They would still have qualified if events in Istanbul had fallen their way, but in the event the game between Galatasary and Sturm Graz finished in a 2-2 draw that meant that both of these sides had qualified, the Austrians as group leaders. In the later stages of the game both sides had played for a draw, a mutually beneficial stand-off, knowing the result from Glasgow. Nonetheless, Rangers, having won their two opening games, had had it in their own hands to qualify. Ironically, the Ibrox men, level on points with the Turks, had the superior goal difference only to lose out on the head-to-head record. Galatasaray would go on to reach the last eight before being eliminated by Real Madrid (3-2, 0-3).

As in previous seasons, finishing third in their group meant entry to the UEFA Cup third round, where they were to face yet another Bundesliga club,

Kaiserslautern. The first game at Ibrox was won by a solitary goal, a twenty-yard piledriver from Jorg Albertz in the dying moments of the match. Without the suspended Barry Ferguson and the injured Van Bronckhorst, the performance at Kaiserslautern was disappointing – Rangers went down 3-0 through goals from Miroslav Klose, Andreas Buck and Vratislav Lokvenc and once more were out of Europe before Christmas. The Germans, meanwhile, progressed as far as the penultimate round before succumbing to Spanish side Deportiva Alaves (1-5, 1-4).

2000/01 European Champions' Cup, second qualifying round, first leg
Wednesday 26 July 2000, Ibrox Stadium, Glasgow
Rangers 4 (Dodds 2, Johnston, Albertz pen) FBK Kaune 1 (Zuta)
Attendance 45,974
Klos; Ricksen, Vidmar (Miller); Moore, Wilson (Dodds), B. Ferguson; Johnston,
Reyna, Johansson (McCann), Wallace, Albertz
Second qualifying round, second leg
Wednesday 2 August 2000, Dariaus ir Gireno Sporto Centro Stadione, Kaune
FBK Kaune 0 Rangers 0
Attendance 4,000
Klos; Ricksen (Kanchelskis), Vidmar (Porrini); Konterman, Amoruso,
B. Ferguson; Reyna, Tugay, Dodds, Wallace (Johnston), Van Bronckhorst
Third qualifying round, first leg
Wednesday 9 August 2000, Herfolge Stadion
Herfolge 0 Rangers 3 (Albertz, Wallace, Amoruso)
Attendance 3,523
Klos; Porrini, Van Bronckhorst; Konterman, Amoruso, B. Ferguson; Reyna,
Dodds (Kanchelskis), Wallace (Miller), Albertz, McCann (Johnston)
Third qualifying round, second leg
Wednesday 23 August 2000, Ibrox Stadium, Glasgow
Rangers 3 (Wallace, Johnston, Kanchelskis) Herfolge 0
Attendance 34,141
Klos; Ricksen (Kanchelskis), Van Bronckhorst; Konterman, Amoruso,
B. Ferguson; Reyna, Dodds (Johnston), Wallace, Albertz (Vidmar), McCann
Champions' League Group D
Matchday one
Tuesday 12 September 2000, Ibrox Stadium, Glasgow
Rangers 5 (Mols, De Boer, Albertz, Van Bronckhorst, Dodds) Sturm Graz 0
Attendance 49,317
Klos; Ricksen, Numan; Amoruso, Konterman, B. Ferguson; Johnston
(Kanchelskis), De Boer (McCann), Mols (Dodds), Albertz, Van Bronckhorst
Matchday two
Wednesday 20 September 2000, Stade Louis II, Monaco
AS Monaco 0 Rangers 1 (Van Bronckhorst)

Attendance 11,161

Klos; Reyna (Vidmar), Numan; Amoruso, Konterman, Tugay; Johnston,

B. Ferguson, Mols (McCann), De Boer, Van Bronckhorst

Matchday three

Wednesday 27 September 2000, Ali Sami Yen, Istanbul

Galatasaray 3 (Bulent Akin, Hakan, Jardel) Rangers 2 (Kanchelskis,

Van Bronckhorst)

Attendance 20,954

Klos; Reyna, Numan; Amoruso, Konterman, Tugay; Johnston (Kanchelskis),

B. Ferguson, Mols (Dodds), De Boer, Van Bronckhorst

Matchday four

Tuesday 17 October 2000, Ibrox Stadium, Glasgow

Rangers 0 Galatasaray 0

Attendance 49,603

Klos; Reyna, Vidmar (Wilson); Porrini, Konterman, B. Ferguson; Kanchelskis,

Tugay, De Boer, Lovenkrands (McCann), Albertz

Matchday five

Wednesday 25 October 2000, Arnold Schwarzenegger Stadion, Graz

Sturm Graz 2 (Yuran, Prilasnig) Rangers 0

Attendance 15,400

Christiansen; Porrini (Negri), Numan; Amoruso, Konterman, B. Ferguson;

Kanchelskis, Tugay, De Boer, Wallace (Dodds), Van Bronckhorst (McCann)

Matchday six

Tuesday 7 November 2000, Ibrox Stadium, Glasgow

Rangers 2 (Miller, Mols) AS Monaco 2 (Da Costa, Simone)

Attendance 50,228

Christiansen; Vidmar, Numan; Amoruso, Wilson, B. Ferguson; Ricksen, De Boer

(Wallace), Mols (Tugay), Miller, Albertz (McCann)

UEFA Cup, third round, first leg

Thursday 30 November 2000, Ibrox Stadium, Glasgow

Rangers 1 (Albertz) 1. FC Kaiserslautern 0

Attendance 47,279

Klos; Reyna, Numan; Amoruso, Wilson, Konterman; De Boer (McCann),

B. Ferguson, Mols (Wallace), Miller, Albertz

Third round, second leg

Thursday 7 December 2000, Fritz-Walter-Stadion, Kaiserslautern

1. FC Kaiserslautern 3 (Klose, Buck, Lokvenc) Rangers 0

Attendance 28,757

Klos; Ricksen (McCann), Numan; Amoruso, Wilson, Konterman; Reyna, Tugay

(Dodds), Wallace, Miller (Mols), Albertz

TEN

Politics

Rangers' efforts in Europe under Dick Advocaat had increased the UEFA co-efficient of Scotland to such an extent that now two clubs – obviously Rangers and Celtic – were able to enter the 2001/02 Champions' League. Celtic, having won the championship under Martin O'Neill in his first season, went into the third qualifying round, whereas Rangers, as runners-up, would go into the second qualifying round. There, they would face Maribor of Slovenia, the club's first ever visit to that young country. Maribor were certainly an accomplished and attractive side with a reasonable track record – they had qualified for the Champions' League in season 1999/2000, eliminating both Belgian Champions KAA Gent and Olympique Lyon of France en route. They had not disgraced themselves there, winning in Kiev and drawing at Leverkusen. By no stretch of the imagination was this a formality for Rangers, but as it happened, the Ibrox men won comfortably 3-0. In many ways, the game in Slovenia was decided by the opening goal by Tore Andre Flo after thirty-eight minutes. Heads went down at the loss of an 'away' goal and Maribor were never a threat thereafter. Norwegian international Flo had arrived in Glasgow in mid-season during the previous campaign for a Scottish record transfer fee, that stands to this day, of £12.5 million. An astonishing attendance in excess of 50,000 – with many more locked outside – turned up at Ibrox for what many regarded as a mere formality with Rangers 3-0 ahead. Unfortunately, it was clear from the opening minutes that the home players themselves felt likewise, with Maribor having come to Glasgow claiming they had no chance in the return leg, indeed fearing a drubbing, but those statements were made to look like kidology after seventeen minutes when a Stipe Balajic through-ball saw Vanja Starcevic shrug off a weak challenge from Bert Konterman before rifling a low shot past Stefan Klos for the opening goal.

The Slovenian Champions were visibly lifted by the unexpected score and the feeling spread around the stadium that perhaps this was not such a formality after all. Konterman must have felt the loneliest man in the ground, as he was booed – not for the first time – when he next took possession of the ball.

Maribor grew in confidence with the goal, and there could be little doubt that a second for the visitors would put the outcome of the tie back in the melting pot, but in the fifty-fourth minute, to great relief inside the stadium, Rangers levelled when Neil McCann created space for himself on the left with some superb close control, played a one-two with Claudio Caniggia before squaring the ball across goal where Flo had the easiest of chances to net.

Four minutes later the tie was secure when Ricksen released Stephen Hughes only for Simeunovic to block the teenager's effort, Caniggia seizing on the loose ball to put Rangers 2-1 ahead.

The die was cast, with Rangers in control, and after seventy-three minutes Ricksen was again the instigator of a flowing move involving Flo and Caniggia, the Argentinian netting with an angled drive for goal number three.

Apart from Flo's three goals in the tie, the remaining goals came from other new signings in the form of Argentinian international (and World Cup star) Caniggia from Dundee and Christian Nerlinger from Borussia Dortmund. Rangers' 6-1 aggregate took them into the third qualifying round where, although seeded, they had the misfortune to be drawn against one of the most dangerous unseeded clubs in the draw, Turkish Champions Fenerbahce, thus returning to Istanbul for a second time in ten months. Fenerbahce, on the Asian side of the Bosphorus, were principal rivals to the two clubs on the European side, Galatasaray and Besiktas – formidable opponents for anyone, especially in Istanbul.

The first leg at Ibrox ended goalless with Rangers handicapped when substitute Michael Mols was ordered off following a clash with Samuel Johnston. Mols had raised his hands after being assaulted off the ball, sparking utter mayhem, with Turkish goalkeeper Rustu Recber running fully fifty yards to floor the Dutch striker with a right hook. Incredibly, Swiss referee Urs Meier showed Mols a red card, but both Johnson and Recber merely yellow. It was an astonishing decision by the official, who must have been the only one in the ground to miss the goalkeeper's assault – although exactly what he saw to merit a yellow was equally mystifying. Just to rub salt in the wound, within seconds Recber produced a stunning save from a Flo header. Fenerbahce had perhaps had the better of the first half, but the home side piled on the pressure in the closing stages without making the vital breakthrough.

The return leg in Istanbul, in the Fenerbahce Stadium, saw Rangers concede an early goal when Him Revive, an Israeli playing in Turkey, scored with a twenty-yard free-kick in the fourth minute. Rangers, hustling for an away goal at least, lost a second goal to a breakaway after seventy-one minutes from Serhat Akim. The visitors responded immediately, Fernando Ricksen succeeding with a low drive from twenty yards. From then on Rangers were on top. A second goal and a 2-2 result would take Rangers through. Inside the last ten minutes, Caniggia had a strong penalty claim denied when he went down in the penalty area, but Pierluigi Collina, the Italian referee considered the best in the world, waved it away. Rangers' feelings about his decision were formulated by Dick Advocaat. When asked if he was looking for a penalty award from the incident he said, 'Not from this referee'. Rangers continued to press the Turks. In the dying seconds Konterman's low fifteen-yard drive was cleared off the line. Once more Rangers had failed to qualify for the Champions' League. Once more they had to settle for second best – entry to the UEFA Cup.

The first-round UEFA draw set Rangers against Russian side Anzhi Makhachkala, in southern Russia. 'The worst cup draw in Rangers' history' was this author's immediate observation. Not everyone agreed on that first day, yet as soon as the draw was made, the club anticipated problems. Makhachkala was situated on the Caspian Sea, located in the Russian Republic of Dagestan in the heart of a war zone close to Grozny, Chechnya. Dagestan had been an area of all sorts of terrorist activities – clearly a very dangerous place to visit. The Foreign Office had advised British citizens not to travel to Dagestan. In fact, the city of Makhachkala was not as close to Grozny, the capital of Chechnya, as Vladikavkaz, where Rangers had played some five years earlier. The difference was that Makhachkala was in Dagestan and, in any case, the situation had escalated considerably since 1996. The Foreign Office advised Rangers not to travel.

The club found it impossible to take out adequate insurance for the trip and there were reported threats from Chechnyan rebels that they would launch a missile attack on the Dinamo stadium while the game was in progress. Rangers sent a reconnaissance in the persons of Campbell Ogilvie, director/secretary and Laurence McIntyre, security chief. They visited Makhachkala and received very warm hospitality there. This did not alleviate their concerns nor, accordingly, those of the club. A formal request was made to UEFA that the fixture be switched to a different venue, possibly Moscow. UEFA, having taken their own advice, refused and insisted that Rangers travel to Dagestan. The key difference between the two sets of advice was that Rangers were listening to the Foreign Office and NATO, while the Swiss-based UEFA were consulting the Swiss Government and the Geneva-based Red Cross. The tie was scheduled for Thursday 13 September 2001.

As an aside, a group of fans who wanted to travel to Dagestan and were obviously quite prepared to meet the risks involved were refused visas to travel by the Russian Consulate in Edinburgh, a refusal based on the grounds that it was not safe for Western citizens to do so. This raised the question that if it was not safe for British citizens, how could it be safe for British footballers to travel? Because of safety concerns, large elements of the media, who normally travel in force with Rangers, had withdrawn their representatives from the club's charter flight. After much soul-searching the club chairman, David Murray, having noted the advice of his own security people, the Foreign Office and the British Embassy in Moscow, made the positive decision – Rangers would not travel to Dagestan. However, he did not declare this publicly. Consequently, the club cancelled their charter flight. Under UEFA regulations, a visiting club is required to be in the match venue city at least twenty-four hours before kick-off. Effectively, by the evening of 12 September 2001, Rangers would have failed to meet their obligations under existing UEFA regulations. The inevitable outcome would have been that not only would the club have been thrown out of the competition, but almost certainly in addition would have been suspended from European competition for at least two years. This would have had a drastic impact on the club, both financially and in a playing sense. However, world events were to decide that this deadline would not come into effect.

Two days before the scheduled game, the World Trade Centre in New York City was attacked and destroyed by Al Qaeda terrorists. Hijacked, suicidal aircraft were flown into the twin towers, bringing them down, and killing thousands of people. UEFA suspended all fixtures for Wednesday 12 and Thursday 13 September. The games scheduled for the evening of 11 September did go ahead as scheduled. The other games were postponed and rearranged for a week later. In itself, this made no change to the Rangers' situation, but it did give them time for pressuring UEFA into changing their attitude and switching the first leg to a neutral venue, or a semi-neutral venue, in Moscow. Debate had raged for three weeks over the attitude of Europe's governing body, with the Nyon-based organisation taking soundings from both the Red Cross and the Swiss Government, and coming in for deserved criticism over a 'head in the sand' attitude that beggared belief.

Crucially, however, there were further terrorist attacks close to Makhachkala in the intervening days so that, finally, UEFA relented almost at the eleventh hour on the morning of Tuesday 18 September and decided that the tie would no longer be two-legged, but would be played as a one-off game at a neutral venue. That venue was to be Warsaw, the Stadion Legia, and played on Thursday 27 September.

In a perfect world, politics would play no part in sport but only the most naïve would expect such idealism. UEFA spokesman Rene Eberle, speaking to the media in Warsaw, was at pains to point out that it was NATO Governments who were advising against their citizens visiting Dagestan, and that as the governing body of European football his employers had to be seen to be fair and even-handed in such a difficult diplomatic situation. Yet UEFA had for many years ensured that Greek and Turkish clubs – to use just one example – are not drawn against each other.

The UEFA official was also quick to stress that he had himself visited Makhachkala in June 2001, receiving 'hospitality unmatched anywhere in Europe', and was satisfied that all the arrangements had been made to ensure that a UEFA Cup fixture could go ahead as scheduled. 'UEFA must represent every national body and club within its orbit equally,' he was at pains to stress.

To be fair, it must be recognised that Russian clubs visit Makhachkala on a regular basis in domestic competition – one Moscow journalist recalled to the author that he had in the last year visited the city on nine occasions without any problem. One might also add that the antics of certain Scottish newspapers did Rangers no favours whatsoever; publishing the telephone and fax numbers of UEFA so that readers might swamp their offices with nuisance calls served only to antagonise the Swiss officials.

It is only right that UEFA allow access to their competition to every affiliated nation under their umbrella and equally the poverty of an area should never be allowed to debar it from playing host to European fixtures, but the safety and safe passage of visitors – whether they are officials, players or supporters – must surely be paramount. If the authorities tell fans that it is not safe for them to visit Dagestan – as happened in this instance – then how on earth can it be safe for the official party?

Mercifully, UEFA finally came to the right decision, although questions remain over the puzzling decision to reschedule the fixture as a one-off tie, particularly given the recent precedent of both Leeds United and Leicester City having games moved away from Belgrade to Holland and Austria respectively, yet still being allowed to play host to their opponents in Britain.

Although Rangers had been denied the income from a full house at Ibrox for the second leg, the relief at the club was nevertheless tangible – they had gone to the very edge of the precipice in defying UEFA and refusing to travel to Dagestan and were now cleared to compete in the tournament. The game itself in Warsaw was far from memorable – a poor, tense game in difficult circumstances. Rangers, to their great relief, finally won with a Konterman goal after eighty-five minutes, a low, long shot drilled though the Anzhi defence following a Russell Latapy free-kick. Rangers were through to the second round. Few connected with Rangers would not have settled for the eventual outcome even as late in the day as Monday 17 September (the day before the eventual decision was made), for the sad but undeniable fact is that were it not for 9/11 Rangers would have been expelled from the competition and facing a probable two-year ban. All true football fans will, however, feel genuine sympathy for Anzhi, their players, officials and fans who were denied the opportunity to welcome Rangers to their city in their inaugural European tie through no fault of their own. Perhaps the day will come when the Ibrox men will be able to travel to Makhachkala.

To no one's surprise the second-round ballot saw the Ibrox men paired with familiar opponents in the shape of Dinamo Moscow. Not the kindest of draws, but then Rangers were not UEFA's favourite club at that moment in time.

Nevertheless, Rangers had a comfortable passage over the two matches. In the first leg at Ibrox, an eighth-minute opener settled any nerves when a Claudio Reyna free-kick was headed against the upright by Craig Moore, only for Lorenzo Amoruso to force the ball home with an angled drive.

There was no further scoring before the break, but during the interval the heroes of Barcelona were introduced to the 45,000 crowd.

The Muscovites had much the better of the opening stages of the second half, controlling the midfield, but the goal when it arrived came totally against the run of play at the other end, £6.5 million England international full-back Michael Ball opening his account for the Light Blues with a curling twenty-five-yard free-kick on the hour that found the net with the aid of a deflection.

Rangers got their second wind with the goal and it was one-way traffic as the home side dominated, De Boer heading goal number three from a Reyna free-kick after seventy-nine minutes. Four minutes later, a flowing move between substitute McCann and Numan saw the Dutchman's cross turned behind by Caniggia with the goal gaping.

A 3-0 lead nevertheless seemed secure, but in the ninetieth minute the Russians scored a priceless away goal when slackness in the home defence allowed Rolan Gusev to turn a Kharlachev cross into the net, completely changing the complexion of the tie.

Manager Dick Advocaat was absolutely livid at this turn of events – a 3-0 result would have been an excellent score, money in the bank so to speak, to take to Russia. A fourth goal was not so important but suddenly 3-1 was a less secure lead.

Rangers, however, did better in Moscow; the second leg in the Dinamo Stadium saw the tie virtually won in the opening fifteen minutes, with goals from Ronald de Boer and Barry Ferguson. In the end Rangers won 4-1, putting together a healthy 7-2 aggregate. The 'Little General' (Dick Advocaat) returned from Moscow in triumph.

Remarkably, at this stage Rangers had never been beated by a Russian team in Europe nor, indeed, had they ever lost on aggregate to clubs from the old Soviet Union. It was a remarkable record and one highlighted by the fact that two days earlier, in the same stadium, the great Real Madrid had lost 2-0 to Lokomotiv in the Champions' League. In seven trips to Moscow in European competition, Real Madrid had not won one game.

Rangers, through to the third round of the UEFA Cup, found themselves with very different opposition and very different travel problems – they were to face Paris Saint-Germain, a top-class European side in one of Europe's greatest capitals. The first leg at Ibrox ended goalless. Rangers were without Shota Arveladze who had been cup-tied when playing for Ajax against Celtic, but might well have won the first match with Caniggia and De Boer both missing good chances in the first half. Again, Rangers finished with ten men; again Ricksen was sent off. PSG, with a certain Ronaldinho in their ranks, had a good grip in midfield, controlling the pace of the game and were certainly not in Glasgow to defend, although Rangers created the better chances. The night ended goalless and Rangers now faced a daunting task in Paris.

Two weeks later, in the Parc des Princes, a massive Rangers support estimated at 12,000 of a 35,000 crowd, sustained the team. Once again the game finished goalless after extra time, Ronald de Boer missing a golden opportunity to win the game and the tie after 116 minutes when a penalty kick was awarded, goalkeeper Lionel Letizi (a Ranger five years later) felling Caniggia. De Boer skied the ball over the bar, maintaining, with brother Frank, the family curse on penalty kicks. One recalls a European Championship semi-final in Amsterdam for Holland against Italy. Rangers, however, did progress in Paris, winning the penalty shoot-out. This match, incidentally, was Claudia Reyna's last for the club. The American captain joined Sunderland for £4.75 million and replacing him in the Ibrox midfield the following summer would be Mikel Arteta who had played for the Parisians in both games, although he was at the time on loan from Barcelona.

Now in the last sixteen of the UEFA Cup, Rangers were set to play Dutch giants Feyenoord. Before the tie, Dick Advocaat stepped down as manager, to be succeeded by Alex McLeish. The first leg at Ibrox on 21 February was a passionate encounter on a windswept night when the weather conditions were so bad they had many older fans recalling such occasions as Real Zaragoza and Atletico Osasuna. There were unsavoury scenes prior to kick-off when the visiting fans rioted, rushing the Rangers' support in an attempt to provoke violence. Thankfully, there was no retaliation and Strathclyde's finest quelled the trouble. Nevertheless, these were the worst scenes seen at Ibrox for many years.

The game took some time to warm up, the capacity crowd looking on in frustration as Feyenoord settled comfortably into the flow of the game. Rangers failed to establish any measure of control in the middle of the park where they desperately missed the injured De Boer.

The first half ended goalless and in frustration for a Rangers side who had found the conditions to be just as difficult as their Dutch opponents but the game exploded within seconds of the restart when Pierre van Hooijdonk (once of Celtic) committed a quite disgraceful over-the-top tackle on Hughes that without question merited a red card. Astonishingly, French referee Eric Poulat appeared to ignore the tackle altogether before belatedly administering a yellow to the former Celt.

Feyenoord were certainly not in Glasgow to defend and Stefan Klos remained the busier goalkeeper. Midway through the second half he had to be on his guard to deny Van Hooijdonk from a twenty-five-yard free-kick, but the opening goal was only delayed a further four minutes when Shinji Ono – Feyenoord's Japanese midfielder – found the net with the aid of a deflection from all of twenty-five yards, the ball dipping over Klos who would have saved the effort but for the deflection.

Rangers had been lacking in penetration, but in the eightieth minute Glenn Loovens hauled down Peter Lovenkrands for a clear penalty. Barry Ferguson took full responsibility as captain, proving to many doubters that he is made of the right stuff, and promptly sent Edwin Zoetebier the wrong way from the spot to level matters at 1-1.

There was a flurry of yellow cards in the closing stages, including that of Ricksen in the eighty-third minute for an innocuous tackle on Robin van Persie. Five minutes later, the Dutch player retaliated with an abominable karate kick on the Ranger, yet received merely a yellow card.

The 1-1 result, including the away goal, made Feyenoord favourites to win the tie in their own Stadion Feyenoord, nicknamed 'de Kuip' (the Tub), where Rangers would be cheated of victory by a Feyenoord side that proved themselves masters at influencing the referee.

Two free-kick goals from Van Hooijdonk – who should not even have been playing – turned a dramatic tie in the home side's favour, but the simple truth is that neither decision was in any way a foul in the first place. The Feyenoord players, rather like the Celtic pair Chris Sutton and Henrik Larsson, were adept at winning free-kicks in that danger zone, the edge of the penalty area. Feyenoord's away goal advantage had been cancelled after twenty-five minutes when McCann volleyed home a quickly taken Barry Ferguson free-kick. Eleven minutes later a contentious free-kick awarded to the home side some twenty-two yards out, when Pierre van Hooijdonk backed into Scott Wilson, presented Feyenoord with the chance to find the net with a curling effort. Two minutes later the gamble to play De Boer failed when he was substituted for Mols, obviously suffering a recurrence of his foot injury.

Feyenoord took the lead on the stroke of half-time in identical circumstances to the first goal, this time a free-kick being awarded when Vidmar won the ball fairly against Van Persie. The award was – as with the first goal – ridiculous, but that didn't stop Van Hooijdonk producing an identical effort to put Rangers 2-1 down at the interval. One question which many Light Blue followers were asking, however, was just how many goals had Klos conceded from free-kicks during the present campaign?

Things went from bad to worse in the opening seconds of the restart when the Ibrox men were caught cold in the very first attack. A Van Persie effort struck an upright, the rebound falling to Van Hooijdonk whose cross was headed home by Kalou.

Rangers appeared to be on the way out, yet within seven minutes they were thrown a lifeline when a Konterman pass released Mols who was hauled to the ground by Patrick Paauwe. A clear penalty and a red card for the Dutch defender. Barry Ferguson did the necessary from the spot and suddenly the visitors were in with a real shout against depleted opposition.

The scoreline should have been levelled after sixty-two minutes when Caniggia showed great skill in controlling the ball and turning a defender before squaring for Lovenkrands who somehow shot wide from some fifteen yards.

Rangers too were reduced to ten men in the seventy-second minute when McCann received a second yellow card for dissent, protesting about a free-kick awarded against him when Brett Emerton had clearly fouled him. German referee

Herbert Fandel – who had been conned by the home side all evening – had clearly forgotten that McCann was already on a yellow card, as he merely flashed the same colour in his direction, only to quickly realise his mistake and send the Ranger off. It was nevertheless an act of sheer stupidity on the part of McCann who must certainly have known he had already been booked. The home crowd received a tremendous lift from the incident, but Rangers nevertheless continued to press forward, Mols seizing on a long ball out of defence to beat the offside trap, only to slice his shot into the side netting. It was all Rangers in the closing stages, but that elusive third goal was denied to them.

Ronald De Boer, the target of abusive and sickening chants from the home fans, was blunt in his assessment of the match official: 'The referee was horrendous'.

Feyenoord incidentally went to the final with the distinct advantage of it being staged on their own ground where they beat Borussia Dortmund 3-2.

2001/02 European Champions' Cup, second qualifying round, first leg
Wednesday 25 July 2001, Stadion Ljudski vrt, Maribor
NK Maribor 0 Rangers 3 (Flo 2, 1 pen, Nerlinger)
Attendance 6,100
Klos; Ricksen, Numan; Moore, Amoruso (Ferguson), Konterman; Caniggia
(Mols), Reyna, Flo, Latapy, Nerlinger (McCann)
Second qualifying round, second leg
Wednesday 1 August 2001, Ibrox Stadium, Glasgow
Rangers 3 (Caniggia 2, Flo) NK Maribor 1 (Starcevic)
Attendance 50,045
Klos; Ricksen, Vidmar; Moore, Konterman, Ferguson; Latapy (Wilson), Hughes,
Flo, Caniggia (Dodds), Nerlinger (McCann)
Third qualifying round, first leg
Wednesday 8 August 2001, Ibrox Stadium, Glasgow
Rangers 0 Fenerbahce 0
Attendance 49,472
Klos; Vidmar, Numan; Moore, Wilson, Konterman; Ricksen, Hughes, Flo,
Caniggia (Mols 45), McCann
Third qualifying round, second leg
Wednesday 22 August 2001, Sukru Saracoglu, Istanbul
Fenerbahce 2 (Revivo, Serhat) Rangers 1 (Ricksen)
Attendance 18,272
Klos; Vidmar (Ross), Numan; Amoruso, Wilson, Konterman; Kanchelskis
(Caniggia), Ricksen, Flo, De Boer, Reyna (Hughes)
UEFA Cup, first round
Thursday 27 September 2001, Stadion Legia, Warsaw
Rangers 1 (Konterman) Anzhi Makhachkala 0
Attendance 4,200

Klos; Ricksen, Numan; Moore, Amoruso, Ferguson; Latapy (Hughes), Konterman, Flo (Caniggia), De Boer, McCann (Lovenkrands)

Second round, first leg

Thursday 18 October 2001, Ibrox Stadium, Glasgow

Rangers 3 (Amoruso, Ball, De Boer) Dinamo Moscow 1 (Gusev)

Attendance 45,008

Klos; Ricksen, Numan; Moore (Ball), Amoruso, Ferguson; Reyna, Konterman, Flo (McCann), De Boer, Caniggia

Second round, second leg

Thursday 1 November 2001, Dinamo Stadium, Moscow

Dinamo Moscow 1 (Gusev) Rangers 4 (De Boer, Ferguson, Flo, Lovenkrands)

Attendance 6,000

Klos; Ricksen, Numan; Moore, Amoruso, Ferguson; Reyna, Konterman, Flo (Mols), De Boer (Lovenkrands), Caniggia (Latapy)

Third round, first leg

Thursday 22 November 2001, Ibrox Stadium, Glasgow

Rangers 0 Paris Saint-Germain 0

Attendance 49,223

Klos; Ricksen, Numan; Konterman, Amoruso, Ball (Lovenkrands); Reyna, Ferguson, Flo, De Boer (Ross), Caniggia (Latapy)

Third round, second leg

Thursday 6 December 2001, Parc Des Princes, Paris

Paris Saint-Germain 0 Rangers 0

Attendance 35,000

Rangers won 4-3 on penalties

Klos; Ross (Vidmar), Numan; Moore, Amoruso, Ferguson; Reyna, Konterman, Flo (Latapy), De Boer, Lovenkrands (Caniggia)

Fourth round, first leg

Thursday 21 February 2002, Ibrox Stadium, Glasgow

Rangers 1 (Ferguson pen) Feyenoord 1 (Ono)

Attendance 49,041

Klos; Ricksen, Numan; Konterman, Amoruso, Vidmar; Hughes (Latapy), Ferguson, Flo (Mols), Caniggia, Lovenkrands

Fourth round, second leg

Thursday 28 February 2002, Stadion Feyenoord, Rotterdam

Feyenoord 3 (Van Hooijdonk 2, Kalou) Rangers 2 (McCann, Ferguson pen)

Attendance 45,000

Klos; Vidmar (Flo 74), Numan; Amoruso, Wilson, Ferguson; Caniggia, Konterman, De Boer (Mols 38), Lovenkrands, McCann

Rangers, in the UEFA Cup again in 2002/03, were drawn against Viktoria Zizkov from Prague – not one of the top names in Czech football. For that reason many observers thought that this would be a formality, a walkover for the Scots, overlooking the fact that Czech football in general was of a very high standard, plus the fact that Viktoria had failed to win the Czech League by a single point, otherwise they would have been in the Champions' League. In their final away game to Slavia Prague, they needed one point to clinch the title but lost 1-0 to an eighty-fourth-minute goal from Pavel Kuka. Rumours of match fixing were rife. Nothing was proven, but two players never played for Zizkov again!

The Light Blues thus faced opponents who, perhaps unknown outside the Czech Republic, were certainly going to be formidable. Despite all the warnings, it was clear that Rangers underestimated them. The first leg in Prague, switched from Zizcov's own stadium to the national stadium, the Strahov, saw Rangers play very poorly and go down 2-0. An early sixth-minute goal from Alesi Piko and a goal on the hour from Ludak Stracemy at a time when Craig Moore was off the field because of injury, were enough to down Rangers. Barry Ferguson, critically, failed with a first-half penalty, his first such miss for the club, and Shota Arveladze had a last-minute goal disallowed for an infringement that was not immediately obvious to anyone except the referee. It would have made a critical difference – 2-1 down would have been infinitely better than 2-0.

The return before a packed house at Ibrox, with thousands more locked outside, saw Rangers all out to overturn the two goals, something they had never done before. Two Ronald de Boer goals after forty-two and fifty-eight minutes tied the aggregate score, the first when Ferguson found Fernando Ricksen, then cleverly dummied the Dutchman's wall pass, releasing De Boer who slotted the ball home, the second when Ricksen's imaginative pass found Arveladze whose low drive was parried by goalkeeper Pavel Kucera, the ball being turned home by De Boer. De Boer, in superb form throughout that season, saw his header from a Mikel Arteta cross in the dying minutes strike the crossbar, denying him his hat-trick and Rangers a place in the next round. It meant extra time. Substitute Neil McCann put the home side ahead on aggregate after ninety-seven minutes when a superb Arteta pass released De Boer on the right, his low cross being rifled home from point-blank range. Rangers were well on top at this stage and manager Alex McLeish, clearly believing the tie won, decided to replace the outstanding De Boer with Claudio Caniggia. The Dutchman departed to a standing ovation, but, disastrously, four minutes later, abject carelessness in defence saw a crucial away goal ceded to Marcel Licfa. Rangers positively besieged the Zizkov goal during the second period of extra time, resulting in goal-line clearances, strikes against the woodwork and miraculous saves from Kucera. It was an age-old pattern. With the sands of time running out, there was one bizarre incident when, with Mikel Arteta poised to take a corner, Jan Buryan felled Moore inside the box. The referee red-carded the Czech, and awarded the Ibrox men a penalty kick before realising that he couldn't do so since the ball was out of play. Manager Alex McLeish afterwards slaughtered Greek referee Athanassios Briakos: 'This was his first European tie, and it certainly showed.'

In the final analysis, however, the blunt truth is that the tie was lost in Prague. This was a defeat that was a disaster both in footballing and financial terms as Rangers suffered their earliest exit from Europe for some five years. Alex McLeish had enjoyed a good start to his Ibrox career on the domestic front, but had now lost two ties out of two in Europe.

2002/03 UEFA Cup, first round, first leg
Tuesday 17 September 2002, Stadion Strahov, Praha
FK Viktoria Zizkov 2 (Piko, Stracemy) Rangers 0
Attendance 3,427
Klos; Ross, Muscat; Malcolm, Moore (Konterman), Ferguson; Caniggia, Ricksen, R. De Boer (Mols), Arveladze, Lovenkrands
First round, second leg
Thursday 3 October 2002, Ibrox Stadium, Glasgow
Rangers 3 (De Boer 2, McCann) Viktoria Zizkov 1 (Licka)
Attendance 47,646
Klos; Ricksen, Numan; Amoruso, Moore, Ferguson; Arteta, Konterman (Muscat), R. De Boer (Caniggia), Arveladze, Lovenkrands (McCann)

Rangers had to wait almost twelve months until, as Scottish League Champions (by a margin of one goal), they went into the third qualifying round of the 2003/04 Champions' League, scheduled to meet FC Kobenhavn of Denmark. All was not well at Ibrox, however – gross financial mismanagement over a period of many years had led to an escalating debt that had long since required addressing. Tens of millions had been spent on transfer fees, regardless of the new reality that 'Bosman' had introduced. Accordingly, Arthur Numan, Lorenzo Amoruso, Neil McCann, Claudio Caniggia and most importantly club captain Barry Ferguson all left for pastures new – some for considerable fees, others simply to remove high earners from the wage bill. True, replacements arrived in their stead – but Henning Berg, Paulo Vanoli, Nuno Capucho, Emerson and Egil Ostenstad were all players in the twilight of their careers and it was clear that whereas since the onset of the Souness Revolution Rangers had been shopping in Harrods, now they were shopping at the 'Barras'.

The Danish Champions had still to be overcome and Rangers made a dream start when a dipping Mikel Arteta free-kick after seven minutes deceived Danish goalkeeper Balazs Rabuczki who could only push the ball out into the path of Peter Lovenkrands who swept the ball home. That early strike brought the stadium to life with 47,901 spectators (including a healthy contingent from across the North Sea) inside.

Rangers had the better of the first half and the interval arrived with the home side still 1-0 ahead, but the single goal advantage was wiped out five minutes after

Shota Arveladze's wonder winner in Copenhagen.

the restart when, with little danger apparent, Hjalte Bo Norregaard's thirty-yard drive was deflected into the path of Todi Jonsson who swivelled on the eighteen-yard line before dispatching a low left-foot drive beyond Klos into the net. It was the third consecutive Ibrox European tie in which the home side had conceded an away goal. It was a hammer blow for Rangers who had lost the momentum built up during the first half. Kobenhavn, however, were invigorated by their away goal and began to dominate the midfield. The Light Blues were struggling desperately now against a side who were certainly well organised and hard work-ing. There was no further scoring and the final whistle brought a crescendo of booing from a hugely disappointed home crowd.

A 1-1 draw at home is never to be recommended in Europe and Rangers travelled to Scandinavia very much as underdogs. Yet they gave a sterling per-formance in the Parken Stadion before a 35,000 crowd. Goalless at the interval, Rangers needed a breakthrough and they took the lead after fifty-one minutes when Arteta scored from the penalty spot. Hungarian goalkeeper Balazs Rebeczki parried a thirty-yard Michael Ball free-kick; Michael Mols seized on the loose ball, only to be fouled by Urmas Rooba. After taking this early second-half lead Rangers inevitably found themselves under severe pressure, with central defend-ers Berg and Zurab Khizanishvili outstanding. The Danes came close on several occasions before the score was levelled in the eighty-second minute when a long Bo Svensson pass sent Santos clear on goal and he bundled the ball past Stefan Klos. Extra time seemed inevitable when with just four minutes left on the clock Shota Arveladze scored from a Christian Nerlinger cross, hooking the ball over his shoulder from within the penalty area. This wonderfully acrobatic goal clinched a 2-1 win for Rangers, 3-2 on aggregate.

So, in spite of everything the Ibrox men had qualified for the Champions' League. Their group was to be Manchester United, Panathinaikos of Greece and Stuttgart from Germany – a group surely indigestible by any pretender. The opening match was to be against Stuttgart at Ibrox. The German side had finished second in the Bundesliga the previous season and were very much in contention again when they faced Rangers, who approached the fixture aware that they were without a win in Europe's premier club competition for three years and four games. Interestingly, bottom seeds in the group Stuttgart, under the shrewd leadership of Coach Felix Magath, a European Cup winner as a player with Hamburg in 1983, had visited Glasgow just seven months earlier when they were desperately unlucky to lose 1–3 to Celtic, playing for all of seventy-five minutes with ten men, a handicap that had a decisive influence on the outcome of the tie. There was a tumultuous noise pouring down from the stands from the very instant that the last notes of the Champions' League signature tune died away, with Stuttgart showing a composed and assured attitude even in such a daunting atmosphere. The Scottish Champions had probably had the better of the first half, yet conceded the opening goal in the last minute of injury time when a Marcelo Bordon free-kick from fully thirty yards went straight through the wall, cannoned off the base of the post and rebounded for Kevin Kuranyi to net from close range.

Rangers pressed incessantly as the second half wore on, Stuttgart falling back in defence of their lead, and the scores were level after seventy-three minutes when Nerlinger took advantage of a bad clearance from his countrymen and forced his way through the centre of the German defence and attempted to find Mols only for the ball to break back into the midfielder's path, enabling him to find the net with a low shot. It was the first goal that the Bundesliga side had conceded during the current campaign and Stuttgart visibly wilted under the wall of noise from the packed stadium.

Six minutes later the Light Blues, unbelievably, had the lead when a superb solo effort by Lovenkrands brought the house down. Taking possession wide on the left – and seeing little in the way of options inside – the Dane cut inside before unleashing a dipping twenty-five-yard shot that perhaps caught goalkeeper Timo Hildebrand off-guard. The Ibrox legions erupted, with a memorable and significant victory in sight, and the tension of the occasion was demonstrated when, bizarrely, substitute goalkeeper Allan McGregor was yellow-carded without having set foot on the park, French referee Gilles Veissiere indicating that he had taken too long to return the ball into play from the dug-out. Rangers were to win 2–1 – indeed it should have been 3–1 when deep into injury time Lovenkrands, with an open goal in front of him and after hitting the crossbar, somehow sliced the ball wide! Nevertheless, it was an impressive win against a powerful Stuttgart team to open Rangers' campaign. The second game was in Athens against Panathinaikos, intimidating, daunting, a unique atmosphere in the Apostolo Nikolaidis Stadium, a small ground, tightly confined, spectators breathing down the players' necks, close to the playing field. The capacity was only 16,730, ridiculous for a massively supported club like 'Pana', who had played many of their big European matches in Athens' Olympic Stadium. That particular venue was unavailable at the time, due to reconstruction work going on in advance of the 2004 Olympics. Rangers on the night gave a very professional, disciplined display. They played very well, as indeed they had been doing for most of the season up to the point of this game, on 1 October. They took the lead after thirty-four minutes when the Brazilian midfielder Emerson converted a low right-wing cross from Capucho. Rangers were comfortable with this one-goal lead and their chances of winning the game were greatly enhanced after fifty-six minutes when Ionnes Goumas was shown a second yellow card and ordered off. Rangers appeared to sit back, protecting the lead, and paid the price when Pantelis Konstantinidis headed home a cross from Dmitri Papadopoulos in the dying minutes. The 1-1 draw was a great opportunity missed and would be a result that would come back to haunt the Scottish Champions.

The Athens game had been an historic tie for another reason – it was the very first game in Rangers' history where all thirteen players fielded, i.e. the starting line-up plus two substitutes used, were all non-Scots. The side did not even feature a player born outside the country but who was eligible to play for Scotland, for example Andy Goram, Richard Gough, Stuart McCall.

Facing Rangers that hot and humid evening in Athens incidentally was a certain Sotirios Kyrgiakos who little more than a year later would wear the Light Blue. The central defender suffered a cruciate knee ligament injury in an accidental collision with Stefan Klos and, as a consequence, would miss out on his country's Euro 2004 triumph. Six points from two games would have been impressive. The same evening Stuttgart defeated Manchester United 2-1, to underline Rangers' achievement in overcoming the Germans in the first game, yet in hindsight the Manchester United defeat did Rangers no particular favours. Stuttgart and Manchester United were very much in the running to qualify from the group. Rangers' next two games were against Manchester United and it was crucial that something was taken from them, preferably from both and particularly the first one, at Ibrox. Sir Alex Ferguson was returning to his roots for a massive game, dubbed inevitably the 'Battle of Britain' between the two biggest clubs in the United Kingdom. The home side started well, but suffered a catastrophic loss of the crucial opening goal after four minutes when Phil Neville was allowed to advance unchallenged towards the danger area, Craig Moore failing to halt his progress, and fire a low drive into the corner of the net. The Scottish Champions were giving their English counterparts far too much respect and allowing them too much time and space. As the game went on, however, Rangers forced the visitors onto the back foot but the United defence remained solid until the final whistle, which signalled a first home European defeat in four years.

Professor and student – Sir Alex Ferguson and Alex McLeish at Old Trafford in 2003.

Rangers had played very well and deserved to take something from the match. The defeat was harsh and a draw would have been a fair result. United manager (and former Ranger) Sir Alex Ferguson was delighted to leave Ibrox with a win: 'It was a great game of football and a terrific atmosphere. Rangers have good footballers who gave their all. They have balance, and kept possession very well. I always enjoy coming back to Glasgow, especially when you win.' The return game at Old Trafford was to be a different story – Rangers were comprehensively beaten, at times embarrassingly so, by 3-0. Again an early goal, after six minutes from Diego Forlan, left Rangers out of the game, out of the running, and they must have been thankful that the only goals added by the home side were two Ruud van Nistelrooy strikes in the forty-third and sixtieth minutes, the first when Forlan's drive struck the underside of the bar, the rebound striking Van Nistelrooy and trundling into the net. The Dutchman struck again on the hour when he turned home Cristiano Ronaldo's cross. Rangers had badly missed the experience of the injured Ronald De Boer and Fernando Ricksen but it was a defeat that all too cruelly highlighted the limitations of the current Ibrox squad, weakened so desperately the previous summer. The Ibrox men had worn all blue, as indeed they did on the occasion of their record European defeat (0-6 to Real Madrid, 1963/64), and at times there were many friends of Rangers who feared that a similar scoreline had been on the cards at Old Trafford.

The fifth game in the group saw the Light Blues travel to Stuttgart still, three weeks later, with some kind of chance of qualifying – they required a win in the Gottlieb Daimler Stadion. They played well in Stuttgart without ever looking as though they could win the match. The best chance of the evening fell to Ricksen, clean through after twenty-two minutes following a flick-on by Arveladze. His shot cannoned off the legs of Hildebrandt. Rangers paid for that miss on the stroke of half-time when Timo Wenzel scored after the ball had broken to him from Horst Heltt's free-kick. Rangers were unable to retrieve the situation in the second half. The 1-0 defeat left them out of the Champions' League, requiring a draw at Ibrox against Panathinaikos to ensure that they progressed to the UEFA Cup. The game was a dreadful letdown for a capacity Ibrox crowd. The team started well, taking only twenty-seven minutes for Mols to score with a stunning header from a Ball cross. A goal up at home, and needing only a draw to progress, you would think it almost impossible to fail, but within four minutes the scores were level when appalling defending allowing Raimondas Zutautas to take possession of a Markus Munch pass in acres of space and beat Klos all ends up with a low twenty-five-yard drive.

Rangers fell behind on the hour, Angelos Basinas giving the visitors the lead with a stunning thirty-yard drive that perhaps caught Klos by surprise. The end was nigh after seventy-nine minutes when Epalle sprang the offside trap, releasing Michael Konstantinou who raced clear to coolly net and spell disaster for Rangers. It was a dreadful result, a dreadful Rangers performance (albeit with an injury-ravaged side), capping a miserable season that was not halfway over, a season that had held so much promise. Now they were out of Europe with little to look forward to on the domestic front.

2003/04 European Champions' Cup, third qualifying round, first leg
Wednesday 13 August 2003, Ibrox Stadium, Glasgow
Rangers 1 (Lovenkrands) FC Kobenhavn 1 (Jonsson)
Attendance 47,401
Klos; Ross (Capucho), Ball; Khizanishvili, Moore, Ferguson; Ricksen, Arteta,
R. de Boer (Thompson), Mols, Lovenkrands
Third qualifying round, second leg
Wednesday 27 August 2003, Parken Stadion, Kobenhavn
FC Kobenhavn 1 (Santos) Rangers 2 (Arteta pen, Arveladze)
Attendance 35,519

Klos; Ricksen, Ball; Khizanishvilli, Berg (Malcolm), Ferguson; Arveladze, Arteta, R. de Boer (Vanoli), Mols (Thompson), Nerlinger

Champions' League Group E

Matchday one

Tuesday 16 September 2003, Ibrox Stadium, Glasgow

Rangers 2 (Nerlinger, Lovenkrands) Vfb Stuttgart (Kuranyi)

Attendance 47,957

Klos; Ricksen (Ross), Ball; Khizanishvili, Berg, Vanoli (Lovenkrands); Arteta, Emerson (Capucho), Arveladze, Mols, Nerlinger

Matchday two

Wednesday 1 October 2003, Apostolos Nikolaidis Stadium, Athinai

Panathinaikos 1 (Konstantinidis) Rangers 1 (Emerson)

Attendance 13,718

Klos; Khizanishvili, Ball; Emerson, Berg, Moore; Capucho, Arteta, Arveladze (Nerlinger), Mols, Lovenkrands (Vanoli)

Matchday three

Wednesday 22 October 2003, Ibrox Stadium, Glasgow

Rangers 0 Manchester United 1 (P. Neville)

Attendance 48,730

Klos; Khizanishvili (Ross), Ball; Moore, Berg, Vanoli (Nerlinger); Ricksen, Arteta, Arveladze, Mols, Lovenkrands

Matchday four

Tuesday 4 November 2003, Old Trafford, Manchester

Manchester United 3 (Van Nistelrooy 2, Forlan) Rangers 0

Attendance 66,707

Klos; Khizanishvili, Ball; Moore (Ross), Berg, Vanoli (Burke); Hughes, Arteta, Arveladze, Mols (Capucho), Lovenkrands

Matchday five

Wednesday 26 November 2003, Gottlieb-Daimler-Stadion, Stuttgart

Vfb Stuttgart 1 (Wenzel) Rangers 0

Attendance 50,438

Klos; Ross (Ostenstad), Ball; Khizanishvili, Berg, Vanoli (Mols); Ricksen, Hughes, Capucho, Arveladze, Lovenkrands (Burke)

Matchday six

Tuesday 13 December 2003, Ibrox Stadium, Glasgow

Rangers 1 (Mols) Panathinaikos 3 (Zutautas, Basinas, Konstantinou)

Attendance 48,588

Klos; Ross (Duffy), Ball; Ricksen, Berg, Khizanishvili (Vanoli); Burke (Ostenstad), Hughes, Capucho, Mols, Lovenkrands

Rangers, runners-up in the Scottish Premier League, went into the third qualifying round of the 2004/05 Champions' League and were drawn against old

friends CSKA Moscow, very difficult opponents, and a club whom the Ibrox men had faced in the inaugural campaign of 1992/93. For once, Rangers had made effective use of the 'Bosman' market with the signings of such as Dado Prso, a Champions' League finalist with AS Monaco the previous season, Jean-Alain Boumsong from AJ Auxerre and veteran Scottish midfielder Alex Rae from Wolverhampton Wanderers. The Russians, sponsored by Roman Abramovich, owner of Chelsea, had spent $30 million in signing new players and were going to be formidable opposition. Included in their ranks was a certain Rolan Gusev who had scored in both legs of Rangers' UEFA Cup-tie with Dinamo Moscow three years earlier. The first leg saw the Light Blues go down 2-1 away from home, conceding an early goal when Wagner Love headed home a cross from Arica Olic. Under severe pressure early in the match, after thirty-six minutes they snatched an equaliser. Following dogged work on the left by Prso, Nacho Novo took his square pass and netted at the second attempt after his first shot was blocked. With a 1-1 scoreline Rangers had plenty to be pleased about at half-time, but yet again they conceded an early goal when a shocking lack of concentration at a throw-in let Jiro Jarosik, the Czech international and most expensive player in Russia, score. The 2-1 reverse was hardly an unacceptable defeat against a side of the quality of CSKA in a European tie on a foreign field and Rangers would have been happy to finish the game with that deficit but found themselves in the eye of a storm over an incident involving Alex Rae.

In attempting to win the ball, Rae had made contact with a grounded Moldovan, Sergey Dadu. There was a furore over this incident. The fact that the ball was there to be won was overlooked. There were claims from Moscow that the player had suffered concussion – ignored was the fact that he had carried on playing, finished the game and played for his club the following Saturday in a League match. If he did suffer concussion then this was a recovery to baffle medical science. There was massive coverage of the incident in the Scottish media, certain elements of which took advantage of the fact that this was a stick with which to beat Rangers. It led to a UEFA enquiry in which Rae was quite unjustly suspended for five European games. Dutch referee Jan Wegereef also had some questions to answer. The author had spoken to him at Moscow Airport on the day after the game – he spoke perfectly fluent English – and when asked about the incident advised that he had seen the incident quite clearly, his decision had been a free-kick to Rangers, a decision he stood by. At the UEFA enquiry, he changed his evidence and then claimed he did not have a clear view of the incident.

Rangers could feel hard done by, heavily penalised over this matter. The consequences were that they were without a most influential player for five games, and most importantly, he was to miss the Ibrox return. A full house there saw a most disappointing home performance. They never looked like qualifying for the Champions' League, although the game did erupt in controversy on forty minutes when Novo shrugged off a challenge on the edge of the box before sending a twenty-yard screamer into the roof of the net. Unbelievably, the German referee awarded a free-kick to Rangers, despite the recent FIFA directive that referees have discretion to allow play to continue before making their decision.

CSKA were comfortable, composed on the ball and led after an hour when Wagner Love netted from close range from a Jiri Jarosik cutback, following a Craig Moore error. It was a catastrophic goal to lose and the many who believed that Moore should not have been allowed to cross the Ibrox threshold ever again had their views justified, for his presence in the Rangers team was controversial in itself. The Australian international had actually defied his manager by going off to play in the Olympic Games. Thus his services to the club were denied in the early, critical weeks of the season, in particular in Moscow, where his presence might have made a difference. We shall never know.

Manager Alex McLeish promptly stripped 'Oz' of the captaincy, appointing Stefan Klos as his successor. All this led to a diplomatic furore when Australian Prime Minister John Howard and his government condemned Rangers for victimising the player, stressing that no player should be denied the right to play for his country. The president of the International Olympic Committee, Mr Rogge, likewise denounced Rangers for their attitude. Overlooked in this squabble was the fact that three months earlier, in May, the Australian government itself had advised its citizens not to travel to Athens for the Olympic Games for fear of terrorist attacks.

Moore did go to Athens where his team reached the quarter-final. This was not the first time that he had fallen foul of the Ibrox management and of the supporters. The previous season, as captain, he had declared he would not be extending his contract until he saw the quality of players Rangers were going to be signing. Given all of this it was astonishing that Moore should be brought straight back into the team following Australia's elimination from the Olympic competition in Athens. Many Rangers fans felt that instead of being brought back into the team, he should have been shown the door. It is inconceivable that this could have happened in Bill Struth's day. The final irony is that it was Moore's error that brought CSKA their vital goal. Rangers levelled matters on the night after eighty-six minutes when, with memories of Roger Hynd and Colin Jackson from earlier European campaigns, substitute Marvin Andrews was thrown up front in a bid to unsettle the Russian defence, the move paying dividend when Boumsong's long ball was nodded down by Andrews allowing Steven Thompson to net from the edge of the box.

Suddenly Rangers were pouring forward in search of a second goal that would mean extra time, and two minutes later a free-kick some twenty-five yards out saw Gregory Vignal's low drive produce a superb one-handed save from Akinfeev, the rebound falling to Andrews who alas sent his effort wide. The final whistle soon afterwards meant that a Russian club had eliminated the Ibrox men for the first time and CSKA had qualified for the Champions' League. In truth, the Russians always looked the more accomplished side and on the balance of play over the two legs deserved to progress. The victory was a measure of revenge for their coach, none other than Valerie Gazzaev, who had eight years earlier suffered a humiliating defeat at the hands of Rangers whilst coach of Alania Vladikavkaz. By the campaign's close the Russians had underlined their quality by annexing the UEFA Cup with a 3-1 win over Sporting Lisbon in their own backyard.

The defeat was a financial catastrophe for Rangers and it was clearly essential that they should get into the group stages of the UEFA Cup. There was a new format for this competition – a knockout round involving eighty clubs, reducing to forty divided into eight groups of five. That meant two home, two away matches against four different clubs. CS Maritimo were Rangers' opponents in the first round, a club based on the island of Madeira (which Rangers had never visited before); this was opposition not to be dismissed, lying as they did second in the Portuguese League. Rangers' performance in Funchal was poor, going down to a twenty-second-minute Manduca goal. Klos might have done better – he had parried a shot from Leo Lima, with Manduca netting the rebound. Rangers were quite dreadful in the second half and were fortunate to leave the island only one goal down.

The story of the return match at Ibrox was one of constant pressure against an accomplished and very disciplined Portuguese defence. It was a night of unbelievable tension as the fate of the two clubs and perhaps also that of Gers manager Alex McLeish hung in the balance before a near-capacity crowd of 47,360. The breakthrough eventually came after sixty-nine minutes when Vignal's cross was touched on by Thompson for Prso who swivelled to sweep the ball into the net, to the immense relief of the capacity crowd. A second Prso goal in the eightieth minute was erroneously disallowed for offside. Extra time brought no goals and featured constant Rangers pressure and chances spurned. It went to penalty kicks and Rangers were successful in the shootout. Thus they went into the promised five-team group, the others being old friends Auxerre from France, Grazer from Austria, Amica Wronki from Poland and AZ Alkmaar of the Netherlands. Rangers' first game was to be in Poland, in the small town of Wronki to be precise, close to the city of Poznan. Amica – a white goods company – sponsored the team, based in Wronki, not much more than a village built around the factory. As it turned out, the Poles were to become the whipping boys of the group, Rangers winning 5-0 in the opening group fixture. Grazer AK visited Ibrox for the second game. The Austrians had played Liverpool in a Champions' League qualifier earlier in the season and had been unlucky to go down. They came to Ibrox having amassed four points from their two opening games – an excellent 0-0 at Auxerre and a home win over Amica, 3-1. A goalless first half might have gone either way, but Rangers were comprehensive winners in the second half, finishing it off 3-0. The deadlock was broken after fifty-seven minutes when a Ricksen free-kick from the left found Novo unmarked at the far post to sweep the ball into the net. The Light Blues were now in the ascendancy, but time and again were defied by Austrian goalkeeper Andreas Schranz. Victory was secured after eighty-five minutes when yet another Ricksen free-kick found Prso at the far post, his header across goal being stabbed goalwards by Hamed Namouchi only to be blocked on the line by Gernot Plassnegger. Time appeared to stand still until Arveladze squeezed the ball over the line to make it 2-0. The goal of the game was left until the dying seconds when Khizanishvili found Novo wide and deep on the right. A mazy run took Nacho to the goal line, his low cross being turned into the net by Namouchi. Six points from two matches left Rangers in control of the group.

Their third fixture was to be a visit to Holland to face AZ Alkmaar, who had also won their opening matches, beating Auxerre 2-0 at home and Amica Wronki by 3-1 in Poland. Ironically, the Dutch were seeded bottom in the group, a ranking that belied their outstanding form throughout the season. Not one of the big three Dutch clubs – Ajax, PSV Eindhoven and Feyenoord – they were still a team to be feared. Their small ground, the Alkmaarderhout, held just 8,372 fans and was packed for the visit of Rangers. Alkmaar is an ambitious club. They were building a new stadium with sponsorship behind them and one had a feeling that this was a club going places. Their coach was the experienced Co Adriaanse.

The Dutch led courtesy of an early, sixth-minute goal from Denny Landzaat. Rangers had their chances – Novo missed a very good one in the first half – and in the second with ten minutes left were denied a clear penalty when a Stephen Hughes cross was handled by Barry van Galen. The referee turned a blind eye to this; Rangers might have had a draw but, over the piece, the Dutch side probably deserved to win. One game remained in the group, Rangers versus Auxerre at Ibrox with the Light Blues aware that a draw would guarantee qualification for the next round of the UEFA Cup. Not to lose to Auxerre was the mantra, but sadly the Auxerre game was just as big a disappointment as had been the Panathinaikos game one year earlier. The day did not get off to the best of starts when the news broke that Graeme Souness had bid £8 million for Rangers' French defender Jean-Alain Boumsong. In the event, an unsettled Boumsong would leave Rangers in January, and his performance against Auxerre was a clear indication that his mind was elsewhere. Souness, manager of Newcastle United in the Premiership, had already raided Rangers when manager of Blackburn Rovers in taking Messrs Ferguson, Amoruso and Tugay south. Premiership clubs often seem to have money to burn, such is their income from lucrative Sky television deals. Souness clearly rated the defender – signed on a 'Bosman' from, ironically, Auxerre the previous summer – very highly indeed.

The game itself was yet another major letdown for the loyal, capacity Ibrox crowd. There were certain team selections and tactics from Alex McLeish that were inexplicable. Ricksen had been the midfield dynamo, the engine of the team throughout the season, arguably Rangers' Player of the Season. He was moved from midfield to right-back with Khizanishvili, who had been right-back, moved to midfield. It was a move that patently did not work and it was a tactical and man-management error on the part of the Ibrox boss. Similarly, the exclusion of Alex Rae, named only as a substitute with Bob Malcolm taking his place in midfield, was a move that surely puzzled every onlooker.

Rangers yet again lost an early goal, this time in the ninth minute when, in a lightning breakaway following a Rangers corner, a swift Auxerre counter-attack saw Kanga Akale feed Benjamin Mwaruwari whose cross evaded Khizanishvili and fell to Kalou who struck the crossbar with his first effort before turning home the rebound. Rangers fought their way back into the game, missing several clear chances. At half-time Alex McLeish admitted his error and switched the two players back into their rightful positions. Unfortunately, this was not done soon enough – immediately after the restart Kalou netted his second from an Akale cross, with the defence found wanting. The home side fought on to the end, but never looked like retrieving the situation and a crescendo of booing and jeering greeted the final whistle. Auxerre certainly had been a fine side but for the second successive year Rangers had gone into a final group match requiring only a draw to progress in European competition and on both occasions were beaten, at home. Perhaps the most telling comment of the night came from wily Auxerre Coach Guy Rous who commented: 'I was surprised it was so easy.'

2004/05 European Champions' Cup, third qualifying round, first leg
Tuesday 10 August 2004, Lokomotiv Stadium, Moskva
CSKA Moskva 2 (Wagner Love, Jarosik) Rangers 1 (Novo)
Attendance 19,000
Klos; Ross, Vignal; Boumsong, Khizanishvili, Ricksen; Lovenkrands (Thompson),
A. Rae, Arveladze, Novo, Prso
Third qualifying round, second leg
Wednesday 25 August 2004, Ibrox Stadium, Glasgow
Rangers 1 (Thompson) CSKA Moskva 1 (Wagner Love)
Attendance 49,010
Klos; Ricksen, Vignal; Boumsong, Moore, Hughes; Arveladze, Mladenovic
(Andrews), Prso, Novo, Lovenkrands (Thompson)
UEFA Cup, first round, first leg
Thursday 16 September 2004, Estadio Barreiros, Funchal, Madeira
CS Maritimo 1 (Manduca) Rangers 0
Attendance 4,000
Klos; Ross, Vignal (Vanoli); Boumsong, Moore, Ricksen; Burke, Mladenovic,
Prso, Novo (Lovenkrands), Arveladze
First round, second leg
Thursday 30 September 2004, Ibrox Stadium, Glasgow
Rangers 1 (Prso) CS Maritimo 0

Attendance 47,360

Rangers won 4-2 on penalties

Klos; Ross, Vanoli (Vignal); Boumsong, Khizanishvili, Malcolm (Hughes); Novo, Ricksen, Prso, Thompson, Burke (Arveladze)

Champions' League Group F

Matchday one

Thursday 21 October 2004, Stadion Amica, Wronki

KS Amica Wronki 0 Rangers 5 (Lovenkrands, Novo, Ricksen, Arveladze pen, Thompson)

Attendance 4,500

Klos; Khizanishvili, Vignal; Boumsong, Andrews, Malcolm; Burke, Ricksen, Prso (Thompson), Arveladze (Namouchi), Lovenkrands (Novo)

Matchday two

Thursday 25 November 2004, Ibrox Stadium, Glasgow

Rangers 3 (Novo, Arveladze, Namouchi) Grazer AK 0

Attendance 46,453

Klos; Khizanishvili, Vignal (Ball); Boumsong, Andrews, Malcolm; Namouchi, Ricksen, Prso, Novo, Lovenkrands (Arveladze)

Matchday three

Thursday 2 December 2004, Stadion Almaarderhout, Alkmaar

AZ Alkmaar 1 (Landzaat) Rangers 0

Attendance 8,343

Klos; Khizanishvili, Ball; Boumsong, Andrews, Malcolm (Hughes); Ricksen, A. Rae, Prso, Novo, Lovenkrands (Namouchi)

Matchday four

Wednesday 15 December 2004, Ibrox Stadium, Glasgow

Rangers 0 AJ Auxerre (Kalou 2)

Attendance 48,847

Klos; Ricksen, Vignal; Boumsong, Andrews, Malcolm; Namouchi (A. Rae), Khizanishvili (Hutton), Prso, Novo, Arveladze

ELEVEN

The Enduring Dream

A sensational last-day title triumph on 22 May 2005 meant that Rangers went into the third qualifying round of the following season's Champions' Cup – there to face old rivals Anorthosis Famagusta of Cyprus. The venue was not Famagusta but Nikosia, the only divided capital in Europe, a decision imposed by UEFA decree due to the inadequacy of Anorthosis' floodlights in their adopted and temporary home of Larnaca (where the Ibrox men had played in 1995).

Alex McLeish had enjoyed a summer spending spree in France, signing Jose Pierre Fanfan from Paris Saint-Germain, Brahim Hemdani from Olympique Marseille and Julien Rodriguez, who had played alongside Dado Prso for AS Monaco in the Champions' League final two years earlier. Barry Ferguson had returned to Ibrox the previous January, and another signing at that time had been Thomas Buffel from Feyenoord, a quality forward with a considerable pedigree.

Rangers, wearing all blue, faced opponents who arguably had the better of proceedings in the first half, but the deadlock was broken after sixty-four minutes when Nacho Novo rifled the ball home after Fernando Ricksen's overhead volley from a Prso cross had been parried by Antonis Giorgallides. Six minutes later it was 2-0 when Ricksen demonstrated great composure to net from Prso's reverse pass. A team, however, is always at its most vulnerable immediately after scoring, and so it proved instantaneously when Nicolaus Frousos netted from a Leonidas Kampantais lay-off following a Rodriguez error. The game finished 2–1 to the Scottish Champions, an excellent result by any reckoning, but the return had still to be negotiated. The Cypriots provided an early threat but Buffel it was who provided a superb opening goal when he moved on to a Novo flick before sweeping the ball high into the far corner of the net as he moved away from the goal in the thirty-eighth minute. Rangers thereafter were always in command, adding a second in the fifty-seventh minute when Prso won possession some twenty-five yards out before turning one way then the other as he advanced and rifled the ball into the net.

Rangers had qualified for the Champions' League for a seventh occasion, the draw pairing them with Internazionale Milano, Porto and Artmedia Bratislava who had eliminated Celtic in round two (5-0, 0-4).

The Portuguese side were visitors to Glasgow on matchday one, remembered with great fondness by all friends of Rangers for Seville 2003 when they comprehensively outplayed and outclassed Celtic. They were now coached by an old friend from AZ Alkmaar, Dutchman Co Adriaanse, who had spent £65 million on new players. It was to prove one of the great European nights at Ibrox – a night when Rangers silenced the prophets of doom that had encircled the club. The campaign got off to the perfect start with a 3-2 win in a thrilling game that surged from end to end throughout. Somewhat against the run of play, Rangers opened the scoring after thirty-four minutes when Ricksen's cross found Peter Lovenkrands who hooked the ball home past the advancing Vitor Baia. The 48,599 spectators were in good heart at the interval, but it took Porto just two minutes after the restart to level matters when Pepe headed Cesar Peixoto's inswinging corner home. It was end-to-end stuff now, but the Light Blues regained the lead after fifty-eight minutes when a Ferguson free-kick broke to Hamed Namouchi whose overhead flick saw both Prso and Vitor Baia jump for the ball, the Ranger forcing the ball over the line. Inswinging corners had been troubling Rangers all night – witness the first goal – and yet another from Cesar Peixoto was chested over the line by Pepe in the seventy-first minute, with Julien Rodriguez turning his back on the ball to shadow another forward on the goal line.

In an incredible night there was, however, yet another twist in the tail, Sotirios Kyrgiakos back-heading a long through-ball from Ferguson into the net via an upright. The night was won, the win providing the perfect answer to the mounting criticism that manager Alex McLeish and his team had faced over difficult domestic results in recent weeks.

The Stadio Guiseppe Meazza – or San Siro – is, of course, one of the great cathedrals of world football, but tragically for the game the visit of Rangers was, by dint of UEFA decree, categorised as a 'closed doors' fixture although the presence of various sponsor's guests hardly equate with one's understanding of such a regulation. The disciplinary move was enforced (for four home matches) due to crowd trouble in the previous season's quarter-final tie against their city rivals AC Milan that had led to its abandonment after seventy-three minutes.

In the ghost-like atmosphere, Rangers acquitted themselves well, defying the prophets of doom who had predicted a heavy defeat; indeed, they certainly should have taken the lead after nine minutes when Lovenkrands, just six yards out, volleyed over from a Hamed Namouchi cross. Inter, however, were presented with a glorious opportunity to open the scoring in the thirty-sixth minute when Greek referee Kyros Vassaras judged that goalkeeper Ronald Waterreus had brought down Julio Cruz following an Olivier Bernard error. It was a poor decision, as the

One of the most bizarre settings ever encountered by a Rangers team: an almost empty Stadio San Siro hosts a Champions' League clash with Internazionale in 2005.

Dutch goalkeeper had clearly touched the ball, but in the event Cruz struck the post with the penalty. Three minutes into the second half, David Pizzaro struck with a twenty-five-yard free-kick that was deflected past Waterreus. Rangers kept battling to the end, but Inter were too professional to concede anything.

On the same night, Artmedia had turned the group on its head with a shock 3-2 win in Porto, and the Slovaks were to visit Ibrox three weeks later. It was a night where the Light Blues failed to capitilise on a whole host of chances, visiting goal-keeper Juraj Cobej defying the Scottish Champions time and time again, and the goalless draw left the outcome of the group very much in the balance, all the more so as Porto had secured their first win with a 2-0 home success over Inter.

To Bratislava Rangers ventured two weeks later for the first time since 1959. The venue was the very same stadium where the Scots had triumphed almost half a century earlier – Stadion Tehelne pole, home of Slovan.

The visitors got off to a dream start after two minutes when a Hemdani free-kick found Kyrgiakos at the back post, his header across the face of goal being nodded into the net by Prso. That lead, however, lasted a mere five minutes – Balazs Borbely taking advantage of hesitation in the Ibrox defence to turn the ball home from close range following a Fodrek corner. Rangers were belying stuttering domestic form to dominate the first half and regained the ascendancy two minutes before the interval when Steven Thompson headed home a Prso cross. The break found the Scottish Champions, unbelievably, group leaders, with Porto a goal to the good in the San Siro. Defensive blunders continued to haunt the Light Blues, however, Artmedia equalising on the hour when Jan Kozak's twenty-five-yard drive found an empty net with both Waterreus and Rodriguez stranded. Rangers squandered chances right to the end: in the eightieth minute an Oliver Bernard cross struck the crossbar, the rebound falling to Ricksen whose chip across the face of goal was somehow headed wide by Lovenkrands. A second consecutive draw, linked with Inter's 2-1 victory over Porto, meant that Rangers' fate hung in the balance – they could still finish in any of four positions in Group H. Meanwhile, domestic form went from bad to worse; taking the Bratislava fixture into account the Ibrox club had failed to win in six consecutive fixtures prior to their trip to Portugal, including two successive Celtic Park reversals in League Cup and League.

There were an estimated 6,000 Gers fans inside the Estadio do Dragao on matchday five – the magnificent new ground had been constructed for Euro 2004, replacing the dated Estadio das Antas where the Ibrox men had suffered defeat some twenty-two years earlier. On this occasion, manager Alex McLeish did not have his problems to seek – there was no Rodriguez, Buffel, Nieto, Novo or Prso and accordingly the under-pressure boss set his stall out to play an ultra-cautious 4-5-1 set-up.

Porto attacked from the start, but Rangers held firm until Lisandro provided the breakthrough on the hour with a header from a Bosinga cross. A home win appeared inevitable – yet the introduction of youngsters Chris Burke and Ross McCormack turned the game, the latter volleying home after Ricksen's deep cross to the far post had been headed back across goal by Burke. Porto desperately surged back – but the visitors' goal miraculously survived an eighty-eighth-minute scramble when Waterreus twice and Ian Murray somehow blocked Almeida from a Quaresma cross.

So now it was all down to matchday six at Ibrox – all to play for, with Inter Milan due at Ibrox having already secured first place in the group. Nevertheless, the Italians opened the scoring after twenty-eight minutes when an inswinging corner from Sinisa Mihajlovic found Adriano who was offered a free header. Ibrox was silenced, but only temporarily, for within eight minutes Rangers were level when a slide-rule pass from Thomas Buffel released Lovenkrands who coolly advanced on goalkeeper Francesco Toldo before slotting the ball home. The Italian giants were comfortable on the ball, their class, skill and vision all too apparent to knowing observers, but the home side gave as good as they got, and the scores were still level as the dying embers of the game approached. Word had reached Glasgow that Artmedia and Porto remained goalless in Bratislava – a result that would send Rangers through. There being no further scoring at either venue, the Light Blues were through to the last sixteen – and beleaguered manager Alex McLeish thus became the first Scottish club boss to guide his charges beyond the group stages of Europe's premier competition, an achievement he rightly regarded as one of the finest of his managerial career.

Diego Forlan nets a controversial second goal for Villarreal at Ibrox, 2006.

Rangers found themselves paired with Spanish aces Villarreal in the last six-teen, a name that perhaps did not carry the glamour of the likes of Barcelona, Real Madrid or Valencia but one who had proven themselves formidable opponents, eliminating Celtic from the UEFA Cup in 2003/04, when they reached the semi-finals.

The first leg at Ibrox saw two contentious and critical decisions by French referee Eric Poulat materially affect the outcome. Villarreal were undoubtedly technically superior opponents but on a passionate night before 49,372 spectators the Scottish Champions never stopped battling. On such occasions, the home side is always taking extra precautions in order to prevent the loss of a crucial away goal, yet Rangers made a nightmare start after six minutes when Dado Prso, so often a talismanic figure for the Light Blues, inexplicably handled the ball in midair following a Juan Roman Riquelme corner, leaving M. Poulat with little choice but to award a penalty that Riquelme himself converted.

The scores were level after twenty-one minutes when – out of the blue – Lovenkrands curled home a twenty-yard left-foot shot following a mazy Chris Burke run. The 'Yellow Submarine' regained the lead in the thirty-fifth minute with the most controversial goal seen at Ibrox for many a year, Riquelme's cross breaking off Javier Gonzalo into the path of Diego Forlan who was at least six yards offside as he swept the ball into the net. Unbelievably, the French referee and his linesman both allowed the goal to stand.

Villarreal were excellent on the ball, retaining possession with their classic close-passing game. At the heart of virtually every attack by the Spanish club was the Argentinian midfielder Riquelme, a superb talent. A superb run by Buffel after eighty-one minutes produced an unexpected equaliser, his cross being deflected into his own net by Juan Pena. Five minutes later, Rangers were denied a stonewall penalty when Prso's back-header was blatantly handled by Pena, but astonishingly M. Poulat saw nothing amiss.

A 2-2 draw left the Light Blues with a mountain to climb in El Madrigal – but inspired by a massive travelling support of some 15,000 Gers fans the visitors took a twelfth-minute lead when Lovenkrands was on hand to finish off a Buffel–Ferguson move after the Dane had dispossessed Josico. Rangers held the advantage at the interval, but within four minutes of the restart Villarreal were in pole position in the tie again when Arruabarrena finished off a Riquelme–Forlan move at the back post. The Scottish Champions fought on to the end and substitute Kris Boyd missed a golden opportunity to net a second goal in the seventy-fifth minute when he failed to connect with a Burke cross.

Rangers were out and Villarreal would go on to reach the last four before being eliminated by Arsenal.

2005/06 European Champions' Cup, third qualifying round, first leg
Tuesday 9 August 2005, Gsp Stadium, Nikosia
Anorthosis Famagusta 1 (Frousos) Rangers 2 (Novo, Ricksen)
Attendance 16,990
Waterreus; Fanfan, Ball; Rodriguez, Andrews, Murray; Ricksen, Ferguson, Prso (Thompson), Buffel (Lovenkrands), Novo (Burke)
Third qualifying round, second leg
Wednesday 24 August 2005, Ibrox Stadium, Glasgow
Rangers 2 (Buffel, Prso) Anorthosis Famagusta 0
Attendance 48,500
Waterreus; Ricksen, Ball; Rodriguez, Fanfan, Murray (A. Rae); Buffel (McCormack), Ferguson, Prso (Thompson), Novo, Lovenkrands
Champions' League Group H
Matchday one
Tuesday 13 September 2005, Ibrox Stadium, Glasgow
Rangers 3 (Lovenkrands, Prso, Kyrgiakos) Porto 2 (Pepe 2)
Attendance 48,599
Waterreus; Ricksen, Bernard; Kyrgiakos, Rodriguez, Murray; Namouchi (Novo), Ferguson, Prso, Jeffers (Thompson), Lovenkrands (Buffel)
Matchday two
Wednesday 28 September 2005, Stadio Giuseppe Meazza, Milano
Internazionale Milano 1 (Pizzaro) Rangers 0
Attendance 2,000
Waterreus; Ricksen, Bernard; Rodriguez, Kyrgiakos, Murray (Nieto); Namouchi (Thompson), Ferguson, Prso, Buffel (Jeffers), Lovenkrands

Matchday three

Wednesday 19 October 2005, Ibrox Stadium, Glasgow

Rangers 0 Artmedia Bratislava 0

Attendance 49,018

Waterreus; Ricksen, Bernard; Kyrgiakos (Andrews), Rodriguez, Ferguson;
Namouchi (Burke), Hemdani, Prso, Nieto (Thompson), Lovenkrands

Matchday four

Tuesday 1 November 2005, Stadion Tehelne pole, Bratislava

Artmedia Bratislava 2 (Borbely, Kozak) Rangers 2 (Prso, Thompson)

Attendance 20,000

Waterreus; Hutton, Bernard (Murray); Rodriguez, Kyrgiakos, Ferguson; Ricksen,
Hemdani, Prso, Thompson (Jeffers), Lovenkrands

Matchday five

Wednesday 25 November 2005, Estadio do Dragao, Porto

Porto 1 (Lisandro) Rangers 1 (McCormack)

Attendance 39,439

Waterreus; Ricksen, Murray; Kyrgiakos, Andrews, Ferguson; Namouchi, A. Rae
(Thompson), Jeffers (McCormack), Hemdani, Lovenkrands (Burke)

Matchday six

Tuesday 6 December 2005, Ibrox Stadium, Glasgow

Rangers 1 (Lovenkrands) Internazionale Milano 1 (Adriano)

Attendance 49,170

Waterreus; Ricksen, Murray; Kyrgiakos, Andrews, Ferguson; Burke, Malcolm,
Lovenkrands, Buffel, Namouchi

First knockout round, first leg

Wednesday 22 February 2006, Ibrox Stadium, Glasgow

Rangers 2 (Lovenkrands, Pena o.g.) Villarreal 2 (Riquelme pen, Forlan)

Attendance 49,372

Waterreus; Hutton, Smith; Rodriguez, Kyrgiakos, Ferguson; Burke, Hemdani,
Prso (Boyd), Lovenkrands (Novo), Namouchi (Buffel)

First knockout round, second leg

Tuesday 28 March 2006, El Madrigal, Villarreal

Villarreal 1 (Arruabarrena) Rangers 1 (Lovenkrands)

Attendance 23,000

Waterreus; Hutton, Murray; Kyrgiakos, Rodriguez, Ferguson; Burke (Novo),
Hemdani, Lovenkrands, Buffel (Boyd), Namouchi

Postscript

No club anywhere in the world has annexed more trophies than Rangers Football Club but there have been eras when the Light Blues have struggled to compete with the very best in Europe. Rangers as a club can hold their own against any of the great institutions anywhere across the globe, but whilst few would dispute that is true off the field of play, there have been occasions over the past half-century when that has not been reflected on the pitch. The reasons behind this are many and varied – no club can realistically expect to compete at the highest level for such a prolonged period of time as fifty years, but primarily the great clubs of Europe no longer compete on a level playing field. The introduction of the Champions' League brought a new level of wealth to the major European leagues of Spain, Italy, Germany, England and France. Television revenue and commercial sponsorship have resulted in the rich getting richer.

For a club to triumph in Europe, as Rangers did in 1972, it required just nine games to achieve the dream. Today, that potential number of games has doubled. Indeed, today one might have to fulfill nine fixtures before Christmas. If Rangers are ever to repeat the glories of a bygone age then it will take either a unique combination of talent on the field of play or a change in the logistical circumstances off it.

Today the club has a new manager, born and bred in Europe, in the form of Frenchman Paul Le Guen who has an excellent CV, having enjoyed outstanding success with Olympique Lyon. He attracted interest from several major European clubs before agreeing to join Rangers. The coming years will dictate whether Le Guen can achieve the success in the European arena that the club once enjoyed.

Fifty years ago only a very limited number of fans had the means to travel abroad. Half a century on, thousands 'Follow Follow' to certain games. Rangers have played four matches in European finals (including, of course, the 1960/61 two-legged affair with Fiorentina) and a select band of fans were present at all four – one thinks of Ross Bowie, Bob Moffat, John Paton and Joe Walsh, all sadly no longer with us, and of Andy Bain. The author attended just the two – Fiorentina at Ibrox and Barcelona – but many did achieve three, including Ian Loch and Les Melrose. Three European finals in eleven years – will we ever see another?

Other titles published by Stadia

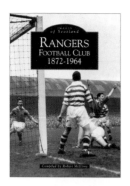

Rangers Football Club 1872-1964
ROBERT MCELROY

Rangers is a club with a tradition and history that is second to none. This collection of over 200 old photographs illustrates memorable moments from the first ninety years of a remarkable story. From humble beginnings on Glasgow Green, to the all-conquering team of the early sixties, the formative and subsequent years of Rangers Football Club are chronicled in unsurpassed pictorial detail.

0 7524 1191 8

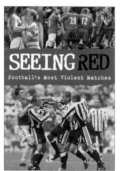

Seeing Red Football's Most Violent Matches
PHIL THOMPSON

It is a fact that football and fighting are all too frequent bedfellows. Competitive spirit leading to anger – and then to violence – is not a new facet to the game. This book explores some of the most violent games of all time. Violent challenges, tactics of foul play and ill-conditioned manners, they are all here. Upfront and honest, this is a telling insight into the ugly side of the beautiful game.

0 7524 3778 X

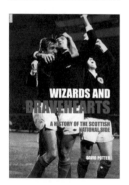

Wizards and Bravehearts A History of the Scottish National Side
DAVID W. POTTER

The history of Scotland's national football team from 1872 is full of highs and lows, thrills and heartbreaks, passion and pride. Read the stories – including the 1920s when they were indubitably the best in the world, the sad under-performances of the 1950s and '60s and the disasters of Argentina in 1978. This is a must for every Scottish football fan.

0 7524 3183 8

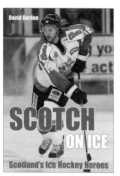

Scotch on Ice Scotland's Ice Hockey Heroes
DAVID GORDON

Throughout the sport's history, many of the finest ice hockey players produced by these islands have hailed from Scotland. Individuals like Billy Fullerton and 'Tuck' Syme, for example, were as outstanding in their chosen sport as any hero of football or rugby. Illustrated with many rare images, this book provides a fascinating commentary on the evolution of ice hockey in Scotland and the UK, and a lasting tribute to some of the sport's most exceptional talents.

0 7524 3901 8

If you are interested in purchasing other books published by Stadia, or in case you have difficulty finding any Stadia books in your local bookshop, you can also place orders directly through the Tempus Publishing website

www.tempus-publishing.com